Joshua Tree & Palm Springs

JENNA BLOUGH

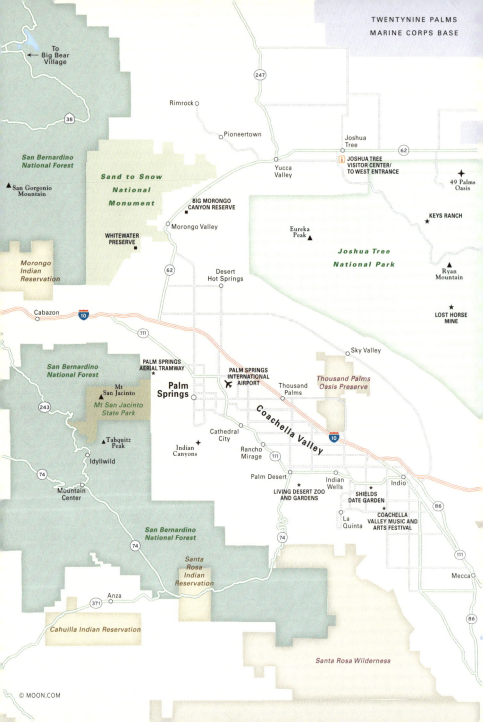

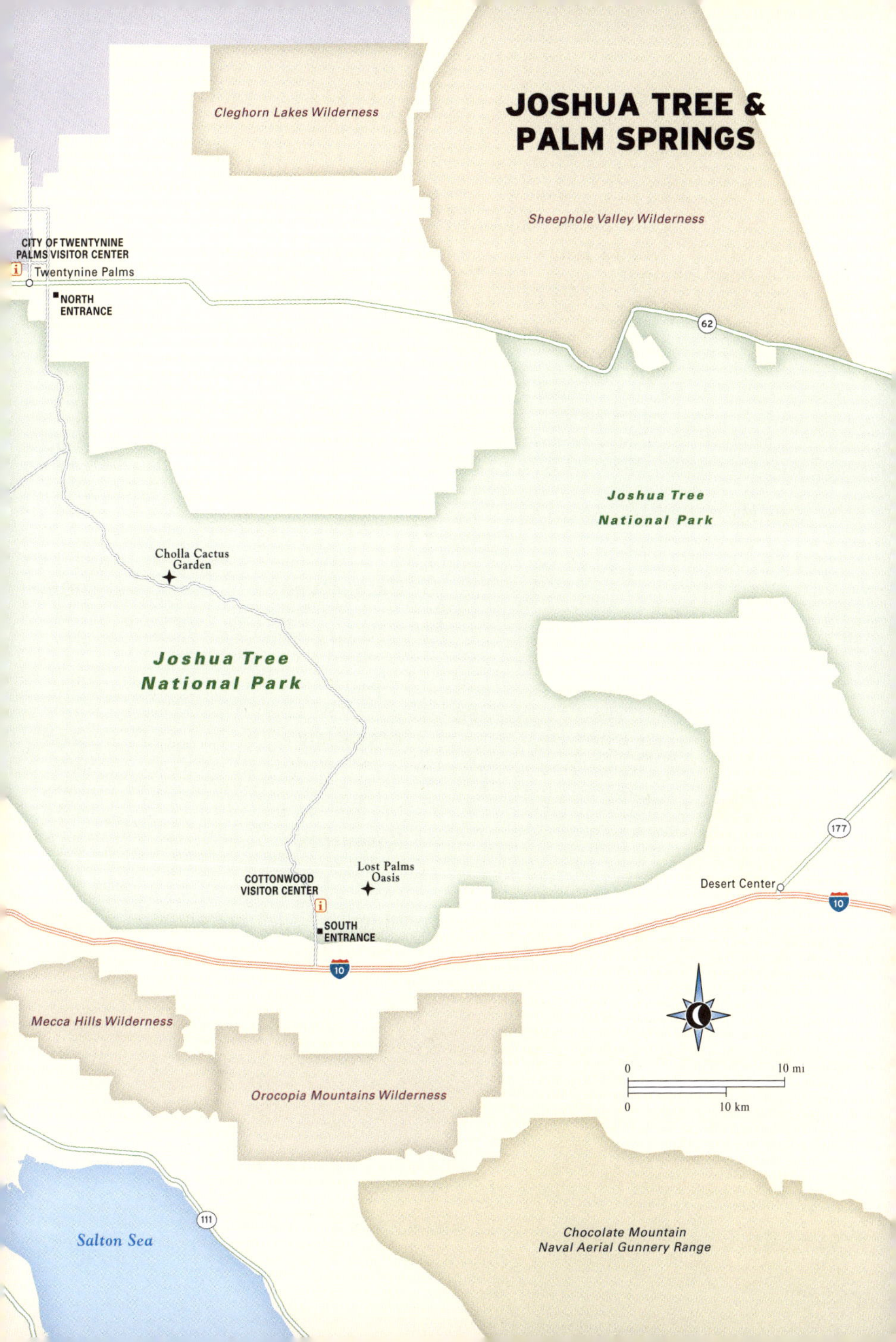

JOSHUA TREE & PALM SPRINGS

Cleghorn Lakes Wilderness

Sheephole Valley Wilderness

CITY OF TWENTYNINE
PALMS VISITOR CENTER
Twentynine Palms

NORTH
ENTRANCE

62

*Joshua Tree
National Park*

Cholla Cactus
Garden

*Joshua Tree
National Park*

177

Lost Palms
Oasis

COTTONWOOD
VISITOR CENTER

Desert Center

10

SOUTH
ENTRANCE

10

Mecca Hills Wilderness

Orocopia Mountains Wilderness

0   10 mi

0   10 km

111

Salton Sea

*Chocolate Mountain
Naval Aerial Gunnery Range*

Contents

Welcome to Joshua Tree & Palm Springs 7
5 Top Experiences 9
Planning Your Trip 14
• Palm Springs Loves a Party 15
Best of Joshua Tree & Palm Springs ... 18
• Day Trips from Palm Springs 19
Joshua Tree Camping Trip 21
Best Hikes 23
• Best Spa Experiences 25
Retro Palm Springs Weekend 26

Joshua Tree National Park 28
Exploring the Park 32
Sights 35
Scenic Drives 39
Sports and Recreation 43
Camping 67
Information and Services 72
Transportation 73

Around Joshua Tree 74
Yucca Valley, Pioneertown, and
    Landers 79
Joshua Tree 89
Twentynine Palms 97
Sand to Snow National Monument ... 101

Palm Springs and the Coachella Valley 113
Sights 116
Sports and Recreation 125
Entertainment and Events 136
Shopping 142
Food 146
Bars and Nightlife 151
Accommodations 153
Transportation 158
Information and Services 160
The Coachella Valley 160
Mount San Jacinto State Park and
    Wilderness 173

Background 185
The Landscape 185
Plants and Animals 190
History 194
Government and Economy 199
People and Culture 199

Essentials 202
Transportation 202
Travel Hub: Los Angeles 205
Travel Tips 211

Resources 217
Suggested Reading 217
Internet Resources 219

Index 220

List of Maps 224

hiking in the Wonderland of Rocks

WELCOME TO

Joshua Tree
& Palm Springs

Despite being such near neighbors, the spiky swath of Joshua Tree National Park and the sleek urban chic of Palm Springs appear to have little in common. Their link is the California desert, where relentless sunshine and rocky landscapes evoke a sense of the unknown.

Joshua Tree is wild, eroded, and fantastical. Its surreal rock formations were cooked up through millions of years of erosion, sedimentation, and continental collisions to form hulking, toothy piles of granite. The namesake Joshua trees, with their jagged silhouettes, run rampant among the jumbled piles of boulders. This is the high desert—gorgeous in spring and fall, searing hot in summer, and cold enough in winter that snow sometimes dusts the agave.

The resort town of Palm Springs got its start in the 1920s, and its popularity escalated as a getaway for the Hollywood Rat Pack. Today, it's a stylish time capsule with impeccable mid-century architecture, luxury resorts, boutique hotels, and retro gems tucked against the rocky foothills. In a landscape of drama and leisure, the gleaming blue of its plentiful swimming pools competes with the crystal-blue sky.

Joshua Tree was my first experience with the California desert, and I could hardly believe something so magical existed—the right blend of rustic, funky, and chic. I went to Palm Springs that same summer and navigated my way to a classic mid-century boutique hotel, where all the guests in the pool knew each other and welcomed us with Bloody Marys.

It's these contrasts that shape Joshua Tree and Palm Springs: The confluence of nearly perpetual sun, well-watered canyons, and bubbling hot springs backdropped by snowcapped mountains and a scoured desert make any visit here unique.

hiking through rock formations in Joshua Tree

5 TOP EXPERIENCES

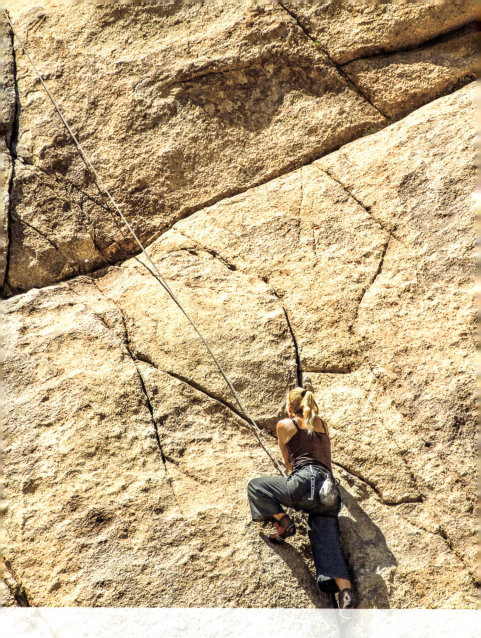

1 **Hiking and rock climbing** Joshua Tree's iconic rock formations, hidden waterfalls, fan palm oases, stunning canyons, and twisted boulder piles (pages 43 and 63).

2 Browsing the chic Uptown Design District for **vintage finds,** from caftans and denim to lamps and glassware (page 142).

3 Taking a **scenic drive** through Joshua Tree's dramatic landscape (page 39).

4 Exploring **mid-century modern architecture** inspired by the laid-back Palm Springs lifestyle and the modern clean lines of the desert (page 138).

5 **Pool-hopping** between Palm Springs's stylish boutique resorts (page 140).

Planning Your Trip

WHERE TO GO

Joshua Tree National Park
Dusty desert roads, jagged boulder piles, and spiky Joshua trees draw droves of **hikers, rock climbers,** and day-trippers to this otherworldly geologic landscape. Tour the **historic mines** and **ranches** of desert dreamers, wander amid strange cacti and colorful **wildflowers,** and take in the views from scenic peaks.

Around Joshua Tree
Peppered along the northern border of Joshua Tree National Park are the gateway towns of **Morongo Valley, Yucca Valley, Pioneertown, Landers, Joshua Tree, Twentynine Palms,** and **Wonder Valley.** All offer unique accommodations and alternatives to camping in the park, as well as local saloons, live music, and epic desert art worthy of exploration.

Palm Springs
Palm Springs is a charmed escape, filled with preserved mid-century architecture, non-stop pool parties, and lounges to release your inner Rat Pack. Take a whirlwind flight up the **Palm Springs Aerial Tramway,** wander amid Picassos and Warhols at the **Palm Springs Art Museum,** or simply park yourself poolside and soak in the rays. Surrounding Palm Springs is the **Coachella Valley,** best known for the popular Coachella Valley Music and Arts Festival. In under an hour, you can escape the desert heat of the searing valley floor with a quick tram ride or a short drive to **Mount San Jacinto State Park** and the artsy, rustic mountain town of **Idyllwild.**

Gonzalo Lebrija's *History of Suspended Time (A monument for the impossible)* at the Palm Springs Art Museum

Palm Springs Loves a Party

Palm Springs knows how to throw a party. Palm Springs and the Coachella Valley have several signature events throughout the year, from music festivals to modernism events. Plan your trip around these weekends or take note to avoid these times if you're looking for a low-key getaway.

- Palm Springs's signature event, **Modernism Week** celebrates mid-century modern architecture, design, and culture with tours, exhibits, and parties over a packed two weekends in February. In October, the city hosts a second Modernism Week to kick off the resort season (page 136).
- The **Palm Springs International Film Festival** draws thousands of visitors to screen more than 200 films over 12 days in January (page 137).
- Downtown Palm Springs blocks off streets every November to host **Pride Weekend,** with music, entertainment, and host hotels, to celebrate diversity and foster pride in the LGBTQ+ community (page 141).
- The **Coachella Valley Music and Arts Festival** draws iconic music headliners and hundreds of thousands of festivalgoers to this three-day music festival over two weekends in April (page 162).
- **Stagecoach** music festival brings hot names in country music to the Coachella Valley stage on the last weekend in April every year (page 162).

KNOW BEFORE YOU GO

High Season (Oct.-Apr.)

October-April is the high season for both Palms Springs and Joshua Tree National Park, with spring being the busiest time of year. Advance reservations for hotels in Palm Springs and campsites in Joshua Tree are a good idea during big events like **Modernism Week** and the **Coachella Valley Music and Arts Festival.**

The **Coachella Valley Music and Arts Festival** (www.coachella.com) takes place over two three-day weekends in April. Advance ticket sales begin in May for the following year with tickets historically selling out before the lineup is announced in January. Attendees have the option of tent camping on-site or staying at lodging in one of the Coachella Valley towns. Bundled tickets with tent camping or hotel packages are available to reserve when you buy festival passes. Partner hotels are located in nearby towns, including Palm Desert, La Quinta, Rancho Mirage, and Indio (5-13 mi/8-21 km from the festival) as well as Palm Springs (23 mi/37 km from the festival). The festival offers prepaid shuttles at stops throughout the Coachella Valley, including Palm Springs, so that festivalgoers don't have to drive. On festival weekends, breakfast spots in Palm Springs and other desert cities can be busier than usual, and hotel prices inflate. The festival runs Friday-Sunday, so freeway traffic in and out of Palm Springs is most heavily impacted the Thursday before Coachella and the Monday after Coachella on both weekends in April. Traffic between LA and Palm Springs can be bumper-to-bumper at these times, and the two-hour trip between Palm Springs and LA can take as long as five hours. To avoid festival traffic, avoid driving on these days, or leave well before noon.

At only 479 ft (146 m) above sea level, Palm Springs's low elevation means that temperatures are fairly mild in **winter.** The months of October-April are the most temperate, with temperatures ranging from the high 60s to the low 90s (20-34°C) during the day.

Low Season (May-Sept.)

Summer is the low season, with **brutally hot temperatures** holding fast in the triple digits (over 38°C) for much of June-September. Some businesses in Palm Springs have **limited hours,** though the resort town remains a destination, compensating with pool parties and lower hotel rates. Joshua Tree National Park remains open, with average highs in the 100s (38-43°C) and temperatures not dipping lower than the high 70s (25°C) at night. Recreational activities are extremely limited and can even be dangerous.

The San Jacinto Mountains and the town of **Idyllwild** offer a cool retreat during these searing months.

Transportation

Palm Springs International Airport (PSP; 3400 E. Tahquitz Canyon Way; 760/318-3800; https://flypsp.com) serves the resort town and can save you the 3-4-hour drive from Los Angeles. The airport has fewer airline options, however, and fares may be higher than at larger airports. International travelers may want to fly into **Los Angeles International Airport** (LAX; 1 World Way, Los Angeles; 424/646-5252; www.lawa.org) and spend a few days in LA before renting a car for the drive east along I-10.

There is no public transportation in Joshua Tree National Park. Exploration of the Coachella Valley and Joshua Tree National Park will require **your own vehicle.**

Entrance Stations

Joshua Tree National Park (www.nps.gov/jotr) has three entrance stations open year-round. The entrance fee ($30 vehicles, $25 motorcycles, $15 bikes or on foot) is good for seven days. The Annual Park Pass is $55, and season pass-holders are often offered a shorter line at entrance stations.

- **West Entrance** (Hwy. 62 and Park Blvd.) is accessed from the gateway town of Joshua Tree and sees the heaviest visitation.
- **North Entrance** (Hwy. 62 and Utah Tr.) is in the gateway town of Twentynine Palms and is a good alternative during high season, when lines are long at the West Entrance.
- **South Entrance** (off I-10) accesses Cottonwood Spring and sees the fewest visitors.

Visitor Centers

The **Joshua Tree Visitor Center** (6554 Park Blvd., Joshua Tree; 760/367-5500; 7:30am-5pm daily) is in the town of Joshua Tree on Park Boulevard before the park's West Entrance and offers a bookstore, restrooms, and a café.

The **Joshua Tree National Park Visitor Center** (74485 National Park Dr., Twentynine Palms; 760/367-5500; 8:30am-5pm daily) is located in downtown Twentynine Palms and offers a bookstore, drinking water, restrooms, and an EV charging station. The **Cottonwood Visitor Center** (Pinto Basin Rd.; 760/367-5500; 8:30am-4pm daily) is at the South Entrance near Cottonwood Spring and offers a bookstore, drinking water, restrooms, and a nearby picnic area.

The **Palm Springs Visitors Center** (2901 N. Palm Canyon Dr.; 760/778-8414; www.visitpalmsprings.com; 10am-5pm daily) is housed in the 1965 Tramway Gas Station, near the entrance to the aerial tramway.

Reservations

Camping reservations (877/444-6777; www.recreation.gov; $20-25) in Joshua Tree National Park are required at five campgrounds—Black Rock, Indian Cove, Cottonwood, Jumbo Rocks, and Ryan; demand is especially high in spring. Campgrounds tend to fill all weekends October-May. If you're planning a weekend camping trip in the park during this time, make reservations ahead of time or have alternate overnight plans. First-come, first-served sites are available at Belle, Hidden Valley, and White Tank but are limited and tend to fill fully by **Thursday afternoon.** During the summer months, some sites and sections of Indian Cove, Black Rock, and Cottonwood Campgrounds close. White Tank and Belle Campground close temporarily. Only three campgrounds—Black Rock, Indian Cove, and Cottonwood—have **drinking water.**

Visiting the historic **Keys Ranch** in Joshua Tree is by reservation only. Book your tour through www.recreation.gov or by calling 877/444-6777 at least one day in advance.

In Palm Springs, you'll want to book accommodations well in advance during spring events (**February-April**).

downtown Twentynine Palms

BEST OF Joshua Tree & Palm Springs

Day 1: Travel Day

Traffic to Palm Springs can be a beast, especially as you head into the weekend and especially coming from Los Angeles. Set yourself up for a full day of relaxing on Day 2 by making Day 1 a travel day. Your only goal is to check into your hotel of choice, whether it's the classic **Ingleside Inn,** stylish rustic-chic **Sparrows Lodge,** or the luxuriously exuberant **Parker Palm Springs.** Late-night drinks and eats can be hard to come by in Palm Springs, but they are available in a handful of spots including the **Paul Bar, The Reef,** and **The Tropicale.**

Day 2: Palm Springs

Wake up and rejoice that you are in sunny Palm Springs, then get yourself to the sidewalk line at **Cheeky's** to wait for fresh Bloody Marys and brunch specials like Blondie's eggs Benedict, homemade cinnamon rolls, and a bacon flight.

Palm Springs and the Coachella Valley are surrounded by epic desert beauty. Nowhere is this more evident than during a hike through **Indian Canyons.** The **Lower Palm Canyon Trail** visits the world's largest fan palm oasis, while **Tahquitz Canyon** offers a short but scenic stroll to a rare desert waterfall, great for a post-brunch walk.

If you need something to tide you over until dinner, enjoy delicious Cuban deli delights at **Chef Tanya's Kitchen,** good for casual lunch and pickup orders.

Dinner is on the tropical patio at **The Tropicale,** with its throwback supper club feel and Pacific Rim menu, or opt for steaks in the dark lounge at **Mr. Lyon's** upscale modern steak house.

Wind down the night at **Seymour's,** the intimate, dimly lit speakeasy located behind the curtain at Mr. Lyon's, or try **Bootlegger Tiki** for flocked wallpaper, deep booths, and layered rum drinks.

Day Trips from Palm Springs

Palm Springs can be a base camp for day trips to the Coachella Valley, Sand to Snow National Monument, San Jacinto Mountains State Park, and Joshua Tree National Park. Drives within 1.5 hours of Palm Springs allow you to experience shaded desert oases, forested mountain peaks, outsider art installations, charming mountain towns, and the famous cracked boulders of Joshua Tree National Park.

- **Joshua Tree National Park** (1 hour) can be explored as a day trip from Palm Springs, with scenic stops and hikes along Park Boulevard, Joshua Tree's main road, which winds through the iconic Joshua tree forest and rock formations (page 28).
- The charming village of **Forest Falls** (1 hour) is nestled in a canyon on the edge of the San Gorgonio Wilderness, making for a scenic mountain drive with opportunities to picnic and hike (page 105).
- Visit the crystal-clear waters of the Whitewater River, remarkable for its rocky desert location in the **Whitewater Preserve** (25 minutes). Hiking trails, including a small section of the Pacific Crest Trail, offer river access and canyon views, while a wading pond is fun for families (page 107).
- The **Thousand Palms Oasis Preserve** (30 minutes) highlights desert landscapes along the San Andreas fault, including shaded palm oases and eroded mud hills (page 163).
- Accessed from the mountain town of Idyllwild, **Mount San Jacinto State Park and Wilderness** (1 hour 20 minutes) has forested hikes like the Ernie Maxwell Scenic Trail and Tahquitz Peak, with long vistas as a reward for the climbs (page 173).
- **Idyllwild** (1 hour 20 minutes) has a picturesque downtown with shops, restaurants, and local art for strolling in cooler summer temperatures or winter snow (page 178).

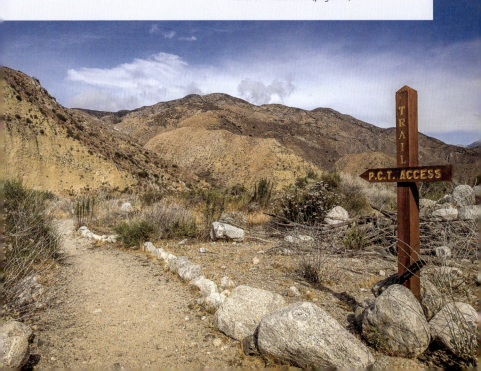

Pappy & Harriet's Pioneertown Palace

Day 3: Joshua Tree Day Trip

Today you will explore Joshua Tree. Pack a cooler with drinks, snacks, lunch, and water and head to the South Entrance at Cottonwood Spring (1 hour). Stop at the Cottonwood Visitor Center for maps and tips and then check out scenic **Cottonwood Spring,** where you can take a short hike around the spring or a longer hike to the **Mastodon Mine** or **Lost Palms Oasis.** Continue north along Pinto Basin Road to soak in the stark landscape of the Sonoran Desert with a stop at the **Cholla Cactus Garden.**

At the intersection with Park Boulevard, take a left to head west and watch as the landscape shifts into the dramatic Mojave Desert with its signature spiky Joshua trees and otherworldly boulder piles. Enjoy a scenic drive along Park Boulevard into the popular **Hidden Valley** region of the park, stopping off to explore the short nature trails at **Barker Dam, Cap Rock,** and **Skull Rock.**

Your trip through the park will end at the West Entrance in the town of Joshua Tree, just in time for dinner with other hikers, rock climbers, and locals at the casual **Joshua Tree Saloon,** with a menu that includes burgers, salads, sandwiches, and tacos. The back patio is good for kids and dogs.

If you're early enough and up for a wait, head up to **Pappy & Harriet's** restaurant and saloon, a former Wild West movie set in aptly named Pioneertown. Debrief your day, people-watch, and enjoy the funky surroundings while digging into the hearty Tex-Mex menu at this one-of-a-kind spot.

From either place, the drive back to Palm Springs is about 45 minutes.

Day 4: Palm Springs

Get back into the swing of Palm Springs by celebrating with brunch at **Pinocchio in the Desert,** where the bottomless mimosas draw a packed patio crowd.

After brunch head to the **Uptown Design District** for vintage shopping. Browse the wares at **The Shops at Thirteen Forty-Five,** where the stunning architecture matches the vintage clothing and accessories inside, then pick up a home accessory at **Phylum** to bring a bit of Palm Springs with you.

The afternoon is spent relaxing poolside, soaking up your last day in Palm Springs.

For dinner check out one of the downtown's upscale Mexican spots. **Clandestino** offers a curated Latin American menu and margarita flights in view of the art museum. **Tac/Quila** sets street tacos and ceviche against 1970s-inspired swank along the downtown strip.

Day 5: Travel Day

Enjoy the last moments of your hotel's amenities while you pack. On the way out of town, enjoy a low-key lunch at **The Heyday.**

Joshua Tree Camping Trip

The landscape of Joshua Tree National Park is mesmerizing—from the spiky trees to the scoured desert and jumbled boulders begging to be climbed. A visit here typically means camping, with extra time spent exploring the funky sights of the surrounding desert towns. Bring **water** and **your own vehicle** and plan a two-night camping trip to visit this desert wonderland **October-May.**

Day 1

Arrive in the town of Joshua Tree and fortify after your drive with lunch at the nouveau diner **Crossroads Café** for a creative take on diner classics, including plenty of veggie options. The laid-back vibe and fresh plates, ranging from huevos rancheros to buttermilk pancakes, will set you up for making camp and exploring in the park.

After lunch, continue on Highway 62 to the less crowded **North Entrance,** stopping at the **Joshua Tree National Park Visitor Center** to pick up maps before entering the park.

Check in to your reserved campsite at the centrally located **Jumbo Rocks Campground** and set up camp, enjoying your spot amid the iconic

Jumbo Rocks Campground

boulder-strewn scenery. You don't have to venture far from your campsite to find short, scenic hiking trails for the afternoon: **Skull Rock** and **Split Rock** allow you to immerse in the landscape while still getting you back in time for a relaxing camp dinner and stargazing in this International Dark Sky Park.

Day 2

Enough of these easy nature trails! Today, it's time to get those lungs pumping with a more rigorous hike. For epic views, climb **Ryan Mountain** to its 5,457-ft (1,663-m) summit. If you want to explore the park's mining ruins, opt instead for a steep climb to the **Lost Horse Mine.** And for those irresistible boulder piles, the **Willow Hole Trail** offers a scenic out-and-back ramble.

If it's too hot to hit the trail today, hit the road instead on a backcountry drive. The **Geology Tour Road** is accessible to all vehicles for the first 5 mi (8.1 km) of its 19 mi (31 km) through the park's unique geologic formations. The dirt roads crisscrossing the Queen Valley also cut through Joshua tree forest with opportunities to explore the park's cultural history.

After your hike, enjoy a picnic lunch in the park at one of the numerous picnic areas, then enjoy a scenic drive along Park Boulevard into the popular **Hidden Valley** region of the park, making a detour to **Keys View** if you haven't had your fill. Continue north to end in the town of Joshua Tree.

Take a night off from campfire cooking to grab a burger with other hikers, rock climbers, and locals at the lively **Joshua Tree Saloon,** a 20-minute drive west from the Willow Hole Trailhead.

Day 3

Pack up camp and save yourself the dishes by enjoying a late breakfast at the **JT Country Kitchen.** Before you head out of town, browse the shops in Joshua Tree.

Ryan Mountain Trail

Best Hikes

The Palm Springs and Joshua Tree region is home to hidden waterfalls, fan palm oases, stunning canyons, and twisted boulder piles, all begging to be explored. The best season to hit the trail is **October-April;** in the hotter months, plan to start from the trailhead early to miss the heat of the day. If it's too hot, opt instead for the lofty and much cooler San Jacintos, just a short drive (or tram ride) away.

Joshua Tree National Park
Lost Horse Mine
This moderate out-and-back or loop hike scales Lost Horse Mountain in about 4-7.4 mi (6.4-11.9 km) round-trip to visit one of the best-preserved mining sites in Joshua Tree National Park (page 45).

Willow Hole Trail
Admire the spiky Joshua trees and boulder piles on this 7-mi (11.3-km) round-trip flat track into the heart of the **Wonderland of Rocks** (page 46).

Ryan Mountain
This 3-mi (4.8-km) round-trip hike climbs more than 1,000 ft (305 m) in elevation to panoramic views from the wind-scoured 5,457-ft (1,663-m) vantage point atop Ryan Mountain (page 54).

49 Palms Oasis
This easy-to-follow trail is only 3 mi (4.8 km) round-trip yet offers no hint to the secret oasis of native fan palms that awaits (page 57).

Willow Hole Trail

Lost Palms Oasis

Lost Palms Oasis
As the south entrance to Joshua Tree, this exposed trail wanders 7.5 mi (12.1 km) round-trip through desert gardens to the Lost Palm Oasis, a watering hole for bighorn sheep and other wildlife (page 62).

Around Joshua Tree
Red Dome
In **Whitewater Preserve,** a 4-mi (6.4-km) out-and-back scenic walk through a wide canyon ends at the **Whitewater River,** which maintains a surprising and brisk presence across the open desert floor for much of the year (page 107).

Palm Springs and the Coachella Valley
Indian Canyons
Andreas Canyon is an easy—and popular—loop in scenic Indian Canyons near Palm Springs. The shaded trail follows a permanent creek for 2 mi (3.2 km) round-trip through stands of leafy fan palms (page 131).

Tahquitz Peak
This steep 8.6-mi (13.8-km) round-trip trail switchbacks through the manzanita, Jeffrey pine, and white fir forests of the **San Jacinto Wilderness** to reward with breathtaking views from the historic lookout tower at the top of Tahquitz Peak (page 177).

Best Spa Experiences

For the best spa experiences near Palm Springs, head north to the town of Desert Hot Springs, uniquely positioned over both hot and cold mineral aquifers. Homesteader, artist, and traveler Cabot Yerxa (of Cabot's Pueblo Museum) is credited with bringing the mineral springs to the attention of homesteaders and developers when he arrived in Desert Hot Springs in 1913. He discovered hot mineral water outside his door when he dug his first well. He dug another 600 yards (550 m) away and discovered pure cold aquifer water. Development began in the 1930s with the goal of making Desert Hot Springs a spa destination.

Today, boutique mid-century hotels offer calming pools and spas where you can take the waters.

- The stylishly updated **Azure Palm Hot Springs Resort** offers spa packages with access to its swimming and soaking pools, a café, and resort grounds (page 167).
- The Moroccan-themed **El Morocco Inn** offers a courtyard mineral pool, covered hot spa, sauna, and spa treatments for guests and non-guests (page 167).
- The **Miracle Springs Resort & Spa** offers eight mineral pools for day use as well as on-site spa services (page 167).
- **The Spring Resort & Spa** features three mineral pools and a Finnish sauna, as well as massages and body treatments to promote relaxation for guests and day use (page 167).
- The rustic, family-friendly **Sam's Family Spa Hot Water Resort** has a spring-fed swimming pool and hot pools in a parklike setting with RV camping (page 168).

Retro Palm Springs Weekend

Palm Springs's treasure trove of mid-century architecture and reputation as a winter playground for the Hollywood Rat Pack-era elite make the city a stylish resort destination that's perfect for a weekend getaway. Whether you're lounging poolside at a mid-century resort, partying at a ladies weekend, or relaxing at a couples spa getaway, you can soak up Palm Springs's dazzling history and sunshine at this timeless haven.

Friday

Fly into Palm Springs International Airport. Or, if you're driving from LA, hop in the car Thursday night to avoid rush hour and start the weekend early. Spend the afternoon visiting the **Palm Springs Art Museum** or riding the **Palm Springs Aerial Tramway** to the top, where you can take in the refreshing view of the valley below. You can't miss Tramway Road, marked by an iconic building with a cantilevered roofline designed by famed architect Albert Frey in 1965 as the Tramway Gas Station. It now serves as the visitor center.

Back on the desert floor, check in to a chic mid-century hotel such as the freshly restyled **Holiday House,** originally designed in 1951 by noted architect Herbert W. Burns, or the classic 1948 William F. Cody **Del Marcos Hotel** and enjoy some time poolside. For dinner, dine on steak frites at **Mr. Lyon's,** a classic steak house from a bygone era. From the dining room, move to the back room, **Seymour's,** for some of the best cocktails in town—bartenders have classic Hollywood movies on for ambience behind the bar. Alternately, opt for tropical drinks at **The Reef** in the kitschy 1960s Polynesian Caliente Tropics hotel.

Saturday

After a breakfast at **King's Highway,** a former Denny's with Naugahyde booths and original terrazzo floors in the Ace Hotel, check out some of the area's stunning mid-century architecture. Pick up a driving tour map at the **Palm Springs Visitors Center,** itself housed in the Albert Frey-designed **Tramway Gas Station,** and discover the works of **Donald Wexler, William F. Cody,** and **Richard Neutra,** among others. For a sneak peek inside, sign up for a tour of historic **Sunnylands Center and Gardens,** which has hosted everyone from British royalty to Hollywood icons. The afternoon is spent relaxing poolside, of course.

Around dinnertime, enjoy a romantic dinner at **Copley's,** part of the former Cary Grant estate, then continue in the footsteps of the Rat Pack with retro-chic cocktails at **Melvyn's** iconic Palm Springs lounge.

Sunday

To wind down your weekend, head to Palm Springs mainstay **Eight4Nine** for an upbeat send-off in the white and jewel-toned space that was the 1954 post office.

Work out the kinks of mind and body with a massage at one of nearby **Desert Hot Springs's** many day spas before packing your bags for the flight or long drive back to reality.

Sunnylands Center and Gardens

Joshua Tree National Park

Exploring the Park 32
Sights 35
Scenic Drives 39
Sports and Recreation. . 43
Camping 67
Information and
 Services 72
Transportation 73

The stunning, alien landscape of Joshua Tree
both startles and charms.

Powerful geologic forces have whipped the rocks here into twisted shapes and scrambled boulder piles. Among the eroded chaos, spiky Joshua trees reach out in unpredictable angles, forming jagged, moody backdrops against dusty desert roads. This is the Mojave, the high desert: gorgeous in spring and fall, brutal in summer, and dusted by snow in winter.

Farther south the landscape changes yet again, straddling the boundary between the Mojave and Sonoran Deserts. The lower-elevation Sonoran sits austere and arid, with wide alluvial fans to guard its mountain canyons. Instead of Joshua trees, creosote bushes

Highlights

Look for ★ to find recommended sights, activities, dining, and lodging.

★ **Keys Ranch:** Take a ranger-guided tour of the ranch house, buildings, and grounds owned by one of Joshua Tree's most colorful characters (page 35).

★ **Eureka Peak Overlook:** While everyone crowds the popular Keys View overlook, this lightly visited peak offers equally spectacular views (page 37).

★ **Cholla Cactus Garden:** A brigade of fuzzy multihued cacti stretch out to form this surreal desert garden (page 39).

★ **Lost Horse Mine:** Follow an old mining road to this well-preserved stamp mill with rock house ruins and stunning views toward Queen Valley (page 45).

★ **Willow Hole Trail:** This easy trek delves into the heart of the wildly eroded Wonderland of Rocks (page 46).

★ **Ryan Mountain:** A vigorous hike leads to panoramic views of the Pinto Basin, Hidden Valley, and the Wonderland of Rocks (page 54).

★ **49 Palms Oasis:** Hike to this mirage-like fan palm oasis (page 57).

★ **Lost Palms Oasis:** From lush Cottonwood Spring, this trail crosses desert ridges to a secluded oasis of fan palms, with detours to mine ruins and panoramic views (page 62).

★ **Rock Climbing:** The park's boulder-strewn oasis makes it a world-class destination for rock climbers (page 63).

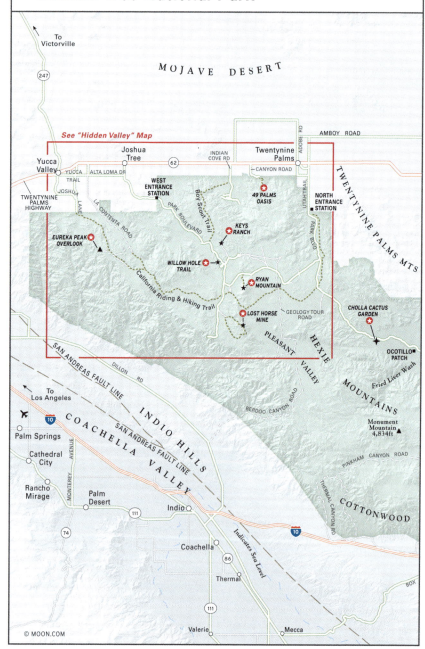

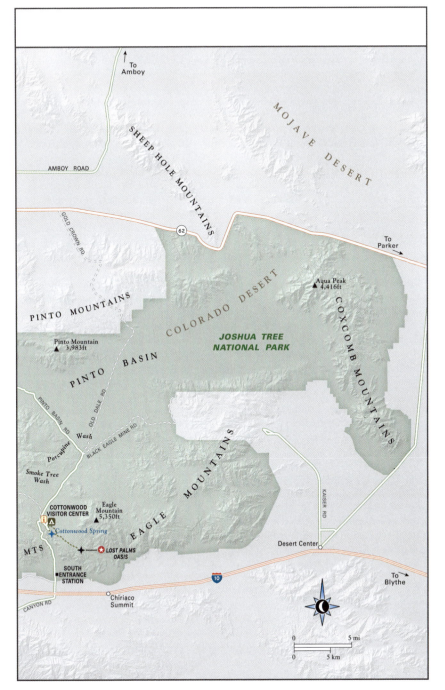

and spindly ocotillos dot the pristine desert wilderness.

Joshua Tree's surreal appeal draws casual day-trippers, spring wildflower hounds, serious hikers, and hard-core rock climbers in droves, all wanting to experience its beauty and strangeness. The park's location near major urban centers like Palm Springs and Los Angeles contributes to its popularity, as does its easy access for locals living in the gateway towns of Joshua Tree and Twentynine Palms. The tiny towns surrounding the park are filled with outsider art, alien-inspired feats of aeronautical engineering, and some of the best live music around.

ORIENTATION

Most visitors spend their time on the west side of the park, where the only paved road access (Park Boulevard) exists. From the West Entrance near the town of Joshua Tree, Park Boulevard delves deep into Hidden Valley (the most popular section of the park, filled with trailheads and campgrounds) to emerge in the town of Twentynine Palms. While the Black Rock Canyon area and Indian Cove offer developed (and reservable) campgrounds, their access does not extend farther into the park. At the South Entrance, Cottonwood Spring offers a less-visited glimpse of the park's Sonoran Desert geography.

PLANNING YOUR TIME

Joshua Tree is doable as a **day trip** from Palm Springs; it's about 1 hour to the Joshua Tree Visitor Center at the West Entrance. From Los Angeles, plan 3-4 hours for the drive and definitely spend the night. Some visitors only spend one day in the park, and most of that in the car driving the Park Boulevard loop into, and then out of, each entrance station. Such limited time affords equally limited exposure to how much the park has to offer—and that involves getting out of the car and onto the trail. Do yourself a favor and plan to spend at least an overnight; **3-5 days** are even better.

Plan your visit during the cooler months of **October-April** (although these are also the most crowded). If you're **camping,** make a reservation well ahead of time to snag a coveted site in the park. Visitors seeking accommodations with luxuries such as running water should book a room at one of the multiple lodging options in the towns surrounding the park entrances—**Yucca Valley, Joshua Tree,** and **Twentynine Palms.**

You'll need a **car,** a full tank of gas, and plenty of patience driving the long distances both on the park roads and between the desert towns. Bring all the **water** you'll need to drink, clean with, or bathe in (at least 2 gallons/9 liters per day of drinking water), as there are no services inside the park.

Exploring the Park

Before exploring the park, stop in the town of Joshua Tree or Twentynine Palms for information, maps, water, and supplies. There are no concessions in the park. The town of Joshua Tree is situated at the park's busiest entrance and offers a visitor center as well as local shops for picnic items and outdoors gear. Twentynine Palms provides a visitor center, a grocery store, and local shops for picnic supplies.

VISITOR CENTERS
Joshua Tree Visitor Center

6554 Park Blvd., Joshua Tree; 760/367-5500; 7:30am-5pm daily; www.nps.gov/jotr; daily year-round

The Joshua Tree Visitor Center is in the town

Previous: Keys View scenic overlook; Joshua trees along the trails in the scenic Wonderland of Rocks; rock climbing in Joshua Tree.

Joshua Tree in One Day

Even with limited time, it's still possible to soak in many of the park's sights and wonders.

MORNING

Start in the **Indian Cove** area with an invigorating and scenic hike to the **49 Palms Oasis** (3 mi/4.8 km) for your first taste of the hidden wonders Joshua Tree National Park has in store. The two-hour hike winds up a rocky canyon with views of the town of Twentynine Palms before emerging above a natural palm oasis tucked into the craggy hills.

After the hike, drive east on Highway 62 and make your way to the park's less-crowded **North Entrance.** Stop by the **Joshua Tree National Park Visitor Center** for a great selection of books, maps, and information, and then head southeast on Park Boulevard to make a loop through the park from east to west. From here on out, it's all about the journey as you marvel at the passing landscape.

Queen Valley

AFTERNOON

On Park Boulevard, drive 10 mi (16.1 km) west (20 minutes) to **Queen Valley,** an excellent destination thanks to its boulder-strewn and Joshua tree-filled landscape and history. A series of networked hiking trails lead to ranching sites, mining remains, and the sites of Native American settlements. The trail to the **Wall Street Mill** (3 mi/4.8 km round-trip, 1.5 hours) leads to a well-preserved ore-processing mill dating from the 1930s, while the remains of the **Desert Queen Mine** (1-3 mi/0.6-4.8 km, 30 minutes) cling to the steep side of Desert Queen Wash. The **Lucky Boy Vista** loop (3.6 mi/5.8 km, 2 hours) traverses an ancient Native American village with views of Hidden Valley. The **Pine City** out-and-back (3 mi/4.8 km, 2 hours) strikes through classic Mojave Desert flora. **Barker Dam** (1.3 mi/2.1 km, 30 minutes) is a popular nature trail leading to the edge of the Wonderland of Rocks and a ranch-era dam created on the site of a Native American settlement. Bring your lunch and picnic at nearby Split Rock or Live Oak picnic areas.

Detour into the park's starker southern landscape with a stop at the **Cholla Cactus Garden** (0.25 mi/0.4 km, 15 minutes).

EVENING

Cap off your time wandering the canyons with a perspective-building drive to popular **Keys View.** This scenic overlook gives sweeping panoramas of the park's southwest, taking in the Santa Rosa Mountains, San Andreas fault, Palm Springs, San Jacinto Peak, and San Gorgonio Peak. The paved observation point is wheelchair-accessible.

For a last hurrah, meander your way northwest along **Park Boulevard** toward the **West Entrance,** passing through the impressive rock formations of **Hidden Valley** on your way; plan one hour for the drive.

of Joshua Tree on Park Boulevard before the park's West Entrance. This fully staffed visitor center offers a well-stocked bookstore with travel guides, nature guides, maps, and gifts. There are restrooms and a café.

Roadrunner Grab + Go
760/974-9290; 7:30am-5pm daily

The Roadrunner Grab + Go is right next door to the visitor center and serves sandwiches, soups, salads, espresso, beer, wine, smoothies, and boxed lunches for dining in or as takeout. This is your last stop for food and beverages before entering the park; there are no concessions within the park.

Joshua Tree National Park Visitor Center
6533 Freedom Way, Twentynine Palms; 760/367-5500; 8:30am-5pm daily

Joshua Tree National Park Visitor Center is en route to the park's North Entrance in the gateway town of Twentynine Palms. The fully staffed visitor center offers a well-stocked bookstore with travel guides, nature guides, maps, and gifts. Water bottle filling stations, restrooms with flush toilets, and EV charging stations are also available.

Cottonwood Visitor Center
Pinto Basin Rd., approximately 7 mi (11.3 km) north of I-10 exit 168; 760/367-5500; 8:30am-4pm daily

Located at the remote South Entrance to the park, the Cottonwood Visitor Center provides check-in for visitors entering through the more sparsely traveled South Entrance. The fully staffed visitor center offers a bookstore with travel guides, nature guides, maps, and gifts. Water, restrooms with flush toilets, and picnic tables are also available. A short botanical garden interpretive loop starts from the visitor center. The visitor center is convenient to the Cottonwood Campground as well as Cottonwood Spring and the Hidden Palms Oasis hiking trail.

Black Rock Nature Center
9800 Black Rock Canyon Rd., Yucca Valley; 760/367-5500; 8am-11am and noon-4pm daily, hours may vary with staffing and in summer

The Black Rock Nature Center is a small visitor center used primarily as a check-in for campers heading to the Black Rock Canyon Campground and other visitors to the Black Rock Canyon area. Park entrance fees may also be paid here. Several trails lead from here, including ones to Warren Peak and

view toward Cottonwood Visitor Center and the campground from the trail

the Panorama Loop through the Little San Bernardino Mountains. The ranger-staffed center has maps, books, and nature guides for purchase. Water, flush toilets, and a picnic area are available.

City of Twentynine Palms Visitor Center

6847 Adobe Rd., Twentynine Palms; 760/358-6324; 10am-4pm Mon.-Fri., 10am-3pm Sat.-Sun.

Located en route to the North Entrance, the City of Twentynine Palms Visitor Center welcomes you to the gateway town of Twentynine Palms and Joshua Tree National Park. The visitor center and gallery features maps to a collection of desert destinations, including Joshua Tree National Park, Mojave Trails National Monument, and Mojave National Preserve, plus maps for navigating back roads and scenic routes. They also offer brochures, local books, Wi-Fi, a gift shop, an electric car charging station, and a community art gallery.

ENTRANCE STATIONS

$30 per vehicle, $25 per motorcycle, $15 bicycle or on foot, $55 annual pass

There are three main entrances into the park:

West Entrance

5 mi (8.1 km) south of Hwy. 62 and Park Blvd.

The West Entrance is accessed from the gateway town of Joshua Tree and sees the heaviest volume of visitors. Lines can be long on busy weekends. Visitors to the park go through a ranger-staffed entrance kiosk to pay entrance fees, while season pass holders are often offered a shorter line. Restrooms are available.

North Entrance

3 mi (4.8 km) south of Hwy. 62 and Utah Trail

The North Entrance is located in the gateway town of Twentynine Palms and sees slightly less traffic and shorter lines. Visitors pass through a ranger-staffed kiosk to pay entrance fees. Restrooms are available.

South Entrance

off I-10, 25 mi (40 km) east of Indio in the Coachella Valley

The South Entrance accesses Cottonwood Spring and sees the fewest visitors. There is no entrance kiosk; instead, visitors entering from the south should stop at the ranger station to pay fees and gather information. Restrooms and maps are available.

Sights

HIDDEN VALLEY

From the park's West Entrance in Joshua Tree, Park Boulevard travels 25 mi (40 km) southeast, making a loop with the North Entrance in Twentynine Palms. This paved stretch is the most popular region of the park, with access to Queen Valley, Hidden Valley, Quail Springs, and the Wonderland of Rocks, as well as the majority of campgrounds and trailheads.

★ Keys Ranch

by reservation only, 877/444-6777 or www.recreation. gov; $10 over age 11, $5 ages 6-11 and seniors, free under age 6

Colorful homesteader, rancher, and miner

Bill Keys was an industrious and resourceful pack rat who fashioned a homestead and a life in the isolated desert. From 1917 to 1969, he and his family carved out a desert domain that included a ranch house, a schoolhouse, a store, and a workshop. Today, visitors can tour the well-preserved ruins of the Desert Queen Ranch, now listed in the National Register of Historic Places.

October-May, park rangers lead 90-minute guided tours of Keys Ranch. This popular tour guides you to a preserved historic homestead near the Hidden Valley Campground. The schedule varies, but tours are usually held once daily Friday-Sunday and offer your only look at these historic remains.

Hidden Valley

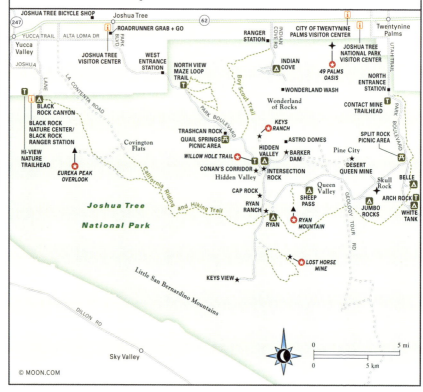

Wonderland of Rocks

view from Indian Cove Campground and Barker Dam Nature Trail parking area

Dubbed the Wonderland of Rocks for reasons that quickly become apparent, this region is characterized by a wildly eroded maze of striking granite rock formations studded with secret basins, gorgeous views, and history. The Wonderland of Rocks covers the area southeast of Indian Cove Campground and northeast of Hidden Valley Campground. Its compelling rock formations are visible to the east and north while driving along Park Boulevard, the main park road. Indian Cove Campground and the parking area for the Barker Dam Nature Trail are the closest driving points into the belly of the beast. The area lures rock climbers and hikers. Four trails (Barker Dam Loop, Boy Scout Trail, Willow Hole, and Wonderland Wash) knife short distances into the Wonderland of Rocks. Rock climbing use trails are signed and established.

Ryan Ranch

Park Blvd.

Ryan Ranch was named after the Ryan brothers, Thomas and J. D., "Jep," who bought interest in the nearby Lost Horse Mine and set up camp at the Lost Horse Well at the base of Ryan Mountain. The homestead ruins date to 1896, but the region had been used by Native Americans prior to the mining era thanks to the availability of water in the area. A short 0.5-mi (0.8-km) stroll leads to the remains of the ranch and its adobe bunkhouse, windmill, and outbuildings. A deeper search of the area reveals a pioneer cemetery and evidence of Native American habitation, including grinding stones. This interpretive site is accessed from a pullout on Park Boulevard between the Ryan Mountain trailhead and the turnoff for Ryan Campground.

Keys View
access via Keys View Rd.

Impressive views spill from the lip of wind-swept Keys View, an observation point in the Little San Bernardino Mountains. Take in a panorama that stretches to the Salton Sea, Santa Rosa Mountains, San Andreas Fault, Palm Springs, San Jacinto Peak, and San Gorgonio Peak. The paved observation point is also wheelchair-accessible. Find it 7 mi (11.3 km) south of the Hidden Valley Campground, a 20-minute detour from Park Boulevard along Keys View Road.

Queen Valley
access via Queen Valley Rd. or Desert Queen Mine Rd.

Queen Valley is like a cross section of Joshua Tree's greatest hits, with Joshua tree stands, mining ruins, Native American village sites, scenic hikes, and views. A series of short dirt roads crisscrosses Queen Valley, chugging through one of the largest pockets of Joshua trees in the park. Mining ruins range from large gold operations, like the Desert Queen Mine, to far humbler affairs marked by the rusty remains of tent encampments. Evidence of Native American settlements dot the boulder-strewn landscape. Established hiking trails follow a series of old mining roads to the **Desert Queen Mine, Lucky Boy Vista,** and the **Wall Street Mine.** To traverse the Queen Valley area, follow the unpaved Queen Valley Road east to its terminus at Pine City.

BLACK ROCK CANYON

The Black Rock Canyon region is in the northwest corner of Joshua Tree, with a campground and several great hikes as well as easy access to the shops and restaurants of Yucca Valley. The Black Rock area is characterized by craggy rolling peaks and piñons, junipers, and oak trees, giving it a different feel from the more popular Hidden Valley section of Joshua Tree. Though the Black Rock Canyon area is located near the West Entrance, there is no direct access into the center of the park.

★ Eureka Peak Overlook

At 5,521 ft (1,683 m), Eureka Peak Overlook offers panoramic views of Joshua Tree and the surrounding valleys. Not only are the views spectacular, Eureka Peak is much less crowded than the very popular Keys View, a paved, drive-up viewpoint in the middle of the heavily visited central section of the park. From the summit, the Coachella Valley, Desert Hot Springs, and the San Jacinto Mountains (including the often snowcapped San Jacinto Peak) lie to the southwest, while views to the north take in the Morongo Valley. Look east into the park and you'll glimpse the Wonderland of Rocks.

Of course, there's a catch: Eureka Peak is not accessed via the park's main entrances. Instead, entry is via a graded dirt road from Yucca Valley (near the Black Rock Canyon Campground) that leads into Covington Flats, ending within a few hundred yards of the peak. It's also possible to hike to Eureka Peak via the trail from Covington Flats (8 mi/12.9 km round-trip) or the Black Rock Canyon Campground (10 mi/16.1 km round-trip).

From Highway 62 (29 Palms Hwy.) in the town of Yucca Valley, take La Contenta Road south. The road quickly becomes dirt and has some sandy places. In normal weather conditions, it should be passable for most two-wheel-drive cars. At 7.8 mi (12.6 km), turn right toward Eureka Peak. At 9.6 mi (15.5 km), turn right again toward Eureka Peak (signed). At 10.9 mi (17.5 km), you reach a small parking area a few hundred yards below the peak.

COTTONWOOD SPRING
off Pinto Basin Rd., north of I-10

Located near the South Entrance to the park, the Cottonwood region encompasses

a visitor center, a campground, and several hiking trails. Cottonwood Spring itself is a fan palm oasis named for a surprising crop of native cottonwood trees that are mixed into the luxuriant vegetation surrounding the spring. Cottonwood Spring has served as a vital water source for centuries, with Native American settlement signs around to prove it. One example of how few and far between such water sources are in the desert: One ill-fated Matt Riley started off with a friend from the Dale Mining District intending to refill their small shared canteen at the spring 25 mi (40 km) away. Beaten down by the heat, the friend turned back and survived. Riley pressed on and died on July 4, 1905, within 200 yards (180 m) of the spring. Your access is a lot easier today. Cottonwood Spring is located on a paved road past the Cottonwood Campground in the vicinity of the Cottonwood Visitor Center.

★ Cholla Cactus Garden

Pinto Basin Rd.

Driving south through the endless landscape of the Pinto Basin, the Cholla Cactus Garden appears like an army of prickly planted teddy bears—their sheer numbers impress in this already surreal landscape. Though these cacti may look fuzzy, their multicolored arms are effective against predators. Urban legend-style photos show hapless visitors covered in cholla (a.k.a. jumping cactus), with segments that have attached themselves to those who got too close. You'll be fine if you keep your hands to yourself and use common sense. A small parking area allows visitors to stop and wander the 0.3-mi (0.5-km) interpretive trail through a surreal crop of this strange flora. The trailhead for this nature walk is located 20 mi (32 km) north of the Cottonwood Visitor Center on Pinto Basin Road.

Scenic Drives

TOP EXPERIENCE

For a paved introduction to Joshua Tree National Park, drive Park Boulevard to access the park's highlights. If you want to get off the pavement, Joshua Tree has several rugged backcountry roads that are best for 4WD vehicles. Many of these roads make for some good biking routes as well. There are also graded dirt roads that still offer scenery and some seclusion but can be navigated by most passenger cars. Note that the speed limit on park roads is 45 mph (72 km/h) or lower.

HIDDEN VALLEY
Park Boulevard

Distance: *25 mi (40 km) round-trip*
Duration: *1-2 hours round-trip*
Start: *West Entrance*
End: *North Entrance*

1: Wonderland of Rocks **2:** Ryan Ranch **3:** Eureka Peak Overlook **4:** Cholla Cactus Garden

Road Surface: *Paved*
Vehicle: *Passenger*
Park Boulevard takes you through the park's most spectacular scenery in a 25-mi (40-km) loop beginning at the West Entrance in Joshua Tree and ending at the North Entrance in Twentynine Palms (you can also do this in reverse). You will pass the fantastical formations of the Wonderland of Rocks and have the opportunity to explore a number of short interpretive trails, some with picnic areas. A detour to Keys View affords a landscape panorama. If you only have a few hours or one day, this is your drive. The paved main road is also a good place to take road bikes.

QUEEN VALLEY
Barker Dam to Pine City

Distance: *3.6 mi (5.8 km) one-way via Queen Valley Road*
Duration: *10 minutes one-way*
Start: *Barker Dam trailhead*

End: *Pine City trailhead*
Road Surface: *Dirt*
Vehicle: *High clearance*

In Queen Valley, a series of short dirt roads crisscross each other, totaling 13.4 mi (21.6 km) to connect Barker Dam with the Pine City backcountry area. Steeped in ranching lore and Native American history, the Queen Valley area also gives rise to thick stands of Joshua trees. The one-lane dirt roads (**Queen Valley Road, Bighorn Pass Road,** and **O'Dell Road**) are accessible to most vehicles, though the narrow roads might make it a tight squeeze for passing. The dirt road is also good for mountain biking.

BLACK ROCK CANYON
Covington Flats

Distance: *10.9 mi (17.5 km) one-way*
Duration: *30 minutes one-way*
Start: *Hwy. 62*
End: *Eureka Peak*
Road Surface: *Dirt and sand*
Vehicle: *High clearance*

The series of dirt roads in Covington Flats gives access to the sweeping views from Eureka Peak, several hiking trails (including the Upper Covington Flats section of the California Riding and Hiking Trail), and some of the largest stands of Joshua trees, junipers, and piñon pines in the park. Covington Flats is situated between Black Rock Canyon and the town of Joshua Tree in the northwestern section of the park. Compared to other sections of the park, this area is lightly traveled and makes for some pleasant scenery-watching. The dirt road is also good for mountain biking.

To access Covington Flats, take La Contenta Road south from Highway 62 in Yucca Valley. A 10.9-mi (17.5-km) drive leads to Eureka Peak and spectacular views of Palm Springs, the Morongo Basin, and the San Jacinto Mountains. The Covington Flats area has signed intersections that make it easy to navigate; while there is occasional sand, the dirt roads are navigable by most cars despite some elevation gain near Eureka Peak. To reach **Eureka Peak,** follow La Contenta Road south from its intersection with Highway 62 in Yucca Valley; the road quickly turns to dirt. After driving 7.8 mi (12.6 km), look for a signed intersection that directs you right toward Eureka Peak. As the road begins to climb, continue straight to a picnic area and the trailhead access in 0.9 mi (1.4 km). At 9.6 mi (15.5 km), another right turn takes you to a small parking area within a few hundred yards of the peak. A left turn here leads south to Upper Covington Flats and access to the **California Riding and Hiking Trail.**

PLEASANT VALLEY
Geology Tour Road

Distance: *19 mi (31 km) round-trip*
Duration: *1-2 hours round-trip*
Start: *Park Boulevard*
End: *Park Boulevard*
Road Surface: *Dirt, with ruts and some sand*
Vehicle: *Passenger cars okay for the first 5 mi (8.1 km), then 4WD beyond*

Geology Tour Road is a pleasant 19-mi (31-km) backcountry drive that descends south into the broad Pleasant Valley and an ancient dry lake. Along the way it gives long views of the dramatic erosion and uplift that have formed Joshua Tree's unique geologic phenomena. This is a good road to take mountain bikes on as well. Pick up a free interpretive pamphlet from the Joshua Tree Visitor Center, which details the route with 16 numbered points of interest. Pamphlets are also available from a small metal box at the start of the drive.

Begin from a signed intersection on Park Boulevard about 2 mi (3.2 km) west of **Jumbo Rocks Campground.** The dirt road knifes south into Pleasant Valley, situated between the Hexie Mountains and Little San Bernardino Mountains. Sights along the way include stark **Malapai Hill,** distinct for its black basalt formation, and Pleasant Valley,

---

1: landscape in Black Rock Canyon 2: views of Malapai Hill and Pleasant Valley from the Geology Tour Road

1

2

with its heavily oxidized rocks (called desert varnish), and the Blue Cut earthquake fault.

As stark as the landscape may seem, the drive will take you past places that saw human—not just geologic—action. **Paac Küvühü'k** (Stop 9) was dammed with concrete by ranchers who were really just bolstering a watering source used by Native Americans in the area for centuries. **Pleasant Valley** (Stop 10) was once home to a periodic lake and cattle-ranching operation when the area was wetter and full of grasses, again on the site of land historically used by Indigenous groups. The steep Hexie Mountains are riddled with **mining shafts** (Stop 12) that date to the late 1800s and early 1900s.

The first 5 mi (8.1 km) of graded dirt road to Paac Küvühü'k are passable by most cars (no RVs) during dry weather. (During wet weather, don't go beyond Paac Küvühü'k in any vehicle, as the road can become flooded or impassable.) Beyond Paac Küvühü'k, the road is labeled **4WD only** by the National Park Service due to deep ruts, sand, and steep grades. There are some rough spots, but you may be able to handle the drive in a compact SUV, depending on your back road driving experience and the current road conditions. Past Paac Küvühü'k, the road completes a one-way loop clockwise along the Hexie Mountain foothills and through Pleasant Valley. From this point you're committed to the drive, a leisurely round-trip that can take up to **two hours.**

Berdoo Canyon Road (4WD)

Distance: 15.3 mi (25 km) one-way
Duration: 1 hour one-way point to point
Start: Berdoo Canyon Road
End: Dillon Road in the Coachella Valley
Road Surface: Dirt, paved last 5 mi (8.1 km) between park boundary and Dillon Road
Vehicle: 4WD

Stemming from the southern tip of the Geology Tour Road, Berdoo Canyon Road continues 15.3 mi (25 km) south to end beyond the park boundary at **Dillon Road** in the Coachella Valley. The unmaintained road heads through Pleasant Canyon and then navigates rugged Berdoo Canyon to the southern park boundary. Outside the park boundary, the final 3.9 mi (6.3 km) of the road passes the remains of **Berdoo Camp,** established for builders of the California Aqueduct in the 1930s. Berdoo Canyon Road requires **high-clearance 4WD.**

COTTONWOOD SPRING
Pinto Basin Road

Distance: 39 mi (63 km) one-way
Duration: 1 hour
Start: Cottonwood Visitor Center, South Entrance
End: Joshua Tree National Park Visitor Center, North Entrance
Road Surface: Paved
Vehicle: Passenger

Joshua Tree National Park is uniquely split across two deserts: the Mojave in the more popular northern section, characterized by the park's signature Joshua trees and monzonite granite boulders, and the Sonoran (or Colorado) Desert to the south, with austere broad valleys and washes—creosote and smoke trees dot the terrain. To beat the crowds and watch the drama of the landscape unfold slowly, start your drive at the park's South Entrance and Cottonwood Visitor Center. The paved highway cuts north through the arid Pinto Basin for 30 mi (48 km), with the Eagle Mountains to the east and Hexie Mountains to the west. Look for the spindly talons of a large **ocotillo patch** and the deceptively fuzzy-looking cholla cactus garden at just under 20 mi (32 km) into your drive. Pinto Basin Road connects with Park Boulevard, the main park drive, at 30 mi (48 km). Continuing north, it is 9 mi (14.5 km) to the Joshua Tree National Park Visitor Center. The paved road is also a good place to take road bikes.

Old Dale Road (4WD)

Distance: 23 mi (37 km) one-way
Duration: 3-4 hours
Start: Pinto Basin Road
End: Old Dale Mining District

Road Surface: *Dirt*
Vehicle: *4WD*

The Old Dale Road begins at a signed intersection on Pinto Basin Road, 6.5 mi (10.5 km) north of Cottonwood Visitor Center. This rugged 23-mi (37-km) unmaintained jeep trail crosses the Pinto Basin for 11 mi (17.7 km), then crawls beyond the park boundary into the eastern hills of the Pinto Mountains and a nest of old mines that make up the **Old Dale Mining District.** (A number of side roads split off to these sites.) The Old Dale Mining District drew prospectors looking for gold from as early as 1881. At peak production in 1898, there were as many as 3,000 miners in the region. Production limped along on a small scale until 1939 and the outbreak of World War II. Today the historic mining district is located on Bureau of Land Management (BLM) land. The main road eventually spills north out onto Highway 62, about 15 mi (24 km) east of the town of Twentynine Palms. This road requires maps and planning. There is no cell service. Carrying a GPS tracker is recommended.

Black Eagle Mine Road (4WD)

Distance: *9.5 mi (15.3 km) one-way*
Duration: *2-3 hours round trip*
Start: *Pinto Basin Road*
End: *Black Eagle Mine*
Road Surface: *Dirt with some sand then rocks*
Vehicle: *4WD*

The Black Eagle Mine Road shares its start with the Old Dale Road off Pinto Basin Road, 6.5 mi (10.5 km) north of the Cottonwood Visitor Center. The road strikes east across the Pinto Basin and into the northwest Eagle Mountains, where it ends at a barricade at the park boundary at just over 9 mi (14.5 km). The road continues beyond the barricade on BLM land near several old mining sites.

Sports and Recreation

TOP EXPERIENCE

HIKING

Joshua Tree offers fantastic hiking in an otherworldly landscape. The park has a range of hikes from easy nature trails to difficult cross-country adventures. Some of the longer trails lend themselves to backpacking (all backpackers overnighting in the backcountry must self-register for a free permit at any backcountry board). For an overview of JTNP trails visit www.nps.gov/jotr/planyourvisit/hiking.htm and download the NPS app for offline maps and additional information.

Regardless of trail length, dehydration is the biggest risk factor while hiking in Joshua Tree. Always carry at least **2 gallons (9 liters) of water per day per person,** especially during strenuous activities, and plan your hike to coincide with cooler times of the day, such as early morning or late afternoon.

Joshua Tree can be a confusing place for hikers because some trails are not well marked, and hikers veer off trail or follow washes instead of trails. Over time, as more people follow these detours, the correct trail can become more difficult to follow. Always follow signs posted by the National Park Service. Also, look for barriers made of natural materials like a line of rocks or a fallen Joshua tree. The park service uses these to maintain trails.

Hidden Valley

This is the most popular area of the park, as it includes access to Queen Valley, Hidden Valley, Quail Springs, and the Wonderland of Rocks. Expect filled parking lots and plenty of company on the trails.

North View Maze Loop

Distance: *6.4 mi (10.3 km) round-trip*
Duration: *4 hours*
Elevation gain: *400 ft (122 m)*

North View Maze Loop

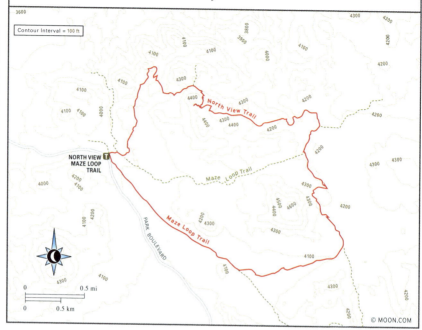

Effort: Moderate
Information and Maps: www.nps.gov/places/north-view-trailhead.htm
Trailhead: Small dirt parking area on the left 1.7 mi (2.7 km) south of the West Entrance. It gives access to the North View, Maze Loop, Window Rock, and Big Pine trails.
Directions: From the West Entrance Station, take Park Boulevard 1.7 mi (2.7 km) south to a small dirt parking area on the left (east) side of the road.

This hike combines the North View and Maze Loops for a spectacular loop trail through fantastical boulder formations, Joshua tree forest, craggy viewpoints, desert wash, and past a window rock. It is also lightly traveled compared to more popular hikes, so add solitude to the mix of reasons to hike here. The trail starts out in a wash heading north toward low hills and a signed intersection. Head left (north) to follow the North View Trail. The trail leaves the wash to wind into the hills, and you are quickly transported to a secluded rock amphitheater surrounded on all sides by towering formations. A few dips in the cracked rock walls allow for glimpses of the desert below. Two spur trails, Copper Mountain View and West Hills, at about 1.7 mi (2.7 km), allow you to catch more views both north and south into the park.

The trail winds down to a deep wash at 2.5 mi (4 km). Cross it and be on the lookout for a signed intersection at 2.7 mi (4.3 km). Here, head right toward the Loop Trail. The next section continues generally south until it reaches the maze. Here the trail cuts directly through rectangular slabs of rock to emerge on flat desert floor on the other side.

Your next landmark will be Window Rock, a prominent peak in front of you as you continue south. Keep looking up and you will see the eagle-shaped hole in the mountain, only visible from a distance. At an intersection, turn right to head west to continue the loop back to the parking area. (Continuing straight adds 1.9 mi/3.1 km as it loops around Window Rock.) The remaining stretch is an enjoyable flat walk through sparse Joshua Tree desert.

Quail Springs Historic Trail

Distance: *6 mi (9.7 km) round-trip*
Duration: *3 hours*
Elevation gain: *243 ft (74 m)*
Effort: *Moderate*
Information and Maps: *www.nps.gov/places/quail-springs-picnic-area.htm*
Trailhead: *Quail Springs Picnic area; look for an unmarked eroded trail on the west side of the paved parking area.*
Directions: *From the West Entrance Station, take Park Boulevard 5.9 mi (9.5 km) south to signed Quail Springs.*

Quail Springs Historic Trail, as it is named on some topo maps, strikes out through peaceful open desert, intersecting with historic routes like the Johnny Lang Canyon (Lang was the original claim-holder for the Lost Horse Mine) and connecting with a network of trails that extend to the park's West Entrance. It is also used to access **Quail Mountain,** the highest peak in Joshua Tree National Park at 5,814 ft (1,772 m).

The first 3 mi (4.8 km) of the trail to the base of Quail Mountain are peaceful and open, crossing what looks like a grassy plain that doesn't necessarily fit into our ideas of boulder-strewn Joshua Tree. The silvery husks of downed Joshua trees burned in a fire further add to the prehistoric savanna feel. The silence is punctuated by the occasional sound of a bird or a car along Park Boulevard, the main road within distant sight for most of the hike, making this place feel that much more secret.

From the picnic area, the trail is clearly defined. One mi (1.6 km) in, the route splits with **Quail Springs wash,** and footprints are visible in both forks. Although the wash (right) will take you in generally the same direction as the trail (due west), the going is easier on the trail. Take the left fork to continue. At 2

mi (3.2 km), the trail crosses the access route to **Johnny Lang Canyon,** veering off to the south (left). Continue straight.

At 2.9 mi (4.7 km) you reach signs indicating that the area used to be **private property.** An out-of-place weathered parking curb as well as sun-silvered timber and metal odds and ends are strewn about. A pile of boulders a few hundred yards to the north marks the site of the 1920s **homestead of John Samuelson,** a Swedish immigrant who was ultimately denied his homestead claim in 1928 by the US land office because of his Swedish heritage. His house burned down in the 1930s.

This is a good turnaround point, or you can continue to Quail Mountain or to eventually intersect with Park Boulevard near the West Entrance. Note: To continue along the Quail Springs Trail requires maps, planning, and possibly a car shuttle at the other end.

★ Lost Horse Mine

Distance: *4-7.4 mi (6.4-11.9 km) round-trip*
Duration: *2-4 hours*
Elevation gain: *450-570 ft (137-174 m)*
Effort: *Moderate to strenuous (very steep, rocky grades climbing Lost Horse Mountain)*
Trailhead: *Far end of the dirt parking area at the end of Lost Horse Mine Road*
Information: *www.nps.gov/jotr/planyourvisit/hiking.htm*
Directions: *From Park Boulevard, take Keys View Road south for 2.4 mi (3.9 km). Turn left onto the signed Lost Horse Mine Road and follow it for 0.9 mi (1.4 km) to the parking area.*

One of the best-preserved mining sites in Joshua Tree National Park, the beautifully weathered stamp mill at the Lost Horse Mine was in operation from 1894 to 1931. The mill's breadth and sturdy construction are a testament to the mine's success as one of the highest producing in Joshua Tree history. The first person to file a claim was Johnny Lang of local lore who, in Wild West campfire tale fashion, had recently had his horses stolen by a gang of local cattle rustlers. The mill and surrounding ruins (look for rock house foundations,

Lost Horse Mine

equipment, and mining tunnels) are the highlight of the out-and-back hike, but the loop offers more surprises and history.

The signed loop trail is located in the middle of the parking lot and directs hikers counterclockwise. The trail climbs (gradually at first and then steeper at 2.5 mi/4 km) around the flank of stark **Lost Horse Mountain** through a mix of Joshua trees, yucca, and juniper, following an old mining road. On the way it crosses paths with the **Optimist Mine;** only a picturesque stone chimney and scattered artifacts remain. Beyond these ruins the trail climbs precipitously, giving way to sweeping views toward the northeast, Wonderland of Rocks, and Queen Valley. At 4.7 mi (7.6 km) the rocky trail hits the ridge below the Lost Horse Mountain Summit, and the **Lost Horse Mine** comes into view below. Take time to check out the area. Although the mill and tunnels are fenced off, remains of rock houses and artifacts make this an interesting place to explore. You've done the hard work—the way back is mostly downhill with pleasant views looking toward Lost Horse Valley. Keep an eye out for additional rock structure remains and mining artifacts.

★ Willow Hole Trail

Distance: *7 mi (11.3 km) round-trip*
Duration: *3-4 hours*
Elevation gain: *Negligible*
Effort: *Moderate*
Trailhead: *Keys West Wilderness backpacking board, off Park Boulevard, 0.6 mi (1 km) east of the Quail Springs picnic area*
Information: *www.nps.gov/thingstodo/hike-willow-hole.htm*
Directions: *From the West Entrance Station, take Park Boulevard 6.5 mi (10.5 km) to the Keys West Wilderness backpacking board trailhead parking.*

The Willow Hole Trail strikes into the heart

Mining History

Word association for visitors to Joshua Tree National Park may evoke spiky Joshua trees, giant boulders, rock climbing, and otherworldly scenery; however, the region also has its share of mining history. Most of us know that the gold rush in California began in 1849, but when the gold began to play out in the Sierra Nevada, prospectors fanned into the deserts.

Mining activity began in the 1870s and peaked in the 1920s and 1930s. Joshua Tree became a national monument in 1936, putting a slowdown on mining as sites came under the protection of the National Park Service. All the usual desert problems, including hot summers, scarce water, limited wood for fuel, and the remoteness of the region made it difficult to get provisions and equipment in and out and to sustain mining operations, even though there was gold in the hills. Gold was the main commodity here, and some hardy souls persevered in finding it. Nearly 300 mines (288 by one scholarly study) were developed in the area that is now

stamp mill at Lost Horse Mine

Joshua Tree National Park. Few of the mines were good producers, and many of these sites are humble and fading back into the desert, marked by mining tunnels, tailings, rusted can dumps, and cleared flat tent sites miners once called home. However, you can visit some of the park's best-preserved sites, with colorful histories, weathered structures, and scattered artifacts all set against the rugged scenery of Joshua Tree's washes and peaks.

WHERE TO SEE MINING HISTORY

- A 4-mi (6.4-km) round-trip hike along the old mining road takes you to the impressive remains of the **Lost Horse Mine,** including a well-preserved stamp mill that once boomed out 24 hours a day as gold and silver ore was crushed (page 45).

- With parts scavenged from the old mining site of Pinyon Well in Pleasant Valley, local rancher Bill Keys used the **Wall Street Mill** to mill ore for different miners in the area. A colorful collection of equipment and junk awaits along this 3-mi (4.8-km) round-trip hike (page 49).

- A series of suspect circumstances landed the ownership of the **Desert Queen Mine** into the hands of an infamous local cattle rustler before rancher Bill Keys ended up with it. Access the picturesque gold mine ruins from a short trail (page 52).

- The biggest drama surrounding the **Mastodon Mine** may be the striking views across the Cottonwood Mountains from this windswept gold mine. The mine is unique for its access to water at nearby Cottonwood Spring, used to feed the mine's processing at the **Winona Mill.** Cottonwoods and other nonnative species at the site mark this time in history (page 61).

of the Wonderland of Rocks. The flat, sandy track and lack of elevation gain mean that your main job is to admire the spectacular scenery. At 1.2 mi (1.9 km) the trail splits at a signed intersection. The left fork continues as the **Boy Scout Trail,** ending at the **Indian Cove Campground** in another 6.4 mi (10.3 km). Most people hike the Boy Scout Trail as a shuttle hike with a car at either end. To continue on the Willow Hole Trail, stay to the right. The trail officially ends unceremoniously in 3.5 mi (5.6 km) in a sandy, boulder-filled wash at so-named **Willow Hole.** As you may have guessed, Willow Hole itself is

Willow Hole Trail

marked by a stand of willow trees. Depending on seasonal rains, the area can be filled with ephemeral pools of water.

Boy Scout Trail

Distance: *8 mi (12.9 km) one-way (arrange a car shuttle at one end)*
Duration: *4-5 hours*
Elevation gain: *1,265 ft (386 m), mostly downhill*
Effort: *Moderate*
South Trailhead: *Keys West Wilderness backpacking board, off Park Boulevard, 0.6 mi (1 km) east of the Quail Springs picnic area*
North Trailhead: *Indian Cove Backcountry Board, near the Indian Cove Ranger Station*
Information: *www.nps.gov/thingstodo/hike-boy-scout-trail.htm*
Directions: *From the West Entrance Station, take Park Boulevard 6.5 mi (10.5 km) to the Keys West Wilderness backpacking board trailhead parking.*

This scenic 8-mi (12.9-km) trail skirts the western edge of the Wonderland of Rocks before it winds through sharp mountains and rocky canyons to end in open desert at the Indian Cove Backcountry Board. With the shifting landscape and elevation along the Boy Scout Trail, the plant zones transition so that you have the chance to move through classic Joshua tree forest and mesquite, piñon, and oak at the higher elevations, yucca and boulder gardens, and creosote and cholla at the lower altitudes. This hike is the most popular overnight backpacking hike in the park. The Wonderland of Rocks to the east is a day-use area only: Campsites must be west of the Boy Scout Trail and require an advance permit. Sections of the trail are indistinguishable or unmarked, especially through washes. Carry a topo map.

The trail begins as a pleasant stroll through Joshua trees along a well-defined sandy track along the western edge of the Wonderland of

Rocks. At 1.3 mi (2.1 km) the trail splits with the **Willow Hole Trail.** Follow the signed junction to the left.

From here the trail climbs slightly before leveling on a high plateau, and the vegetation transforms with piñon, juniper, oak, and cholla cactus. At 3.8 mi (6.8 km) the trail continues into an open wash marked by a **signpost.** For the next 0.5 mi (0.8 km) the trail can be hard to follow through a series of washes. You'll pass a split with the **Big Pine Trail** on your left at 4 mi (6.4 km). Beyond the split, watch for an old concrete cattle trough as a landmark.

The trail exits the wash on the left at 4.4 mi (7.1 km) and winds to the head of a deep canyon with austere desert views. From here the trail descends steeply to the canyon floor and heads right into the wash. Follow the rugged canyon for 1 mi (1.6 km), heading northeast. Yuccas and barrel cactus line your way.

Exit the canyon at 6.2 mi (10 km), bearing right at a signpost. The trail spills into an open bajada. The final leg of the trail crosses open desert to end at the **Indian Cove** Backcountry Board.

Hidden Valley

Distance: 1 mi (1.6 km) round-trip
Duration: 30 minutes
Elevation gain: 20 ft (6 m)
Effort: Easy
Trailhead: Hidden Valley Campground and picnic area, 1.3 mi (2.1 km) north of Barker Dam Road
Information: www.nps.gov/places/hidden-valley-trailhead.htm
Directions: From the West Entrance Station, take Park Boulevard 8.7 mi (14 km). Turn right for 0.3 mi (0.5 km) to the Hidden Valley parking area.

This 1-mi (1.6-km) loop passes through granite boulders to emerge in scenic Hidden Valley, once wetter and grassier and used for cattle grazing during the ranching halcyon of the early-mid-1900s. The well-signed trail circles the small enclosed valley, delving into the monzogranite **boulder piles** with tempting bouldering opportunities.

Barker Dam

Distance: 1.3 mi (2.1 km) round-trip
Duration: 30 minutes
Elevation gain: Negligible
Effort: Easy
Trailhead: Barker Dam parking area; alternate Echo T parking area
Information: www.nps.gov/jotr/planyourvisit/barker-dam-trail.htm
Directions: From the West Entrance Station, take Park Boulevard 8.7 mi (14 km) to Intersection Rock, and turn left toward signed Hidden Valley Campground, Keys Ranch, and Barker Dam. Follow the road 1.5 mi (2.4 km) to the Barker Dam parking area.

Located on the southern edge of the Wonderland of Rocks, the popular 1.3-mi (2.1-km) loop trail winds through boulders to a small pond that can be dry at certain times of year. Ranchers dammed the natural pond for cattle, taking advantage of a site used by Native Americans for centuries. The trail is well marked and easy to follow.

The watering hole is now a stop for migrating birds, bighorn sheep, and other wildlife. This area is also home to the **Disney petroglyphs.** During shooting for a film in the 1960s, a film crew painted over existing Native American petroglyphs to make them more dramatic for the shoot, possibly adding some of their own—a cultural travesty.

Wall Street Mill

Distance: 3 mi (4.8 km) round-trip
Duration: 1.5 hours
Elevation gain: 23 ft (7 m)
Effort: Easy
Trailhead: Barker Dam parking area; alternate Echo T parking area; trailhead for the Wall Street Mill is clearly signed.
Information: www.nps.gov/thingstodo/hike-wall-street-mill.htm
Directions: From the West Entrance Station, take Park Boulevard 8.7 mi (14 km) to Intersection Rock, and turn left toward signed Hidden Valley Campground, Keys Ranch, and Barker Dam. Follow the road 1.5 mi (2.4 km) to the Barker Dam parking area.

When local rancher Bill Keys wanted to build a mill for processing ores from local

Hidden Valley Trail

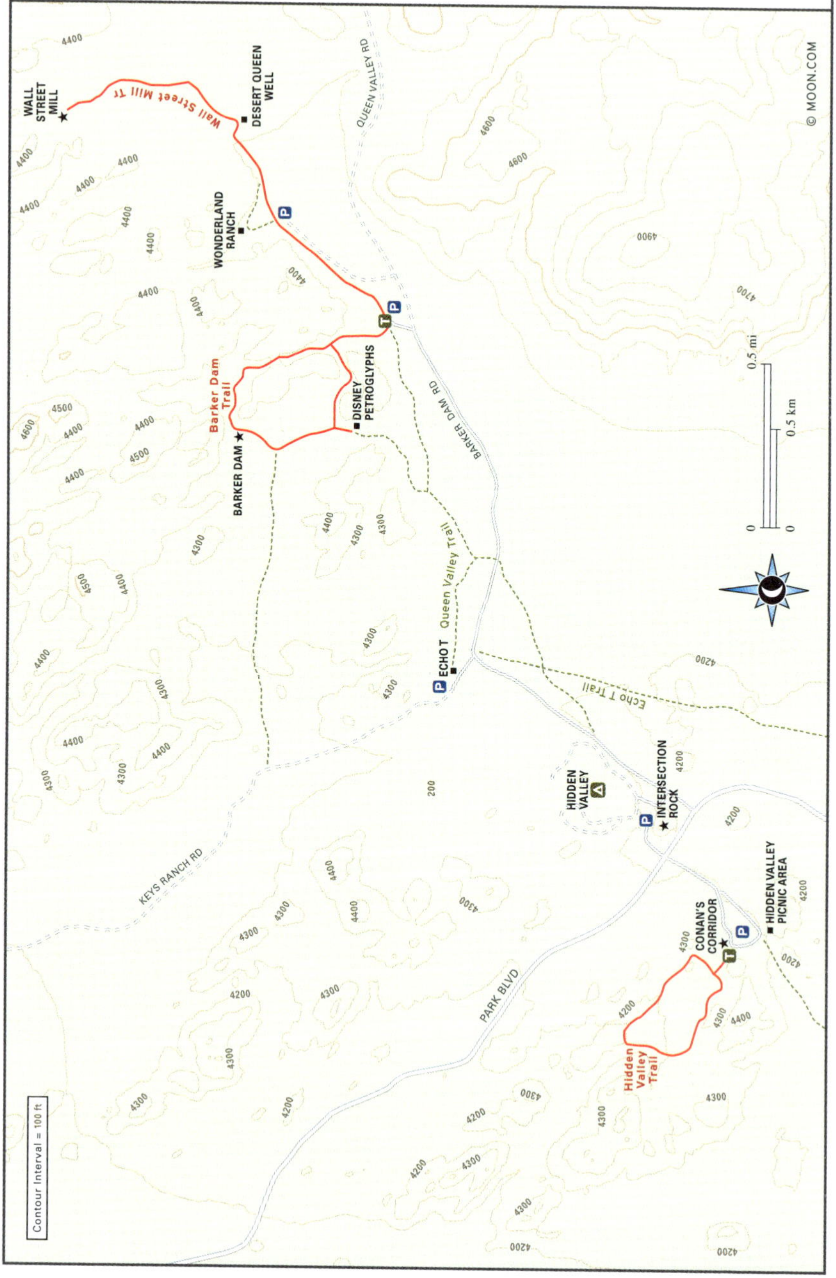

JOSHUA TREE NATIONAL PARK
SPORTS AND RECREATION

© MOON.COM

Contour Interval = 100 ft

mines, he scrounged an existing one and relocated it, tapping into the time-honored desert tradition of moving defunct mining cabins and structures to new, profitable locations. The mill was originally located at Pinyon Well and had been in operation since 1891. Keys rebuilt the mill and used it from 1932 to 1942 to mill ore for different miners in the area. The mill was used briefly in 1949 and again as late as 1966. When Keys died, the National Park Service took over the mill site and has done an excellent job of preserving it. In addition to the mill, you'll find abandoned cars and other equipment and artifacts. The site also used to house a bunkhouse, now gone.

To get to the mill, begin at the marked trailhead for the Wall Street Mill in the Barker Dam parking area. The trail veers east, clearly marked with stone trail boundaries and occasional arrows. In 0.3 mi (0.5 km) the trail hits a second, smaller parking lot then picks up again on the left. At 0.5 mi (0.8 km) an unexpected psychedelic pink marks the remains of the **Wonderland Ranch,** tempting exploration. A short side trip will lead you to the foundations, crumbling walls, and scattered artifacts of the ranch.

Another historic bonus awaits in the form of the **Desert Queen Well** ruins 1 mi (1.6 km) into the hike. A tall windmill, once used to pump water, still stands over piles of weathered timbers and an old tank.

The **Wall Street Mill** is definitely the highlight. Leave time to admire the well and poke around the area.

Wonderland Wash

Distance: 2 mi (3.2 km) round-trip
Duration: 1 hour
Elevation gain: 75 ft (23 m)
Effort: Moderate
Trailhead: Barker Dam parking area; alternate Echo T parking area. Begin at the signed trailhead for the Wall Street Mill.
Directions: From the West Entrance Station, take Park Boulevard 8.7 mi (14 km) to Intersection Rock, and turn left toward signed Hidden Valley Campground,

Keys Ranch, and Barker Dam. Follow the road 1.5 mi (2.3 km) to the Barker Dam parking area.

A use trail past the Wonderland Ranch cuts into the Wonderland of Rocks via a secluded wash and ends at the **Astro Domes,** an impressive pair of granite monoliths popular with rock climbers. Begin at the signed trailhead for the Wall Street Mill. At 0.5 mi (0.8 km), an unexpected crumbling pink structure marks the scattered remains and crumbling walls of the Wonderland Ranch. To the left of the ruins, an unmaintained trail heads east through low boulders into the wash. On the other side, the trail follows the wash northeast. Although the trail dries up at times, follow the wash. You will occasionally have to scramble over low boulders or work your way through foliage. At 0.3 mi (0.5 km) into the wash, cross the remains of a stone dam used by cattle ranchers. Continuing up the wash, you are surrounded by thriving desert vegetation and the striking rock formations of the Wonderland of Rocks. At 1 mi (1.6 km), look for the giant dome of white tank granite, outstanding for its monolithic uncracked state in this maze of jumbled boulder piles. The trail dwindles beyond this, but it is possible to continue deeper into the Wonderland of Rocks. Otherwise, return the way you came.

Pine City Site

Distance: 3 mi (4.8 km) round-trip to Pine City; 4 mi (6.4 km) round-trip to overlook of Pine Canyon
Duration: 2 hours
Elevation gain: 150 ft (46 m)
Effort: Moderate
Trailhead: Pine City/Desert Queen Mine parking area
Information and Maps: www.nps.gov/thingstodo/hike-pine-city-trail.htm
Directions: From the West Entrance Station, take Park Boulevard 8.7 mi (14 km) to the intersection with Desert Queen Mine Road. Turn left on Desert Queen Mine Road for 1.3 mi (2.1 km) to the Pine City/Desert Queen Mine parking area.

"Site," not "city," is the operative word here. Pine City is long gone, marked by piñons and a few scattered mining tunnels. The highlights

JOSHUA TREE NATIONAL PARK
SPORTS AND RECREATION

of this hike are the easy open trail winding through classic Mojave Desert flora, picturesque boulders, and its location off the beaten path of Park Boulevard.

The trail starts at the end of the graded dirt Queen Valley Road, and although the trailhead is less than 1 mi (1.6 km) from Park Boulevard, it offers more solitude than some of the more popular nearby hikes. The trail gains slight elevation as it heads toward the **Pine City site** (1.5 mi/2.4 km) or the **Pine Canyon overlook** (2 mi/3.2 km). The slight elevation makes this an easy desert trek but also gives rise to shifts in desert vegetation along the way. Hearty desert creosotes give way to yuccas and Joshua trees and eventually junipers and piñons. Cholla and barrel cacti also spike the landscape. At 1.3 mi (2.1 km) you'll see your first pine trees interspersed in a picturesque bay of stacked monzonite boulders. The "city" itself is also marked by these pines at 1.5 mi (2.5 km). Here the trail splits slightly with the left (main) fork continuing another 0.5 mi (0.8 km) to an overlook on the edge of Pine Canyon. The trail down into the canyon is unmaintained beyond the overlook. The right fork continues the extra few hundred yards to Pine City proper.

Desert Queen Mine and Wash

Distance: *1-7 mi (1.6-11.3 km) round-trip*
Duration: *1-5 hours*
Elevation gain: *160-660 ft (49-201 m)*
Effort: *Easy to strenuous*
Trailhead: *Pine City/Desert Queen Mine parking area*
Directions: *From the West Entrance Station, take Park Boulevard 8.7 mi (14 km) to the intersection with Desert Queen Mine Road. Turn left on Desert Queen Mine Road for 1.3 mi (2.1 km) to the Pine City/Desert Queen Mine parking area.*

This steep, rugged wash in Queen Valley saw a lot of mining action from the 1890s until the 1960s. A short trek to the Desert Queen Mine reveals the rust-varnished equipment, mining tunnels, and massive tailings of a successful California gold mine. Continuing down the wash turns up more scattered mining debris and, eventually, scant remains of other,

meaner mining camps, never as rich as the Desert Queen, hinting at a harsh life for miners scraping out a living.

To reach the Desert Queen Mine, take the **unsigned trail** from the Pine City parking area. At 0.3 mi (0.5 km) are the picturesque remains of a **miner's stone cabin** on the right. Continuing straight, you will soon reach an overlook. This is a great stop or a destination. From the overlook, you can see across the wash to the mines on the hillside and the old road snaking along the rocky embankment. Tailings, the huge piles of silvery rock excavated from the mining tunnels, are mounded, monuments to mining, on the wash floor.

To get a closer look at the **Desert Queen Mine's** equipment and tunnels, backtrack to the stone house and follow the road down into the wash and then back up to the mining site.

If this didn't satisfy your itch for exploration, a rugged hike through the wash brings you to a much smaller mining site. From the top of the Desert Queen Mine, return to the wash and turn right (north) to continue exploring the wash. After a few hundred yards, the canyon jogs and the hike trends generally east. The sandy-floored canyon is wild and scenic, with steep walls, clusters of boulders, and scattered mining debris, testament to the power of desert floods. **Two boulder jams** block your way, but they are passable by use trails. After the second boulder jam, the wash widens, and you'll see tailings from the **Gold Hill Mine.** The miners' small tent community of John's Camp was located on a long, low shelf on the right side 3 mi (4.8 km) from your starting point in the wash below the Desert Queen Mine. Return the way you came.

Lucky Boy Vista

Distance: *3.6 mi (5.8 km) round-trip*
Duration: *2 hours*
Elevation gain: *150 ft (46 m)*
Effort: *Moderate*
Trailhead: *Pine City/Desert Queen Mine parking area. Trailhead is unsigned at the south end of the parking area, on the right just past the parking entrance.*

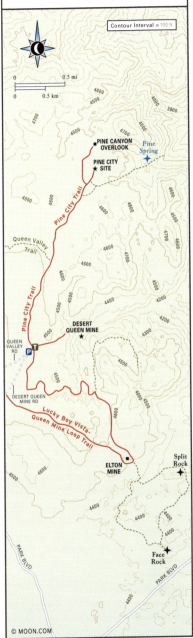

Information: www.nps.gov/places/lucky-boy-loop-trailhead.htm

Directions: From the West Entrance Station, take Park Boulevard 8.7 mi (14 km) to the intersection with Desert Queen Mine Road. Turn left on Desert Queen Mine Road for 1.3 mi (2.1 km) to the Pine City/Desert Queen Mine parking area.

What makes the Lucky Boy Vista such a nice hike is its combination of views, Native American history, mining history, solitude, and the pleasant walk through boulder-strewn desert piñon and yucca gardens. Heads up: There are a number of use trails, old mining roads, and washes crossing this area near the Desert Queen Mine, so it is easy to veer off your route if you're not paying attention. Carry a map and compass and know how to use them.

Start from the Pine City/Desert Queen Mine parking area. The sandy trail is clearly defined but unmarked. It starts by heading south and then curves through a series of washes lined with striking stacked rock formations. Look for signs of the Native American village that once inhabited this site in the form of a pair of **morteros** (stones used to grind and process food) along this stretch. At 0.8 mi (1.3 km), the trail forks. The left (north) trail heads toward the Desert Queen Mine and Wash. Rock scrambling is required. To reach the Lucky Boy Vista, turn right (south) and follow the trail. Continue to head south-southeast over the next 1 mi (1.6 km). You will pass through a **gate,** a holdover from the era of mines and private property. Beyond the gate, the trail forks and begins to climb slightly. Take the left fork to follow the old mining road. The **Elton Mine site** is easily identifiable from its shuttered mining tunnels at about 1.5 mi (2.4 km). The trail continues past the mine site to pause on a lofty plateau with views of Split Rock—the **Lucky Boy Vista.** Follow the return trail.

At 2.6 mi (4.2 km) the trail forks at an easy-to-miss **No Camping post.** Stay straight (west) to complete the loop. Turning right will take you back to where you started the trail. At 3.1 mi (5 km) you will reach the **Desert**

Queen Mine Road. Turn right for the last 0.5 mi (0.8 km) to complete the loop.

Cap Rock

Distance: 0.4 mi (0.6 km) round-trip
Duration: 30 minutes
Elevation gain: Negligible
Effort: Easy
Trailhead: Parking area at intersection of Park Boulevard and Keys View Road
Information and Maps: www.nps.gov/jotr/learn/nature/cap-rock-trail.htm
Directions: From the West Entrance Station, take Park Boulevard 10.4 mi (16.7 km) to the intersection with Keys View Road. Turn left into the Cap Rock parking area.

At first glance the Cap Rock nature trail seems like just another gorgeous destination—a flat, easy trail leads through whimsically eroded boulder formations, most notably a flat cap-like rock balanced on top of a spectacular formation. But there are a few things that set this spot apart. First, it's **wheelchair-accessible.** The trail is wide, flat, and made of hard-packed sandy dirt. Second, although it may be hard to imagine with the paved parking area and interpretive signs, Cap Rock played backdrop to a rock and roll drama. In 1973, country rocker **Gram Parsons** died of a drug overdose at a motel in nearby Joshua Tree. His friends, trying to fulfill his wishes, brought his body out to Cap Rock and set it on fire so that he could be cremated in his beloved Joshua Tree. The site still attracts fans of the cult-famed rocker.

★ Ryan Mountain

Distance: 3 mi (4.8 km) round-trip
Duration: 1.5 hours
Elevation gain: 1,070 ft (326 m)
Effort: Moderate
Trailhead: Signed parking area on Park Boulevard east of Ryan Campground
Information: www.nps.gov/thingstodo/hike-ryan-mountain.htm
Directions: From the West Entrance Station, take Park Boulevard 12.2 mi (19.6 km) to the turnoff for Ryan Mountain.

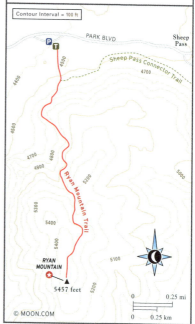

Although only 3 mi (4.8 km) round-trip, this trail climbs a little more than 1,000 ft (305 m) in elevation over its 1.5-mi (2.4-km) ascent to the summit. Hikers are rewarded with panoramic views from the 5,457-ft (1,663-m) wind-scoured vantage point where a **giant cairn** marks the peak. Soak in views of Pinto Basin, Hidden Valley, Wonderland of Rocks, and a bird's-eye view of Ryan Ranch and the Lost Horse Well. This is one of the most popular hikes in the park. While it's short on solitude, it's long on vistas.

Skull Rock

Distance: 1.7 mi (2.7 km) round-trip
Duration: 30 minutes-1 hour
Elevation gain: 157 ft (48 m)
Effort: Easy
Trailhead: Across from Jumbo Rocks Campground entrance or inside the campground, across from the amphitheater

Information: www.nps.gov/jotr/planyourvisit/skullrock.htm

Directions: From the West Entrance Station, take Park Boulevard 16.8 mi (27 km) to Park Boulevard parking near the Jumbo Rocks Campground entrance.

Skull Rock, anthropomorphically named for its gaunt eye socket-like depressions, is a popular rock formation along Park Boulevard. The concave hollows, called tafoni, originally began as small pits. Over time they cyclically filled with rainwater and eroded. After your photo op at the skull, follow the 1.7-mi (2.7-km) nature trail as it winds through the scenic boulder- and plant-strewn landscape. From the right side of the skull, the trail hooks over to **Jumbo Rocks Campground,** passing interpretive signs on desert ecology along the way. Turn right when you reach the campground. The trail follows the campground road until it intersects with Park Boulevard. It crosses the road to wind back through more boulders with views of the surrounding desert before it completes the loop at Skull Rock.

Arch Rock Nature Trail

Distance: 0.5 mi (0.8 km) round-trip
Duration: 30 minutes
Elevation gain: 30 ft (9 m)
Effort: Easy
Trailhead: Twin Tanks parking lot
Information: www.nps.gov/thingstodo/hikearchrock.htm
Directions: From the intersection of Park Boulevard and Pinto Basin Road, take Pinto Basin Road 2.3 mi (3.7 km) south to Twin Tanks parking lot.

The highlight of this trail is a delicately eroded arch tucked into a boulder pile formation in the first third of the loop. The trail is a lollipop shape beginning with a line heading east before it winds through **carved rock formations** then return to the starting point at Twin Tanks parking lot. Though the trail is short, several social trails split off from the official trail and can make it hard to follow. Pay attention to where you're going.

Split Rock Loop

Distance: 2 mi (3.2 km) round-trip

Duration: 1 hour
Elevation gain: 133 ft (41 m)
Effort: Easy
Trailhead: Split Rock picnic area
Information and Maps: www.nps.gov/jotr/learn/nature/split-rock-trail.htm
Directions: From the North Entrance Station in Twentynine Palms, head south for 6.7 mi (10.8 km). Turn right into the signed Split Rock picnic area and park in the parking and picnic area at the end of the road. The trail begins next to a giant split rock at the north (far) end of the parking lot.

The family-friendly Split Rock Loop Trail allows you to immerse yourself in the details of the landscape. The hike starts from a small picnic area and winds for 2 mi (3.2 km) through boulders and desert flora. Yucca, paddle cactus, and mesquite are interspersed with the boulders lining your pathway. Look for lizards sunning themselves on the sun-baked rocks.

Contact Mine

Distance: 4 mi (6.4 km) round-trip
Duration: 2-3 hours
Elevation gain: 516 ft (157 m)
Effort: Moderate
Trailhead: Unsigned trailhead on the right (west) side of road 0.5 mi (0.8 km) south of the North Entrance of the park
Information: www.nps.gov/thingstodo/hike-contact-mine.htm
Directions: From the North Entrance Station, take Park Boulevard 0.5 mi (0.8 km) south to an unsigned turnout on the right (west) side of the road.

The hike to the Contact Mine offers austere desert views, solitude, and a glimpse into the desert's mining history. The hike begins in a wide wash. Follow a series of red hiking signs to navigate this open sandy terrain. In a few hundred yards, the trail takes a more solid shape as the wash leads to a hard-packed, rock-lined trail. This is the remains of the old mining road, still clearly etched into the landscape as it cuts through the steep hills. The hike slowly gains in elevation with views of the Pinto Mountains to the east and craggy peaks running south from Twentynine Palms.

As the trail winds around each hill, you expect the mine to come into view. This feeling is even more pronounced since the trail is completely exposed. Hike early or in cooler weather. More than 1.5 mi (2.4 km) in, the mine finally comes into view on the hillside. It is a tantalizing sight. Enjoy this glimpse from a distance; the remains at the site are scant, but there is some machinery and debris from this old gold and silver mine dating to the early 1900s.

Indian Cove

★ 49 Palms Oasis

Distance: *3 mi (4.8 km) round-trip*
Duration: *2-3 hours*
Elevation gain: *360 ft (110 m)*
Effort: *Moderate*
Trailhead: *Parking area at the end of Canyon Road, about 1.7 mi (2.7 km) east of Indian Cove Road, off Highway 62*
Information and Maps: *https://visit29.org/joshua-tree-national-park/top-sights/49-palms-oasis*
Directions: *From Highway 62, turn right onto Canyon Road, signed for 49 Palms Oasis. (It is only signed heading east.) A small animal hospital on Highway 62 is a good landmark. Follow Canyon Road (signed for 49 Palms Oasis) for 1.7 mi (2.7 km) to the trailhead.*

This natural oasis surrounded by **native fan palms** secluded in a rocky canyon is a striking destination. From the trailhead, the trail climbs up over a ridge and then winds down through arid hills. The trail is easy to follow, passing through a flinty landscape that gives no indication of its secret oasis until you are close. You'll see the oasis from a distance, nestled against the jagged hills, before you reach it. There are only 158 fan palm oases in North America, and five in Joshua Tree; this is clearly a special place, used historically by Cahuilla Indians and offering precious habitat for bighorn sheep, quail, and coyotes. Tread lightly in this fragile ecosystem.

California Riding and Hiking Trail

The California Riding and Hiking Trail is a continuous **36-mi (58-km) trail system** cutting across piñon and juniper forests, Joshua tree stands, and creosote-strewn lowlands in the main western section of the park. Long on views and solitude, this trail can be hiked as a **three-day backpacking trip** or broken into smaller day or overnight hikes. For backpacking, you will want to cache water. You must register at designated backcountry boards if you plan to stay out overnight.

There are **six main trailheads** anchoring **five trail sections.** For thru-hiking, the trail is best hiked west to east.

- Section 1: **Black Rock Canyon Trailhead to Upper Covington Flats.** Starting from the Black Rock Canyon Campground, this 7.5-mi (12.1-km) section of the trail hooks through creosote lowlands before it climbs 1,000 ft (305 m), gaining the steepest elevation of the entire hike, to 5,130 ft (1,564 m). From here, the trail rolls downhill to Upper Covington Flats.

- Section 2: **Upper Covington Flats to Keys View.** This is the remotest section of the trail, and the trail here can be overgrown. Its 10.8 mi (17.4 km) traverse a series of washes and ridges offering panoramic views before descending into the Joshua tree groves of Juniper Flats and then the Lost Horse Valley to end at Keys View trailhead. Nearby Ryan Campground also provides trail access on the eastern end of this section.

- Section 3: **Ryan Ranch to Geology Tour Road.** This 6.5-mi (10.5-km) section of the trail veers close to the ruins of Ryan Ranch and the Lost Horse Well south of Ryan Mountain before climbing to the Geology Tour Road trailhead.

- Section 4: **Geology Tour Road to Pinto Basin.** From Geology Tour Road, the next section is the shortest, clocking in at 4.4 mi (7.1 km) to end up at the Pinto Basin Trailhead (Twin Tanks parking between

1: view from the top of Ryan Mountain **2:** Barker Dam **3:** 49 Palms Oasis **4:** abandoned car along the Wall Street Mill trail

Belle and White Tank Campground). Its manageable distance and light elevation gain make it a candidate for a day hike. Views of Jumbo Rocks and the Pinto Basin make it worth the effort.

- Section 5: **Pinto Basin to North Entrance.** The final 7.3-mi (11.8-km) stretch skirts Belle Campground and offers sweeping views of Twentynine Palms as it continues north to end just south of the north park entrance.

Black Rock Canyon
Hi-View Nature Trail

Distance: *1.3 mi (2.1 km) round-trip*
Duration: *1 hour*
Elevation gain: *320 ft (98 m)*
Effort: *Easy*
Trailhead: *Near Black Rock Campground*
Information and Maps: *www.nps.gov/jotr/ planyourvisit/black-rock-area-hiking.htm*
Directions: *Immediately before the entrance to Black Rock Campground, turn right onto a dirt road and drive 0.8 mi (1.3 km) to a parking area.*

For such a short trail, you'll be rewarded with panoramic views and desert knowledge. To hike the trail, follow the intermittently steep grade clockwise. Take in the sweeping views of the Yucca Valley to the northeast, Black Rock Canyon and campground to the south, and the San Bernardino Mountains to the west. See if you can spot the highest peak in the San Bernardino Mountains, snowcapped San Gorgonio Mountain at 11,503 ft (3,506 m).

The trailhead can also be reached from a spur trail connecting from the **Black Rock Ranger Station,** where interpretive brochures are available. The trailhead can also be reached by driving past the ranger station to a small parking area. Note that some maps show this trail as High View Nature Trail.

Panorama Loop

Distance: *6.6 mi (10.6 km) round-trip; 8.8 mi (14.2 km) round-trip to add Warren Peak*
Duration: *3-5 hours*
Elevation gain: *1,120 ft (341 m)*

Effort: *Strenuous*
Trailhead: *Black Rock Canyon Backcountry Board, or the southern end of the campground near site 30*
Information and Maps: *www.nps.gov/jotr/ planyourvisit/black-rock-area-hiking.htm*
Directions: *From Highway 62 in Yucca Valley, turn south onto Avalon/Palomar Avenue for 2.9 mi (4.7 km). Turn left onto Joshua Lane for 0.9 mi (1.4 km). Turn right and then left to follow San Marino Drive. San Marino becomes Black Rock Canyon Road. Follow Black Rock Canyon Road 0.3 mi (0.5 km) south of San Marino Road. Just before a split in the road, look for a small dirt parking area and the Black Rock Canyon Backcountry Board on the left, just past the campground entrance. Follow park signs.*

Hike this crown of peaks—five in all—and you'll be rewarded with sweeping views extending from the Salton Sea to Mount San Jacinto and the Yucca Valley. Starting from the well-marked trailhead, travel south along a sandy trail that can feel like walking on a desert beach. The trail splits at 0.3 mi (0.5 km); head right to follow a sign pointing toward **Black Rock Canyon.** For the next 0.5 mi (0.8 km), you'll hike Black Rock Wash through open desert and a Joshua tree forest framed by a serrated landscape of ridges and peaks. The trail is easy to follow but splits into smaller washes and use trails at times. Pay attention to official trail markers (**PL** for Panorama Loop; **WP** for Warren Peak), as well as stone boundaries that mark the trail.

At just under 2 mi (3.2 km), you'll reach the base of the foothills and **Black Rock Spring.** The spring usually does not have standing pools, but the ground may be damp. Oaks and other vegetation are abundant here (a good sign of water), and the area can be swarmed with flies, another giveaway. From Black Rock Spring, the trail narrows and cuts through the region's signature black rock formations.

At 2 mi (3.2 km) the trail splits at a **signed intersection.** A straight left continues into the first loop entrance to hike the Panorama Loop clockwise, but we are going to follow the loop counterclockwise. (The trail can be hiked in either direction, but hiking it counterclockwise gives you a slightly gentler grade

Black Rock Canyon

JOSHUA TREE NATIONAL PARK
SPORTS AND RECREATION

going uphill and a steeper hike downhill.) Stay right to reach the second loop entrance in 0.4 mi (0.6 km). From the **second intersection,** continuing straight (right) takes you to Warren Peak in 0.6 mi (1 km). If you're up for it, I highly recommend this 1.2-mi (1.9-km) round-trip detour to get the full eyeful and bragging rights. Six peaks in a day? Sure! If you're only following the Panorama Loop, this will be a left turn at the intersection.

The 3-mi (4.8-km) Panorama Loop begins by climbing a steady grade through the foothills, following the remains of an old road. The grade tops out at a sharp ridge with spectacular views to the southeast across the Coachella Valley—you can see all the way to the Salton Sea on a clear day. Across the valley to the southwest are the impressive San Jacinto Mountains and Mount San Jacinto. At 5,154 ft (1,571 m), this ridge marks the highest point in the hike (including Warren Peak).

From here the trail continues to be one big reward as you wind your way along four more peaks on an open ridge that gives you an eyeful far across the Yucca Valley. Once you've made your way back down to the canyon floor (6.6 mi/10.6 km), turn right to follow the Black Rock Canyon wash the final 2 mi (3.2 km) to the trailhead.

Warren Peak

Distance: 6.3 mi (10.1 km) round-trip
Duration: 3-5 hours
Elevation gain: 1,070 ft (326 m)
Effort: Strenuous
Trailhead: Black Rock Canyon Backcountry Board, or the southern end of the campground near site 30
Information and Maps: www.nps.gov/jotr/planyourvisit/black-rock-area-hiking.htm
Directions: From Highway 62 in Yucca Valley, turn south onto Avalon/Palomar Avenue for 2.9 mi (4.7 km). Turn left onto Joshua Lane for 0.9 mi (1.4 km). Turn right and then left to follow San Marino Drive. San Marino becomes Black Rock Canyon Road. Take Black Rock Canyon Road 0.3 mi (0.5 km) south of San Marino Road. Just before a split in the road, look for a small dirt parking area and the Black Rock Canyon Backcountry

Board on the left just past the campground entrance. Follow park signs.

At 5,103 ft (1,555 m), Warren Peak is the 10th-highest peak in the park. Considering that the highest peak, Quail Mountain, clocks in only 713 ft (217 m) higher at 5,814 ft (1,772 m), Warren Peak's ranking is more impressive than it might sound at first. The trail to Warren Peak manages to be a moderate hike with a huge view payoff.

Starting from the well-marked trailhead, follow the trail for the **Panorama Loop** (PL; see the previous hike) to the second intersection where it junctions with the trail to Warren Peak (WP). Stay right to continue to Warren Peak. At the next intersection at 2.4 mi (3.9 km), stay straight (right). You're only 0.6 mi (1 km) from Warren Peak, and it comes into clear view. The trail climbs steeply up to the knobby peak, where you're rewarded with panoramic views—the San Jacinto Mountains, Coachella Valley, Yucca Valley, and toward Hidden Valley and the Wonderland of Rocks in the heart of Joshua Tree. When you're done basking in the views, return the way you came. A use trail exiting the peak dead-ends at a ridge; pay attention to where you entered the peak.

Eureka Peak

Distance: 10 mi (16.1 km) round-trip
Duration: 4-5 hours
Elevation gain: 1,535 ft (468 m)
Effort: Strenuous
Trailhead: Black Rock Canyon Campground
Information and Maps: www.nps.gov/jotr/planyourvisit/black-rock-area-hiking.htm
Directions: From Highway 62 in Yucca Valley, turn south onto Avalon/Palomar Avenue for 2.9 mi (4.7 km). Turn left onto Joshua Lane for 0.9 mi (1.4 km). Turn right and then left to follow San Marino Drive. San Marino becomes Black Rock Canyon Road. Take Black Rock Canyon Road 0.3 mi (0.5 km) south of San Marino Road. Just before a split in the road, look for a small dirt parking area and the Black Rock Canyon Backcountry Board on the left just past the campground entrance. Follow park signs.

You definitely need to be in an "it's all about

the journey" mind-set to hike Eureka Peak. The journey is a pleasant one, leaving Black Rock Canyon to navigate a series of mountain canyons, finally arriving at Eureka Peak and its spectacular views of the San Jacinto Mountains and the Coachella Valley extending to the Salton Sea. However, after you've huffed and puffed your way to the top, you may be disappointed to find that a perfectly good dirt road, navigable by most vehicles, stops less than 0.2 mi (0.3 km) from the peak. The idea may dawn on you that you could have had those same spectacular views in a much easier way. The road is lightly traveled, and your chances of solitude on the peak are good no matter how you get there.

For hiking purposes, a network of trails spiderwebs out from Black Rock Canyon, giving you various routes for reaching Eureka Peak. Beginning from the Black Rock Canyon Backcountry Board, follow the **California Riding and Hiking Trail** (CA R&H) for the first 2 mi (3.2 km). It quickly leaves the wash to climb into the foothills. Ignore a trail split at 1.5 mi (2.4 km) to stay left on the CA R&H, climbing to an upper valley. At 1.9 mi (3.1 km), a signed junction indicates the **Eureka Peak Trail** (EP). Turn right to head up the wash. Continue to follow the main wash as it narrows and climbs, ignoring another junction at 2.3 mi (3.7 km). Intermittent signposts for the next 2 mi (3.2 km) indicate that you're on the right path. At 4.3 mi (6.9 km), the trail twists up to the peak, arriving at a ridge just below the summit at 4.9 mi (7.9 km). Turn left for the 5,518-ft (1,682 m) peak.

Retrace your steps when you're done basking in the views. It is also possible to turn the hike into a loop by taking **Covington Road** (the dirt road just south of the peak) to its intersection with the CA R&H. You can follow the CA R&H trail the whole way back to the Black Rock Canyon Backcountry Board.

Cottonwood Spring
Mastodon Peak
Distance: 3 mi (4.8 km) round-trip
Duration: 1.5-2 hours

Elevation gain: 375 ft (114 m)
Effort: Moderate
Trailhead: At a nature trail a few yards east of the Cottonwood Spring sign and staircase; campers follow a signed trail from the eastern end of Loop A.
Information: www.nps.gov/thingstodo/hike-mastodon-peak.htm
Directions: From the Cottonwood Visitor Center, continue 1.2 mi (1.9 km) southeast on the Cottonwood Campground road until it dead-ends at Cottonwood Spring.

Mastodon's rocky peak crowns this loop hike and affords dramatic desert views stretching toward the Eagle Mountains, San Jacinto Mountains, and as far as the Salton Sea. On the way, the preserved remains of the Mastodon Mine add some historical spice to the trail. The peak was named by miners for its resemblance to the prehistoric creature. If you spend enough time in the desert sun, it's possible you'll start to see dubious shapes in the rocks too.

The Mastodon Peak loop is very well signed and clearly established. It begins on a nature trail that leaves from the parking area and heads northwest to a junction at 0.5 mi (0.8 km). Turn right (left leads to the campground) to continue toward the base of the foothills. Just past the junction, concrete foundations mark the site of the old **Winona Mill.** From the base of the mountains, the trail climbs toward the peak and the remains of the **Mastodon Mine** clinging to the hillside below the peak at 1.4 mi (2.3 km). From the mine, there are sweeping views toward the west and the Cottonwood Mountains. George Hulsey operated the gold mine from 1919 to 1932. He was also responsible for building the Winona Mill, used to process ore from the Mastodon Mine and other claims to the north in the Dale Mining District. Continue the loop down the mountain. At the base of the hills the trail forks. To complete the loop, turn right (a left turn will take you to the Lost Palms Oasis in approximately 3 mi/4.8 km). The loop has a strong finish at scenic **Cottonwood Spring.** From the spring, follow the staircase up to the parking lot.

Cottonwood Spring

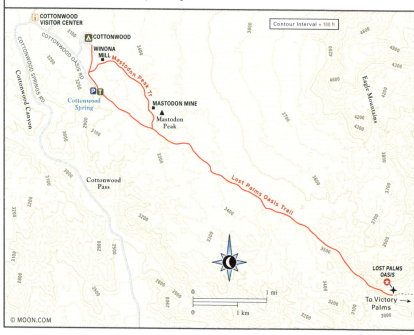

For a longer hike, combine a trip to the Lost Palms Oasis for a spectacular 9.5-mi (15.3-km) trek.

★ Lost Palms Oasis

Distance: 7.5 mi (12.1 km) round-trip
Duration: 4-5 hours
Elevation gain: 460 ft (140 m)
Effort: Moderate
Trailhead: At a staircase leading down to Cottonwood Spring; campers follow a signed trail from the eastern end of Loop A.
Information: www.nps.gov/places/lost-palms-oasis.htm
Directions: From the Cottonwood Visitor Center, continue 1.2 mi (1.9 km) southeast on the Cottonwood Campground road until it dead-ends at Cottonwood Spring.

This trail undulates through striking desert scenery before dropping down to a secluded canyon and the largest collection of fan palms in the park.

The trail is straightforward, making a beeline to the southeast along a well-marked and well-signed route. It starts from scenic **Cottonwood Spring** and ripples over an up-and-down landscape dominated by a series of ridges and washes. The trail is almost completely exposed, flanked by interesting desert gardens, including barrel cacti, ocotillos, and desert willows.

The trail edges into the foothills of the Eagle Mountains before emerging to overlook a steep canyon and the Lost Palms Oasis, tucked on a rugged canyon hillside. The name makes sense in this remote place. The Lost Palms Oasis is a watering hole for bighorn sheep and other wildlife. Over the next 100 yards (90 m), a steep trail continues to the boulder- and palm-strewn canyon floor. Shaded and peaceful, this is a great place to take a break before your return. If you're still feeling like exploring, continue to follow the trail down the canyon. One mi (1.6 km) of picking your way and rock scrambling will bring you to another fan palm stand—the **Victory Palms.**

For a longer hike, add the loop to Mastodon Peak and the Mastodon Mine (adds 2 mi/3.2 km) for a total 9.5-mi (15.3-km) hike.

BIKING

Biking within Joshua Tree National Park is confined to roads that are open to vehicles, but there are some good rides along the park's paved and backcountry roads.

Park Boulevard

For road biking, Park Boulevard offers a great route through the park's most spectacular scenery. The paved road runs 25 mi (40 km) from the West Entrance in Joshua Tree to the North Entrance in Twentynine Palms, with many opportunities for shorter stretches in between.

Pinto Basin Road

Pinto Basin Road, the other main park road, cuts through the Pinto Basin's open desert with scenery that's less rewarding than Park Boulevard but also more lightly traveled. It runs 30 mi (48 km) from its start 4 mi (6.4 km) south of the North Entrance.

Queen Valley

For mountain biking, the short series of dirt roads crossing Queen Valley (the Hidden Valley area between Barker Dam and the Pine City Backcountry Board) totals 13.4 mi (21.6 km) and offers scenic rides through large stands of Joshua trees. The **Geology Tour Road** stretches slightly downhill for its first 5.4 mi (8.7 km) to Paac Kṳv̤ṳhṳ'k; beyond this, it loops 9.8 mi (15.8 km) through Pleasant Valley for a total 20.6-mi (33-km) trip pavement to pavement. Be cautious as the road is sandy and rutted at points.

Bike Rentals

There are no bike rentals available in Joshua Tree National Park.

Joshua Tree Bicycle Shop

6416 Hallee Rd., Joshua Tree; 760/366-3377; www. joshuatreebicycleshop.com; 10am-6pm Wed.-Sun., check website for seasonal hours; $65 per day

Located near the West Entrance in the town of Joshua Tree, Joshua Tree Bicycle Shop is a full-service bike shop that rents bikes and offers repairs and ride recommendations.

TOP EXPERIENCE

★ ROCK CLIMBING

Joshua Tree National Park is famous for its large stands of Joshua trees and scenic desert landscape. Wildly eroded rocks make the park a world-class rock climbing destination. From rock stars to beginners, climbers of all levels are drawn to the park's traditional-style crack, slab, and steep-face climbing and its vast array of climbs. More than 400 climbing formations and more than 8,000 recognized climbs make it a world-class destination.

Climbing Areas

Joshua Tree's unique desert landscape drives thousands of visitors a year to tackle its signature monzogranite boulders and striking rock formations. When other climbing meccas like Yosemite are covered in winter snow and ice, climbers flock to the scene in "J-Tree" (as it's called by this adventure-driven subculture).

Joshua Tree as an international climbing destination built slowly, starting about a decade after it became a national monument in 1936. The first rock climbing groups were organized through the Sierra Club's rock climbing section and met casually to climb in Joshua Tree and nearby areas like Idyllwild. Through the 1950s and 1960s, some of the pioneers of the sport began testing the vertical geological expanses of the region, and themselves, as they sought a connection with the landscape away from mainstream civilization.

The action grew slowly, with these early pioneers establishing and naming first ascents and recording climbs. The gear also started to improve, initially designed and fabricated by climbers to sell out of their vans, some of whom went on to found companies like Black Diamond, Patagonia, and North Face. As the vertical frontier expanded, Joshua Tree established itself as the perfect winter climbing destination while the tight-knit climbing communities pushed to new heights. The community continues to evolve as climbers make the pilgrimage to Joshua Tree. Today, it's hard to go anywhere in the northwestern section of the park without seeing someone rock climbing. Here are a few spots where you can watch the action (or get in on it).

Quail Springs

The Quail Springs picnic area has another, more adventurous side. While families picnic at this scenic spot, rock climbers tackle popular formations like Trashcan Rock, Hound Rocks, and the White Cliffs of Dover. Trashcan Rock is the main draw, hosting a high concentration of easier routes (5.0-5.6) as well as a few moderate routes (5.7-5.9) and a few harder routes (5.10-5.11). The total elevation gain in the Quail Springs area is 3,976 ft (1,212 m).

Intersection Rock

Intersection Rock at the turnoff to Hidden Valley Campground is the most climbed rock in the park, with over 40 climbing routes. Routes range from beginner to expert level. Even if you are not rock climbing, it is a great place to watch the action. The total elevation gain is 4,195 ft (1,279 m).

Hidden Valley Campground

Hidden Valley Campground has a high concentration of quality routes, meaning you don't have to leave your campsite to experience some of Joshua Tree's finest. Hammocks, slacklines, and other horizontal ropes are not permitted in the campground. Hidden Valley Campground has 4,194 ft (1,278 m) of elevation potential.

Wonderland Wash

A use trail along the scenic Wonderland Wash in the Wonderland of Rocks region leads to the Astro Domes, a destination heavy on solitude, and a scenic 30-45-minute journey to reach the dual granite monoliths. Routes range from easy for beginners to very difficult for expert climbers (5.1-5.13) with 4,000 ft (1,220 m) of elevation gain. This is good place to get away from the crowds.

rock climbers on Joshua Tree's monzogranite boulders

Cap Rock

Cap Rock has a lot going for it: a place in rock and roll history (Gram Parsons), a good selection of routes for beginning climbers, a great boulder circuit, and some of the most classic boulder problems in Joshua Tree. Routes cover the large mass of Cap Rock as well as smaller features off the nature trail with 4,200 ft (1,280 m) of elevation.

Conan's Corridor

There are many classic climbing routes at the Jumbo Rocks Campground, but Conan's Corridor, a short walk northwest from the end of the loop, presents some interesting challenges.

Split Rock Region

While you can't climb the official Split Rock itself, the Split Rock region offers many routes next to an easy-to-access picnic area and loop trail.

Climbing Guides

To get in on the action as a first-timer or experienced climber looking to hone your skills, you may want to take a group class or a private guided climb through one of several outfitters in the area. Guides offer a range of experiences from half-day classes to private weekend trips. Guides' websites generally provide a good sense of their offerings and experience level expected. Adventures are customizable based on the experience level and the type of adventure you are seeking. Some experiences are suitable for children as young as three. Gear is provided. Meetup spots vary based on the program and guide service. Some meet at the Joshua Tree National Park Visitor Center while others meet inside the park boundaries at a specified meeting location. Guides provide detailed location instructions on booking. Visitors must have their own transportation to the climbing locations.

When booking, make sure your climbing guide is permitted to work in Joshua Tree National Park. Each guide is required to have certification through Professional Climbing Guides Institute (PCGI), American Mountain Guides Association (AMGA), or similar organization before getting a Commercial Use Authorization (CUA) permit to work in the park. They are also required to be certified in Wilderness First Aid and CPR as well as carry insurance. The guides below are permitted to work in Joshua Tree.

Mojave Guides

760/820-2806; www.mojaveguides.com; half-day $125-290 pp, full-day $180-420 pp

Mojave Guides offers a range of private instruction for individuals, small groups, and large groups in rock climbing and rappelling. Instruction is geared toward all ages and skill levels and covers basic technique, communication, and safe practices. They offer a separate advanced climbing program for experienced climbers. They also offer an inclusive rock-climbing program geared toward LGBTQ+ and nonbinary climbers. To get into Joshua Tree's famous eroded rocks in a different way, Mojave Guides also offers guided hikes and a hybrid hiking and rock scrambling program that explores the park's slot canyons and rock corridors. All necessary equipment is provided.

Cliffhanger Guides

760/401-5033; www.cliffhangerguides.com; 8am-6pm daily; half-day $145-315, full-day $205-420

Cliffhanger Guides offers custom guided rock climbing adventures, with half-day and full-day rates for up to 10 people. Each adventure is fully customized to suit different climbing abilities and adventure needs with experiences that range from play days to technical instruction. They work with everyone who wants to get out there, from beginner to experienced, ages 3-103. Rates include private instruction, all equipment, and gourmet lunch.

Stone Adventures

https://stone-adventures.com

Stone Adventures offers a range of

rock-climbing experiences from beginner to experienced, technical to adventure play days with no age limits. Courses include Gym to Stone, designed to transition climbers from the gym to the outdoors, as well as more technical courses covering trad and multi-pitch climbing. Stone Adventures also has a big family-friendly side, offering family adventure days and kids climbing events for children under age six. They provide kids' gear that includes high performance shoes, full-body harnesses made for shorter builds, and rock-climbing helmets that fit down to the age of one.

Joshua Tree Guides
www.joshuatreeguides.com; classes from $150, guided day trips from $115

Joshua Tree Guides offers daily rock-climbing classes as well as customized guide services. Guide services are offered for groups of 1-5 people. The most popular half-day service is geared toward a range of skills, from beginner to advanced. All necessary climbing gear is provided, including climbing shoes, harnesses, and helmets, and is included in the price. Classes are geared toward moderate-level climbers looking to build endurance, technique, and route-finding skills. Gear is provided for students who need it for the duration of the class.

Outfitters and Gear

To gear up for your rock climbing or other adventures, check out one of the outfitters located on the main drag in Joshua Tree, close to the intersection of Park Boulevard and Highway 62.

Nomad Ventures
61795 29 Palms Hwy., Joshua Tree; 760/366-4684; www.nomadventures.com; 8am-6pm daily

Nomad Ventures is the most extensively stocked of the Joshua Tree outfitters, with a huge selection of climbing gear, an assortment of camping and hiking gear, and a wide selection of guidebooks, including rock climbing guides.

Coyote Corner
6535 Park Blvd., Joshua Tree; 760/366-9683; www.jtcoyotecorner.com; 9am-6pm daily

Coyote Corner is eclectically stocked with gifts and gear ranging from T-shirts, jewelry, novelty items, and books to camping gear.

Climbing Resources
Publications

There are many great rock climbing guides sold in the park's visitor centers, as well as at outfitters outside the park. Classic guides include *The Trad Guide to Joshua Tree* by Charlie and Diane Winger and a number of guides by rock climber and author Randy Vogel (*Rock Climbing Joshua Tree, Rock Climbing Joshua Tree West*). More recent books on the market include *Joshua Tree Rock Climbs* by Robert Miramontes and Bob Gaines's *Best Climbs Joshua Tree National Park*.

Climber Coffee
Hidden Valley Campground; 8am-10am Sat.-Sun. mid-Oct.-Apr.

To keep an ear to the ground about closed routes and any other climbing info, Climber Coffee offers the opportunity to meet Joshua Tree's climbing ranger and share information with other climbers.

HORSEBACK RIDING

With more than 250 mi (403 km) of equestrian trails and trail corridors, horseback riding is a great way to experience Joshua Tree National Park.

Trail Rides
Knob Hill Ranch
760/821-7525; www.knobhillranch.com; $190-450 pp

Knob Hill Ranch offers guided private and group trail rides from their ranch, located less than 2 mi (3.2 km) from the park's Black Rock Canyon area. Riders explore the Black Rock Canyon area in a series of guided rides ranging 1.5-4 hours and suitable for intermediate to advanced riders. A 6-hour guided ride to Eureka Peak is suitable for intermediate to advanced riders. In summer, rides are scheduled for morning (8am) or evening (4pm-8pm), avoiding the afternoon heat. In winter, ride times are flexible. The ranch also offers lessons and custom trail rides. All equipment is provided.

Equestrian Camping

If you bring your own horse, two campgrounds offer equestrian camping with overnight areas for stock animals. Both campgrounds lie along the continuous 36-mi (58-km) **California Riding and Hiking Trail** that extends through Joshua tree forests, washes, canyons, and open lands from northwestern Black Rock Canyon east to the North Entrance. Popular areas for equestrian users include trails near the West Entrance and Black Rock Canyon. Horse trail maps are available for download from the park website (www.nps.gov/jotr/planyourvisit/horseback-riding.htm). Reservations are required for horse camping. Refer to the horse-riding page

for information about contacting the park for reservations.

Ryan Campground
www.nps.gov; $15; no water
Ryan Campground is centrally located in Hidden Valley, adjacent to the California Riding and Hiking Trail. The campground has 31 sites; 4 are designated equestrian sites. Campsites have picnic tables and fire pits, but there is no water available. Reservations are required.

Black Rock Canyon
877/444-6777; www.nps.gov; $20; water available
Black Rock Canyon is located in Joshua Tree's northwest corner, adjacent to the California Riding and Hiking Trail. The large 99-site campground has a separate section for horse owners for staging a ride or camping. Campsites have picnic tables and fire pits, and water is available. Reservations are required.

Camping

There are no hotels or lodges inside the park boundaries. The closest lodgings are just outside the park in the gateway towns of Joshua Tree and Yucca Valley, both via the West Entrance, and Twentynine Palms, at the North Entrance.

INSIDE THE PARK

There are nine NPS campgrounds located within the park boundaries, five of which— Black Rock Campground, Cottonwood Campground, Indian Cove Campground, Jumbo Rocks Campground, and Ryan Campground—accept reservations year-round. Three other campgrounds—Belle Campground, Hidden Valley Campground, and White Tank Campground—are first come, first served.

Belle Campground and White Tank Campground close in summer. Sheep Pass

Campground is a tent-only group campground with six group sites.

Campgrounds in Joshua Tree book well in advance most weekends **October-May.** Reservations can be made up to six months in advance. The first-come, first-served campgrounds start to fill up on Thursday mornings; by Thursday evening, your options are limited. If you can't make it into the park by Thursday afternoon, and you don't have a reservation, you'd better have a contingency plan. There is limited overflow camping on BLM land and private camping available outside the park boundaries.

Only two campgrounds—Black Rock and Cottonwood—have **drinking water.** Even if you are staying at one of these campgrounds, it is wise to bring at least 2 gallons (9 liters) of water per person per day with you into the park.

There are no RV hookups at any of the park

Campgrounds at a Glance

	Location	Sites	Reservations	Amenities
Hidden Valley	Hidden Valley 4,200 ft/1,280 m	44	first come, first served year-round	tent and RV sites; vault toilets; no drinking water
Ryan	Hidden Valley 4,300 ft/1,310 m	31	reservations required year-round	tent and equestrian sites; vault toilets; no drinking water
Sheep Pass	Hidden Valley 4,300 ft/1,310 m	6	reservations required year-round	group-only tent sites; vault toilets; no drinking water
Jumbo Rocks	Hidden Valley 4,400 ft/1,340 m	124	reservations required year-round	tent and RV sites; vault toilets; no drinking water
Belle	Hidden Valley 3,800 ft/1,160 m	18	first come, first served Sept.-May, closed in summer	tent and RV sites; vault toilets; no drinking water
White Tank	Hidden Valley 3,800 ft/1,160 m	15	first come, first served Sept.-May, closed in summer	tent and RV sites; vault toilets; no drinking water
Black Rock Canyon	Black Rock Canyon 4,000 ft/1,220 m	99	reservations required year-round	tent, RV, and equestrian sites; drinking water; flush toilets; dump station
Indian Cove	Indian Cove 3,200 ft/980 m	101	reservations required year-round, 39 sites only in summer	tent and RV sites; access to drinking water; vault toilets
Cottonwood	Cottonwood Spring 3,000 ft/910 m	62	reservations required year-round	tent, RV, and group sites; drinking water; flush toilets; dump station

campgrounds. Black Rock and Cottonwood Campgrounds have RV-accessible potable water and dump stations, and there are spaces that can accommodate trailers under 24 ft (7.3 m) at Hidden Valley, Belle, and White Tank Campgrounds. There is an RV water filling station at the park headquarters in Twentynine Palms.

Hidden Valley
Hidden Valley Campground
44 sites; first come, first served year-round; $15

Central Hidden Valley tends to be the most difficult campground to get a spot in. On the southern end of the Wonderland of Rocks, the campground is popular with rock climbers—and everyone else. Its sites are picturesquely set amid Joshua Tree's signature boulders, and you are right in the heart of the park. The campground can accommodate trailers and RVs under 25 ft (7.6 m), and amenities include vault toilets, fire rings, and picnic tables. There is **no drinking water.**

Reservations are not accepted. To reach

Hidden Valley from the Joshua Tree Visitor Center on Highway 62, turn south onto Park Boulevard and continue 14 mi (22.5 km) to the intersection with Barker Dam Road. The campground will be to the left.

Ryan Campground

31 sites; 877/444-6777; www.recreation.gov; $20, $15 horse camp

Ryan Campground is a scenic campground centrally located between Hidden Valley and Jumbo Rocks with campsites interspersed among boulders and Joshua trees. RVs and trailers up to 35 ft (10.7 m) are allowed.

The adjoining **Ryan Horse Camp** offers four equestrian sites by reservation only. Amenities include vault toilets, fire rings, and picnic tables. There is **no drinking water.**

Reservations are required year-round. To reach Ryan Campground from the Joshua Tree Visitor Center on Highway 62, follow Park Boulevard south for 27 mi (43 km), passing the Hidden Valley Campground. Immediately past the Keys View Road turn-off, the campground will appear on the right.

Sheep Pass Group Camp

6 sites; 877/444-6777; www.recreation.gov; $35-50

Towering rock formations and Joshua trees surround Sheep Pass Group Camp, a tent-only group campground centrally located off of Park Boulevard between Ryan and Jumbo Rocks Campgrounds. Amenities include vault toilets, fire rings, and picnic tables. There is **no drinking water.**

Reservations are required and can be made up to one year in advance. The campground is 18 mi (29 km) south of the West Entrance and 16 mi (26 km) south of the North Entrance.

Jumbo Rocks Campground

124 sites; 877/444-6777; www.recreation.gov; $20

Jumbo Rocks is the largest campground in the park. Despite its size, sites fill up quickly thanks to a convenient location along Park Boulevard and access to plentiful rock climbing opportunities as well as the Skull Rock trail. Popular sites are scenically tucked into the large rock formations for which the campground is named, but the sheer volume of sites leaves little privacy. This lends the place the feel of a small village, which may be good for families or groups. Amenities include vault toilets, fire rings, and picnic tables. There is **no drinking water.**

Reservations are required year-round. To reach Jumbo Rocks from the North Entrance in Twentynine Palms, follow Utah Trail south as it becomes Park Boulevard and continue southwest for 8 mi (12.9 km). From the West Entrance in Joshua Tree, it is a drive of about 24 mi (39 km).

Belle Campground

18 sites; first come, first served Sept.-May, closed June-Sept. 1; $15

Belle Campground is a small, low-key campground with cozy sites tucked amid a pile of rock formations. Amenities include vault toilets, fire rings, and picnic tables. There is **no drinking water.** A few sites can accommodate RVs or towed trailers with an overall combined length of up to 35 ft (10.7 m).

Reservations are not accepted. To reach Belle from the North Entrance in Twentynine Palms, follow Utah Trail south as it becomes Park Boulevard and continue about 5 mi (8.1 km) to the junction with Pinto Basin Road. Follow Pinto Basin Road 1.5 mi (2.4 km) south, turning left onto Belle Campground Road.

White Tank Campground

15 sites; first come, first served Sept.-May, closed June-Sept. 1; $15

The smallest campground in the park, White Tank is a laid-back campground with sites tucked amid scattered rock formations. Sites can accommodate trailers and RVs under 25 ft (7.6 m). Amenities include vault toilets, fire rings, and picnic tables. There is **no drinking water.**

Reservations are not accepted. White Tank is located just south of Belle Campground along Pinto Basin Road, about 7.4 mi (11.9 km) south of the North Entrance.

Black Rock Canyon
Black Rock Canyon Campground
99 sites; 877/444-6777; www.recreation.gov; $25

Black Rock Canyon Campground is in the northwest corner of Joshua Tree, just south of the town of Yucca Valley. Black Rock Canyon has a distinct geographic feel; instead of boulder jumbles, you'll find rolling hills dotted with Joshua trees and yuccas. This is a good campground for first-time visitors, as **drinking water** is available, and the location offers easy access to Yucca Valley for supplies. This campground also offers limited equestrian sites (by reservation only), and trailer and RV sites with a dump station available. Campground amenities include drinking water, flush toilets, picnic tables, fire rings, and a small visitor center with maps and guides.

The access road dead-ends at the campground, and there is no driving access into the rest of the park. A series of hiking trails, including the short Hi-View Nature Trail and the view-filled Eureka Peak, Panorama Loop, and Warren Peak trails, leave from the campground and offer access into the park by foot. The trailhead for the 35-mi (56-km) California Riding and Hiking Trail also starts at the campground.

Reservations are required online (www.recreation.gov) year-round up to six months in advance. To get there from Highway 62 in Yucca Valley, turn south on Joshua Lane and drive 5 mi (8.1 km) into the park.

Indian Cove
Indian Cove Campground
101 sites; 877/444-6777; www.recreation.gov; $20

Indian Cove requires reservations and has **drinking water available** at the ranger station just 2 mi (3.2 km) away. The sites are tucked into spectacular boulder formations and offer both group and RV (under 25 ft/7.6 m) camping options. Indian Cove sits on the northern edge of the Wonderland of Rocks and is popular with rock climbers; the north end of the popular Boy Scout Trail also begins here. Amenities include vault toilets, fire rings, picnic tables, and access to drinking water.

The campground is located off Highway 62, between the towns of Joshua Tree and Twentynine Palms, and is accessed via Indian Cove Road South. The road dead-ends at the campground, so there is no vehicle access into the rest of the park. The nearest park entrance is the North Entrance in Twentynine Palms.

Cottonwood Spring
Cottonwood Campground
62 sites; 877/444-6777; www.recreation.gov; $25

The area around Cottonwood Campground is much more lightly visited than the Hidden Valley region, which makes finding a site here slightly less competitive when booking online. The campsites are scattered across an open desert dotted with creosotes. Though there is little to divide them, the sites are nicely spaced and offer some privacy. The nearby Cottonwood Visitor Center is a fully stocked visitor center and bookstore, while hiking trails to scenic Lost Palms Oasis and Mastodon Peak depart directly from the campground. There are also trailer and RV sites with water fill-up and a dump station.

Cottonwood Group Campground
3 sites; 877/444-6777; www.recreation.gov; $35-40

The Cottonwood Group Campground provides tent-only sites by reservation. Amenities include flush toilets, fire rings, picnic tables, and **drinking water.**

Reservations are required year-round. Cottonwood Campground is located in the Pinto Basin at the South Entrance to the park. From I-10 south of the park, take Cottonwood Spring Road north for about 10 mi (16.1 km). At the Cottonwood Visitor Center, turn right onto Cottonwood Oasis Road and continue 7.5 mi (12.1 km) to the campground on the left.

1: Cottonwood Campground **2:** White Tank Campground

OUTSIDE THE PARK

Campgrounds in the park fill quickly October-May. Outside the park, options include backcountry camping on BLM land or at a privately owned RV park in Joshua Tree. Short-term private camping or glamping sites are also available through www.hipcamp.com.

BLM Camping

Overflow camping is available on Bureau of Land Management (BLM; www.nps.gov/jotr) land both north and south of the park. Consider this camping your last resort. Plan ahead with a campground reservation or alternate lodging plan. Note that BLM camping includes no amenities (toilets, water, fire pits, or drinking water). Fires are allowed in self-contained metal fire pits (provide your own) in the overflow camping south of the park but are not allowed on BLM land north of the park. Bring your own firewood.

North of the Park

For camping north of the park: Drive 4 mi (6.4 km) east of Park Boulevard on Highway 62 and turn left (north) on Sunfair Road. Continue 2 mi (3.2 km) to Broadway, then turn right (east) on Broadway, where the pavement ends. Drive 1 mi (1.6 km) to a one-lane, unmarked dirt road (Cascade) at a line of utility poles running north and south. Turn left (north) onto Cascade and drive 0.5 mi (0.8 km) until you pass a single-lane, unmarked dirt road. Camping is allowed on the right (east) side of that road for 0.5 mi (0.8 km) beginning with the unmarked dirt road.

South of the Park

For camping south of the park: Drive 6 mi (9.7 km) south of the Cottonwood Visitor Center, passing the park boundary sign. Just beyond the aqueduct, turn right or left on the unmarked water district road. Camping is allowed south of the water district road west and east of the Cottonwood Road. South of I-10, Cottonwood Road turns into Box Canyon Road; camping is allowed south of I-10 on both the east and west sides of Box Canyon Road.

Information and Services

RANGER PROGRAMS

Park rangers offer guided hikes, evening programs, and patio talks—many geared toward families—to connect you with Joshua Tree's geography and history. Locations, subject matter, and times vary seasonally. The ranger program schedule is available for download on the park website (www.nps.gov/jotr), or you can pick up a copy at any visitor center.

SERVICES

Services are more conspicuous in their absence. There is **no food** available inside the park. For easy picnic supplies, **Roadrunner Grab + Go** is located in the Joshua Tree Visitor Center near the West Entrance and offers coffee, sandwiches, snacks, salads, and drinks. There are good dining options in the gateway towns along the edge of the park, including Yucca Valley, Joshua Tree, and Twentynine Palms. There are also chain grocery stores in the towns of Twentynine Palms and Yucca Valley.

Water is not widely available within the park; bring at least 2 gallons (9 liters) per person per day with you. Within the park, water may be available at the West Entrance, the Black Rock Campground, the Indian Cove Ranger Station, the Joshua Tree National Park Visitor Center in Twentynine Palms, and Cottonwood Campground at the south end of the park.

There is **limited cell service** in the park. Emergency phones are located at the **Indian Cove Ranger Station** and at the Hidden Valley Campground. In the event of an emergency, dial 911 or call 909/383-5651.

Transportation

The West Entrance to Joshua Tree National Park is located 40 mi (64 km) north of Palm Springs (about an hour's drive) and 145 mi (233 km) east of Los Angeles (plan 3-4 hours for the drive from LA; Friday afternoons can take up to 4-5 hours from LA). The North Entrance near Twentynine Palms is 16 mi (26 km) farther east along Highway 62. The South Entrance is located about 1 hour (60 mi/97 km) east of Palm Springs along I-10 and 4 hours (160 mi/258 km) east of Los Angeles. All roads and entrance stations are open year-round, weather permitting.

There is no public transportation to the park.

CAR

For exploring Joshua Tree National Park, it is best to have your own vehicle for getting to the park and for transportation between gateway towns in the region. To reach the **West Entrance** from I-10 near Palm Springs, head north on Highway 62 for about 30 mi (48 km) to the town of Joshua Tree. Turn south on Park Boulevard and follow the road into the park. To reach the **North Entrance** near Twentynine Palms, continue east on Highway 62 for 16 more mi (26 km) and turn south on Utah Trail. To reach the **South Entrance,** follow I-10 east for 60 mi (97 km) to Cottonwood Spring Road and turn north.

Several major car rental agencies are available in nearby Palm Springs. Car rentals in Yucca Valley are available from **Enterprise** (57250 29 Palms Hwy.; 760/369-0515; www.enterprise.com; 8am-5pm Mon.-Fri., 9am-noon Sat.).

Yucca Valley is also the best place to fuel up before entering the park. Within the park, there are frequent free parking areas near sights and major trailheads.

AIR

The closest airport is the **Palm Springs Airport** (PSP; 3400 E. Tahquitz Canyon Way, Palm Springs; 760/318-3800; https://flypsp.com), served by 12 airlines. The major car rental carriers are located here, including Enterprise, Avis, Hertz, Dollar, and Alamo.

Around Joshua Tree

Yucca Valley, Pioneertown,
and Landers 79
Joshua Tree 89
Twentynine Palms 97
Sand to Snow National
Monument 101

Dotting the northern border of Joshua Tree

National Park are several small towns and sights worthy of a visit in their own right. Creative and unusual works of art, alien-inspired feats of aeronautical engineering, and a Wild West town built as a movie set express the desert's character and freedom. The towns, framed by spiky Joshua Trees and open desert, embrace their carefully cultivated status as both gateway and destination. Bohemian modern is the vibe. Boutiques, art galleries, restaurants, and bars weave together a desert lifestyle vision inspired by the ruggedly beautiful landscape with a dash of upscale mid-century Palm Springs. All of this is accompanied by a "desert rock" soundtrack composed of talented musicians performing nightly on stages across the scenic

Highlights

Look for ★ to find recommended sights, activities, dining, and lodging.

★ **Shopping in Yucca Valley:** Browse vintage, boutique, and home goods shops to outfit your bohemian modern lifestyle (page 83).

★ **Pappy & Harriet's Pioneertown Palace:** Built as part of a Wild West film set, this historic restaurant and saloon serves up excellent barbecue and live music (page 86).

★ **San Gorgonio Wilderness:** Explore the rugged foothills, lofty mountains, and cascading waterfalls west of Joshua Tree National Park (page 103).

Around Joshua Tree

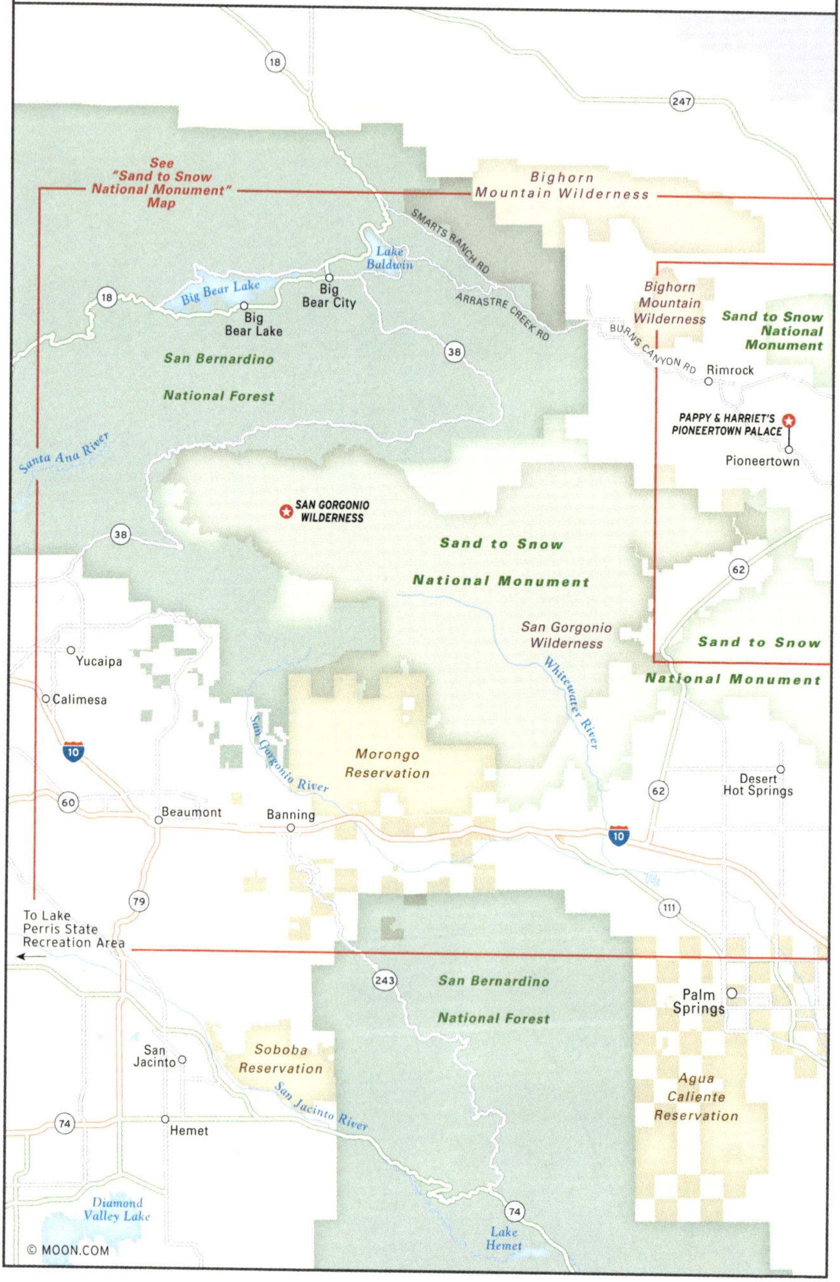

See "Sand to Snow National Monument" Map
Bighorn Mountain Wilderness
SMARTS RANCH RD
ARRASTRE CREEK RD
BURNS CANYON RD
Lake Baldwin
Big Bear Lake
Big Bear City
Big Bear Lake
San Bernardino National Forest
Bighorn Mountain Wilderness
Sand to Snow National Monument
Rimrock
PAPPY & HARRIET'S PIONEERTOWN PALACE
Pioneertown
Santa Ana River
SAN GORGONIO WILDERNESS
Sand to Snow National Monument
San Gorgonio Wilderness
Sand to Snow National Monument
Whitewater River
Yucaipa
Calimesa
San Gorgonio River
Morongo Reservation
Desert Hot Springs
Beaumont
Banning
To Lake Perris State Recreation Area
San Bernardino National Forest
Palm Springs
San Jacinto
Soboba Reservation
San Jacinto River
Agua Caliente Reservation
Hemet
Diamond Valley Lake
Lake Hemet
18
247
38
62
10
60
79
111
243
74
© MOON.COM

valley. It's the Wild West of caftans and cowboy boots, where the phrase *watering hole* means a margarita pop-up, and destination restaurants get write-ups in the *LA Times*. The extreme landscape also inspires connection and seeking, and the area is home to sound baths and meditation retreats, living experiments that blend landscape and architecture.

It is no wonder these towns have such unique character, situated as they are between otherworldly Joshua Tree National Park and the rich natural diversity of the Sand to Snow National Monument. From the clear waters of the Whitewater Preserve improbably cutting through harsh desert to snowcapped San Gorgonio Peak at 11,503 ft (3,506 m), the monument is striking for its range of ecosystems that unfold dramatically across the monument's 154,000 acres (62,320 ha). The cultural history of the ancient Serrano people are also protected in this place; we can see their stories in the volcanic mesas between Big Morongo Canyon and the San Bernardino Mountains.

Here in the towns and in the monument, there is room to immerse and explore a spectacular cross section of Southern California. See live music in an old saloon, shop for pottery, hike to a waterfall, camp in pine forest, then come back down to the desert with its golden glow at sunset.

ORIENTATION

The high desert refers to higher-elevation areas of the Mojave Desert between 2,000 and 4,000 ft (610-1,220 m), distinguished from low desert areas like Palm Springs. It encompasses areas of LA County to the northwest of Joshua Tree to Victorville and Barstow to the north. The term *Hi-Desert* breaks out the towns in the Morongo Basin along the northern border of Joshua Tree National Park, including Yucca Valley, Joshua Tree, and Twentynine Palms, as well as the park itself.

Hi-Desert Towns

The town of **Yucca Valley,** located 13 mi (20.9 km) west of the park's main West Entrance, is the largest town in this area. Funky boutiques and vintage stores compete with big-box stores, grocery stores, and chain hotels for the character of the place. These reminders of 21st-century suburban living feel strangely out of place against the timeless beauty of the desert. However, if you need services, Yucca Valley will likely have what you need. The mostly residential town of **Morongo Valley,** 21 mi (34 km) west of the park's main West Entrance, has a gas station, a Wild West saloon turned spaghetti restaurant, a small breakfast café, an ice cream shop, and the destination-worthy **Cactus Mart.** Most visitors pass through it on the way to Joshua Tree. It is also positioned on the "sand" section of the Sand to Snow National Monument.

Pioneertown, 5 mi (8.1 km) to the north of Yucca Valley, refers to both the Wild West town built as a movie set and the surrounding neighborhood. It is mostly known for **Pappy & Harriet's,** the wildly popular performance venue, restaurant, and roadhouse. Pioneertown also has a few lodge-style hotels and a growing number of vacation rentals.

The tiny outpost of **Landers,** located along Highway 247 (Old Woman Springs Rd.) 15 mi (24 km) north of Highway 62 in Yucca Valley, gets a mention for its destination-worthy restaurant **La Copine** as well as the **Integratron** and unique lodging.

The town of **Joshua Tree,** 7 mi (11.3 km) east of Yucca Valley, is a small artsy outpost that welcomes visitors through the park's main West Entrance, located 5 mi (8.1 km) south. A cluster of charming restaurants and a saloon as well as outfitters, a boutique trading post, and hotels offer a picturesque getaway with a laid-back desert vibe.

Fifteen mi (24 km) east of Joshua Tree, the town of **Twentynine Palms** gives passage to Joshua Tree National Park's quieter North

---

Previous: landscape along a road in Pioneertown; view of the San Gorgonio Wilderness; Pioneertown's Mane Street.

Entrance. The historic 29 Palms Inn anchors the tourism experience here, but Twentynine Palms's downtown is home to a growing number of restaurants and boutiques, adding another hub for shopping and dining. The rest of the small town is scattered across open desert. It's home to a military base and a few functional businesses, including inexpensive motels, a grocery store, and gas stations.

Sand to Snow National Monument

The Sand to Snow National Monument lies to the west of Joshua Tree National Park and its gateway towns. The town of Morongo Valley could be considered the gateway to the sand portion of the monument, which includes the Big Morongo Canyon Preserve and Whitewater Preserve. From any of the Hi-Desert towns, a visit to these preserves will take just a few hours, including the drive, sightseeing, and possibly a short hike. To visit the snow portion requires a full day to include the drive, sightseeing, and a possible hike. Visitors may want to consider making this its own overnight trip to stay in lodging in Big Bear or Angelus Oaks, or camp at one of the US Forest Service campgrounds.

PLANNING YOUR TIME

A cultural scene has grown up around Joshua Tree's gateway towns, making them the primary destination for some visitors. Visitors come to stay in stylish Airbnbs, browse vintage and boutique shops and pop-ups, dine al fresco, drink in saloons, and visit art installations. You could spend a long weekend exploring the area outside the park, perhaps adding a morning hike or a scenic drive.

Plan your visit during the cooler months of **October-May** (although these are also the most crowded).

From the desert towns near Joshua Tree, a visit to the preserves that make up the sand portion of the Sand to Snow National Monument will take just a few hours, including the drive, sightseeing, and possibly a short hike. Visiting the snow portion requires more time and planning. Plan for a full day to drive, sightsee, picnic, hike, and return. Temperatures change drastically from low to high elevations. Plan for as much as a 40-degree temperature drop in the snow portion of the national monument, especially if you are hiking a peak.

You'll need a **car** to cover distances between the desert towns. From the western gateway of Yucca Valley to the eastern gateway of Twentynine Palms is 23 mi (37 km), a 30-minute drive. In between towns there are no services. It's always good practice to have drinking water on hand while traveling through the Hi-Desert towns, especially in summer when temperatures soar.

Yucca Valley, Pioneertown, and Landers

SIGHTS
Pioneertown

53626 Mane St., Pioneertown; https://visitpioneertown. com; daily; free

Created as a Wild West movie set in 1946, Pioneertown was founded by Hollywood investors as a frontier town that served as a backdrop for western movies. Some of the big names that helped establish Pioneertown included Roy Rogers, Gene Autry, Russell Hayden, and the Sons of the Pioneers (which gave Pioneertown its name). The 1940s and 1950s saw Pioneertown as a popular filming destination, with more than 50 films and television shows featuring the stables, saloons, jails, and shops of the main street. As part of the setup, a functioning motel provided quarters for the Hollywood set who were there for filming. When not filming, Pioneertown did double duty as a roadside attraction and tourist spot. Visitors came for the ice cream parlor, the bowling alley, and the motel.

Today Pioneertown continues as a family-friendly attraction. Visitors can wander the main street, taking in the frontier buildings. The original sound stage has been restored and now features live music some weekend afternoons. Visitors can also browse a handful of **retail shops** (open weekends) that feature gifts, soap, skin-care products, clothing, and pottery. And of course, no Wild West town would be complete without a staged **gunfight,** happening on Mane Street most weekends.

The adjacent **Pappy & Harriet's Pioneertown Palace** (53688 Pioneertown Rd.; 760/365-5956; www.pappyandharriets. com; 11am-11pm Thurs.-Fri., 10am-11pm Sat.-Sun., 4pm-11pm Mon.) was originally part of the set as a dusty cantina facade. It was eventually turned into a functioning cantina that served as a biker burrito bar 1972-1982. In 1982, the cantina debuted as Pappy & Harriet's Pioneertown Palace. It is now a wildly popular restaurant, bar, and live music venue.

Getting There
Pioneertown is 4 mi (6.4 km) north of Yucca Valley. From the intersection of Highway 62 and Pioneertown Road, turn left to head north for 4 mi (6.4 km). Pioneertown's Mane Street is located adjacent to Pappy & Harriet's Pioneertown Palace, and the two share parking.

Landers
The Integratron
2477 Belfield Blvd., Landers; 760/364-3126; www. integratron.com; by appointment only Wed.-Sun. Sept.-June; sound bath $55, private groups $1,300-2,000
George Van Tassel (1910-1978) held respectable jobs as an aeronautical engineer for Lockheed Douglas Aircraft and as a test pilot for Hughes Aviation, but arguably his real life's work was as an inventor and UFO advocate.

Van Tassel was the engineer behind the Integratron, a spherical all-wood dome originally intended as an electrostatic generator to promote cellular rejuvenation and time travel. An avowed alien contactee, Van Tassel claimed that extraterrestrials from Venus gave him the formula to build the structure. The building's ship-tight wood construction and dome shape imbued it with an amazing sound resonance.

The current owners of the Integratron haven't yet figured out how to tap into the structure's time travel aspects, but they are intent on rejuvenation (at least for the soul). The only way to enter the Integratron building is by reserving a public **sound bath** (by appointment only). Sound baths last one hour and include 35-40 minutes of crystal bowl harmonies followed by recorded music for relaxation and meditation. Reserving a sound bath also gives you access to the structure's grounds and a display about the history of the Integratron. The grounds and gift shop are available most Thursdays through Sundays for visitors without a sound bath reservation. Call ahead for hours.

Giant Rock
3 mi (4.8 km) north of the Integratron, Landers
Tens of thousands of people attended George Van Tassel's annual Spacecraft Conventions held at Giant Rock, the largest freestanding boulder in the world, coming in at seven stories high and covering 5,800 sq ft (539 sq m) of ground. The spiritually powerful place was a sacred Native American site and meeting place for local tribes until the 1900s.

Van Tassel used to hold weekly meditations in rooms underneath Giant Rock that had originally been dug by a local prospector. From the 1950s to the 1970s, Van Tassel used these meditations to try to attract UFOs. He was eventually successful (according to him) in 1953, when a saucer from the planet Venus landed, and he was invited onto the ship and given the formula for the Integratron. A visit to Giant Rock today shows a sad disrespect for nature and history: Broken glass litters

Hi-Desert Towns

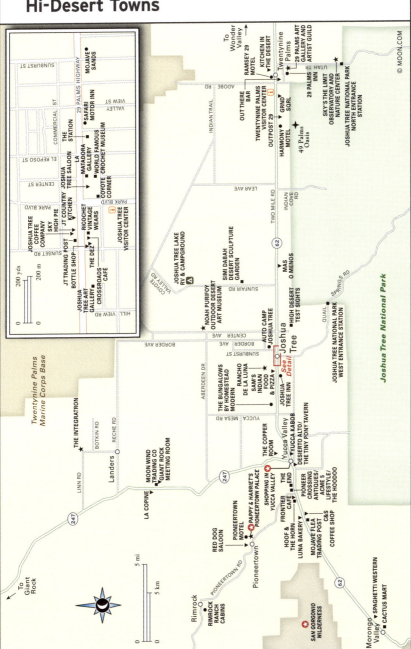

the ground and graffiti detracts from the impressive landmark.

Getting There

The Integratron and Giant Rock are in Landers, north of the town of Yucca Valley. From the intersection of Highway 62 and Highway 247 (Old Woman Springs Rd.), turn left onto Highway 247 and head north for 10.6 mi (17.1 km). Turn right (west) onto Reche Road and continue 2.3 mi (3.7 km). Turn left (north) onto Belfield Boulevard and continue 2 mi (3.2 km) to the Integratron.

SHOPPING

Most of the shops are clustered at the intersection of 29 Palms Highway and Pioneertown Road in Old Town Yucca Valley; a historic curved stucco building (a former pharmacy) marks the distinct junction. There's enough unique boutique clothing, vintage, antique, and lifestyle shops to easily fill an afternoon of browsing.

★ Yucca Valley

Mojave Flea Trading Post

55727 29 Palms Hwy.; https://shoptradingpost.com; 11am-5pm daily

The Mojave Flea Trading Post houses a dreamy collection of vintage and new clothing as well as lifestyle and home goods. The trading post is housed in a standalone adobe near Yucca Valley's Old Town shopping hub and concentrates unique collections of hats, jewelry, vintage, and local designer goods. The shopping here is as great as its sister location in Palm Springs, but with a Hi-Desert vibe.

Hoof and the Horn

55840 29 Palms Hwy.; www.hoofandthehorn.com; 10am-6pm Fri.-Mon., 11am-6pm Tues.-Thurs.

Local tastemakers Adam and Jen preside over the impossibly hip (but not impossibly priced) retail shop Hoof and the Horn, stocking it with a carefully curated selection of women's

and men's new clothing, graphic tees, hats, jewelry, gifts, and housewares, plus some select vintage clothing and vinyl. The perfect leather boots for kicking around in the desert? Check. Flannel shirts to keep you warm and cool at the same time? Check. Tapping into Joshua Tree's reputation as a haven for rock and roll, art, and a bohemian lifestyle, Hoof and the Horn provides your desert chic trappings.

Pioneer Crossing Antiques

55854 29 Palms Hwy.; 760/228-0603; www.pioneercrossingantiques.com; 10am-5pm Fri.-Mon.

Pioneer Crossing Antiques is a charming old-school antiques mall with multiple vendors featuring antiques, collectibles, furniture, knickknacks, and art. The highlight may be their ceramics and pottery offerings: sleek and festively colored Bauer pottery made in Los Angeles and original collector-vintage designs by Joshua Tree artist Howard Pierce (1912-1994).

Acme 5 Lifestyle

55870 29 Palms Hwy.; 760/853-0031; 11am-5pm daily

Acme 5 Lifestyle offers bohemian modern home decor, plants, and furniture for you to take back to your humble abode and make it look as stylish as the Airbnb you just stayed in.

The End

55872 29 Palms Hwy.; 760/418-5536; https://theendyuccavalley.com; 11am-5pm daily

The vintage designer clothing and accessories at The End are the stylish beginning for savvy shoppers who dig a vibrant retro clothing score. It's a colorful stop chock-full of funky patterns and statement jewelry.

The Hoodoo

55866 29 Palms Hwy.; 760/853-0043; https://hoodooyv.com; 11am-5pm daily

Whether the store's name refers to the system of folk magic or the spires of rock that protrude from desert soil, it is into the mystical things in life. Specializing in rock and roll, comics, and tiki, this curiosity shop for

---

1: Pioneertown **2:** the Integratron in Landers **3:** Xêba Botánica **4:** Cactus Mart

the desert wanderer features graphic tees, tiki wares, and gifts—but where it really shines is in its unique collection of vinyl records, comics, and graphic novels.

Cactus Mart

49889 29 Palms Hwy., Morongo Valley; 760/363-6076; https://cactusmart.com; 9am-5pm daily

On Highway 62, 11 mi (17.7 km) west of Yucca Valley, Morongo Valley is a tiny outpost with a café, a gas station, a saloon, and the dig-your-own Cactus Mart. Known for its array of irresistible cacti and succulents, their boutique and gift shop also offers original artwork, hiking and landscape books, candles, jewelry, Joshua Tree Coffee Company coffee, pottery, crystals, gems, and minerals.

Pioneertown
Xēba Botánica

53590 Mane St.; 760/228-9500; www.xebabotanica.com; 10am-sunset daily

Step off dry dusty Mane Street to slather yourself with samples of Xēba Botánica's signature desert balm. The shop is filled with all the products you need to cleanse, tone, and otherwise arm yourself against the arid desert air. The products are consciously made, thoughtfully packaged, and great-smelling.

Soukie Modern Outpost

Mane St.; 310/498-0241; https://soukiemodern.com; 11am-5pm Thurs.-Mon.

Soukie Modern is primarily known for ethically handwoven rugs that mix traditional Moroccan tribal with classic mid-century designs. They have a brick and mortar in Palm Springs with a curated collection of Moroccan goods, vintage Moroccan rugs, and one-of-a-kind rugs woven with traditional techniques. Their outpost in Pioneertown builds on this deep sense of global connection and style to offer home goods, accessories, and clothing.

Landers
Moon Wind Trading Co

1141B Old Woman Springs Rd.; 801/896-4352; https://moonwindtradingco.com; 10am-5pm Thurs.-Sun.

Desert lifestyle boutique Moon Wind Trading Co offers a pitch-perfect selection of new and vintage clothing, beauty and wellness products, and jewelry that may make you want to trade in your entire look for their dreamy desert style. The shop would be in the middle of nowhere except that it's across the street from La Copine restaurant.

FOOD
Yucca Valley
Desierto Alto

55827 29 Palms Hwy.; 760/820-1063; https://desiertoalto.com; 11am-7pm daily

Desierto Alto is a good first stop for your weekend getaway. Located in Old Town Yucca Valley, the shop offers an excellent wine selection, prepackaged cocktails, beer, stylish bar accessories, and gourmet food items including ice cream.

Luna Bakery

55700 29 Palms Hwy.; 442/599-5444; 8am-2pm daily; $4-15

Everything is made from sourdough at this bakery, offering sweet and savory breakfast pastries, cookies, breads, and sandwiches. It's a great stop to grab a quick breakfast or pick up a picnic before heading out for a day of exploring the park. They also have pizza dough for pizza night in at your Airbnb.

C&S Coffee Shop

55795 29 Palms Hwy.; 760/365-9946; 6:30am-6:30pm daily; $6-12

Locals' favorite C&S Coffee Shop offers hearty breakfast and brunch in an old-school diner setting. The heaping plates and early open time set you up for a power breakfast before your morning hike in Joshua Tree. Lunch and dinner add classic diner sandwiches and hearty home-cooked daily specials like meatloaf and fish-and-chips.

Frontier Café

55844 29 Palms Hwy.; 760/820-1360; www.cafefrontier.com; 7am-5pm daily; $5-16

Gourmet coffee shop Frontier Café offers

breakfast sandwiches, oatmeal, and yogurt alongside coffee, espresso, and tea. Lunch adds specialty sandwiches and salads, including vegan options as well as a small but selective beer and wine list in an eclectic, artsy space with a small patio. Pick up Wi-Fi here or listen to some local live music at their location in Old Town Yucca Valley near shopping.

Yucca Kabob

572345 29 Palms Hwy.; 760/820-1644; 11am-9pm Mon.-Sat.; $12-30

Yucca Kabob, a no-frills strip mall eatery in Yucca Valley, serves up seriously delicious shawarmas, pita wraps, kebabs, soups, and salads with plenty of veggie options.

Spaghetti Western

50048 29 Palms Hwy., Morongo Valley; 760/365-9946; 3pm-9pm Thurs.-Fri., 10am-2pm and 3pm-9pm Sat.-Sun., bar until 10pm; $17-43

Located on Highway 62, 11 mi (17.7 km) west of Yucca Valley in the town of Morongo Valley, the cavernous saloon and roadhouse went through several iterations before becoming the cleverly named Spaghetti Western, a business which has, um, stuck. As it turns out, people like spaghetti, especially when the signature sauce includes smoked pepper bacon and San Marzano tomatoes. They also like burgers, live music, and a place that offers happy hour but is also good for families. Look for the giant buffalo on the roof.

The Copper Room

57360 Aviation Dr.; 760/228-0607; 4pm-10pm Mon.-Fri., 10am-10pm Sat.-Sun.; $15-65

The owners of the perfectly curated Pioneertown Motel took Yucca Valley's nondescript airport bar and tapped into its good bones to turn it into the landmark restaurant and lounge it has always wanted to be. Ice-cold martinis and on-tap negronis are served alongside steak house classics with Asian twists. Menu items include fresh spring rolls and a vegetable fried rice to brighten and balance to a classic cheeseburger and a grilled hanger steak.

Pioneertown

Red Dog Saloon

53539 Mane St.; 760/365-6137; https:// reddogpioneertown.com; 10am-10pm Mon.-Thurs., 10am-midnight Fri., 9am-midnight Sat., 9am-10pm Sun.; $4-14

Red Dog Saloon is a welcome addition to Pioneertown, where previously the only game in town was Pappy & Harriet's with its legendary wait times. An Old West-style watering hole opened in 1946, it was shuttered for years until the owners of the Pioneertown Motel brought it back to life. The saloon includes a family-friendly outdoor patio. A low-key menu features tacos and sides. Not low-key? The lightning margarita.

★ Pappy & Harriet's Pioneertown Palace

53688 Pioneertown Rd.; 760/365-5956; www. pappyandharriets.com; 11am-11pm Thurs.-Fri., 10am-11pm Sat.-Sun., 4pm-11pm Mon.; $15-26

People drive many desert miles to the food, drink, and culture oasis that is Pappy & Harriet's Pioneertown Palace. Originally built in the 1940s as part of the Pioneertown Wild West film set, the barbecue restaurant and saloon, which also triples as a music venue, packs in die-hard fans and first-timers every night, managing to stay on the fun side of controlled chaos. The food (burgers, sandwiches, salads, Tex-Mex, steaks, chili, and veggie options) is legitimately good, far surpassing run-of-the-mill bar food. There are no reservations (last dinner seating 9:30pm Thurs. and Sun.-Mon., 10pm Fri.-Sat.). Wait times can be staggering (2-3 hours), but you can wander Pioneertown or grab a drink outside while you wait. Pappy & Harriet's lineup is impressive, snagging groups you might only expect to see in a big city, and gives the whole place a honky-tonk vibe. Lunches are more mellow, and the back patio is a great place for a weekend brunch.

Landers
Giant Rock Meeting Room
1141 Old Woman Springs Rd., Unit A; 442/272-1472; https://giantrockmeetingroom.square.site; noon-11pm Wed.-Sat. and Mon., 11am-11pm Sun.; $14-24

Giant Rock Meeting Room offers pizza, beer, wine, and cocktails in a modern industrial space, meaning you could actually anchor your weekend in the tiny outpost of Landers with the addition of this vacation meal staple. Check out their website for live music and events.

★ La Copine
848 Old Woman Springs Rd.; 760/289-8397; www.lacopinekitchen.com; 11am-4pm Thurs.-Sun.; $16-25

La Copine is not just good by desert standards, it is great by any standard. The nouveau American restaurant is situated in an unlikely remote location near Landers, 10 mi (16.1 km) north of Yucca Valley. The perfectly executed cuisine shines against the chic, spare black-and-white decor of the small restaurant with indoor seating and outdoor patio. Their seasonal menu includes small and large plates with thoughtful dishes like the socarrat (crispy saffron rice, oyster mushrooms, and romano beans) or the chicken piccata with cheesy grits. They also offer one specialty sandwich, for example, a wagyu beef sandwich with horseradish cream and salted cabbage that can be made veggie. Desserts are on par with everything else, including delights like brown sugar beignets and coconut rice pudding. The wine and beer list is just as carefully selected as the fresh, vibrant ingredients. They take a small number of reservations via text one month out; the rest of the space is held for walk-ins. The waiting list opens at 10am, and wait times can be excessive, especially on holidays.

BARS AND NIGHTLIFE
Yucca Valley
The Tiny Pony Tavern
57205 29 Palms Hwy.; 760/820-1644; 11am-1am Mon.-Fri., 9am-1am Sat.-Sun.; $15-24

This eclectic watering hole filled a much-needed gap in Yucca Valley in the sprawling suburban stretch along Highway 62. The drinks are strong and reasonably priced, the velvet paintings add character, and a menu of updated bar food provides balance to the daily drink specials. Kids are allowed inside and on the back patio during the day; after 8pm it's restricted to age 21 and over.

Pioneertown
★ Pappy & Harriet's Pioneertown Palace
53688 Pioneertown Rd.; 760/365-5956; www.pappyandharriets.com; 11am-11pm Thurs.-Fri., 10am-11pm Sat.-Sun., 4pm-11pm Mon.; $15-26, cover charge varies

You don't need a festival to hear great live music at Pappy & Harriet's. Set amid historic Pioneertown, originally built as a Wild West movie set, this saloon, performance venue, and restaurant boasts an impressive music lineup that stands up to offerings in Los Angeles and San Diego. Weekends bring heavy-hitting bands in rock and roll genres, from sludgy desert rock to Americana-influenced. Musicians are excited to play here, and you can feel that energy in this intimate space.

ACCOMMODATIONS
Pioneertown
★ Pioneertown Motel
5240 Curtis Rd.; 760/365-7001; www.pioneertown-motel.com; from $250

Built in the 1940s as part of a permanent Wild West town film set, the Pioneertown Motel offers 19 desert lodge-style rooms. Behind the rustic log cabin facade you'll find sparely styled rooms (queen, king, and twin beds) with exposed concrete floors, reclaimed wood, and a Wild West-chic aesthetic (no TVs or coffeemakers). The motel is situated between the rustic main street of the Pioneertown tourist attraction and the wildly popular Pappy & Harriet's restaurant

1: Giant Rock Meeting Room **2:** Spaghetti Western in Morongo Valley **3:** La Copine **4:** Pioneertown Motel

and saloon. Rooms book quickly with guests coming to see live music at Pappy & Harriet's, and it can be a bit of a party spot depending on what's happening that weekend. Rooms on the back of the property are quieter. Pro tip: On busy weekends, put your name on the Pappy & Harriet's dinner waiting list and then kick back in your room.

Rimrock Ranch Cabins

50857 Burns Canyon Rd.; 760/369-3012; www. rimrockranchcabins.com; $145-350

Tucked away in Rimrock Canyon near Pioneertown, the Rimrock Ranch Cabins offer pitch-perfect 1940s-style accommodations on 10 acres (4 ha) of grounds with hiking trails, a fire pit, and a summer plunge pool. Choose from a refurbished Airstream, one of four cabins, or the four-bedroom lodge. The showstopper is the Hatch House, a stylish corrugated metal-and-glass architectural gem named for its collection of Hatch show prints.

GETTING THERE AND AROUND
Car

For getting around and between the communities of Yucca Valley, Pioneertown, and Landers, having a car is preferable since distances between businesses and towns are long. Gas up in Yucca Valley before heading south into the park or farther east along Highway 62, where services become sparse and the stretches between them greater.

The town of **Yucca Valley** is located at the junction of Highway 62 and Highway 247, approximately 28 mi (45 km) north of Palm Springs. From I-10, take Highway 62 north for 20 mi (32 km). Access to the Black Rock Canyon area of Joshua Tree National Park is via Joshua Lane south for about 5 mi (8.1 km).

Public Transit

Limited public transportation is available in Morongo Basin (which includes the communities of Joshua Tree, Twentynine Palms, Yucca Valley, Morongo Valley, and Landers) in the form of the **Morongo Basin Transit Authority** (760/366-2395; www.mbtabus. com; $1.25-2.50, exact fare only, or download the mobile Token Transit app).

Taxi and Rideshare

There are a few taxi companies in the Yucca Valley region. **Roadrunner Car Service** (760/660-9115; https://roadrunnercarservice. com; noon-midnight daily) is based in Yucca Valley and serves the communities of Yucca Valley, Pioneertown, Joshua Tree, Twentynine Palms, and Morongo Valley. Call to make a reservation or book online. **Desert Sun Cab** (760/475-2310; www.desertsuncab.com) serves Twentynine Palms, Joshua Tree, and Yucca Valley. Reservations are available for drop-off and pickup from Pappy & Harriet's. Cell service is limited, and wait times for a taxi can be long, so plan to book ahead and consider pre-booking your return trip.

Limited rideshares are available in the area powered by **Uber.** Keep in mind that services as well as cell service may be limited.

Joshua Tree

SIGHTS
Noah Purifoy Outdoor Desert Art Museum

63030 Blair Lane, Joshua Tree; www.noahpurifoy.com; sunrise-sunset daily; donation

Artist Noah Purifoy (1917-2004) used found items to create assemblage sculpture that was dubbed "Junk Dada." The title feels dead-on. In the surreal Noah Purifoy Outdoor Desert Art Museum, metal, plywood, porcelain, paper, cotton, and glass are twisted and stacked into sculptures spread across 10 acres (4 ha) of an otherworldly artscape.

Born in 1917 in Snow Hill, Alabama, Purifoy was almost 40 when he received his BFA from Chouinard Art Institute (now California Institute of the Arts). He was the school's first full-time Black student. He spent much of his life in Los Angeles working in public policy and cofounding the Watts Towers Art Center. Using found objects to create sculpture, Purifoy devoted himself to art and social change to become a pivotal American artist.

Purifoy launched his career as a sculptor with his collection *66 Signs of Neon* (1966), assembled from the charred wreckage of debris he collected from the 1965 Watts Riots in Los Angeles. In the late 1980s, he moved to Joshua Tree full-time, creating large-scale art in the Mojave Desert landscape.

The sculptures in this outdoor desert museum are whimsical, political, and comical, with broken pieces and discarded junk mended into recognizable shapes. Made from cheap plywood and gaudy paint, the interior of the brightly colored *Carousel* is jammed with computer monitors, discarded office machinery, and analog artifacts. Other sculptures, such as *Shelter* and *Theater,* are reminiscent of abandoned mining camps and Wild West towns, resuscitated once again into a cobbled together reminder of the American Dream scattered across rocky desert.

In 2015, several of Purifoy's sculptures were featured in an exhibition at the Los Angeles County Museum of Art. It's a testament to the strength of his sculpture that the pieces held their own even when removed from their

Noah Purifoy Outdoor Desert Art Museum

A Rock and Roll Pilgrimage

Harmony Motel, where U2 stayed while shooting photos for *The Joshua Tree* album

Joshua Tree's mystical piles of boulders, spiky lonely Joshua trees, and vast sky have long been a mecca for musicians from LA and elsewhere seeking inspiration. Musicians grow up here, creating a distinct sound to try to fill the open spaces and spare landscape that can make humans take stock of their place in the cosmos. Any way you look at it, Joshua Tree has a serious rock and roll résumé.

JOSHUA TREE INN
61259 29 Palms Hwy.

Follow this pilgrimage through Joshua Tree by starting at Room 8 in the Joshua Tree Inn. On the night of September 18, 1973, country rocker **Gram Parsons** overdosed on alcohol and morphine at age 26. Parsons has since attained cult status for his timeless music as well as the

desert context and featured in a more sterile museum space.

Getting There
From Highway 62 in the town of Joshua Tree, turn north onto Yucca Mesa Road and drive 4 mi (6.4 km) to Aberdeen Drive. Turn right (east) and continue another 4 mi (6.4 km) to Center Street. Turn left (north) onto Center Street and make the next right onto Blair Lane, a dirt road.

ENTERTAINMENT AND EVENTS
Art Galleries and Events
Downtown Joshua Tree is home to several galleries open year-round. The town hosts an art walk the **second Saturday** of each month (5pm-9pm), when local galleries have their monthly openings. For participating galleries and other events check out the Joshua Tree Visitors Guide (https://joshuatree.guide). In addition, larger installations can be found on studio space or private land dedicated to art across the desert.

Joshua Tree Art Gallery
JTAG; 61607 29 Palms Hwy.; 760/366-3636; www.joshuatreeartgallery.com; noon-5pm Fri., 10am-5pm Sat., noon-5pm Sun.

Joshua Tree Art Gallery, an artist-run fine art

strange events following his death. His body was on its way to Louisiana for burial in the family plot when friends, acting on Parsons's predeath request to have his body set on fire in the desert, managed to follow through on a drunken plan that involved borrowing a hearse and stealing his body and coffin off the tarmac at Los Angeles International Airport. Hightailing it to what was then Joshua Tree National Monument, they promptly doused his body with gasoline and lit it on fire near Cap Rock. There is a small shrine at the Joshua Tree Inn and at the site of the "cremation."

HARMONY MOTEL

71161 29 Palms Hwy., Twentynine Palms

Dublin-based **U2**'s cinematic chart-topping album *The Joshua Tree* evoked the open spaces of the American West with its iconic cover. The Joshua tree on display was actually closer to Death Valley, but you can still follow in their footsteps with a visit to the funky, low-key Harmony Motel where they stayed during their desert sojourn.

U2's 1987 album, distinctive as it was, fit squarely into a long line of musicians trying to connect with the quintessential American West experience. **The Eagles** shot their 1972 debut album cover in what was then Joshua Tree National Monument, tripping out around a campfire in a band-bonding visit to the desert. In the 1970s, **John Lennon** recorded the rare *Joshua Tree Tapes*, including "Imagine" and "Come Together." In a faded 1960s video, Doors front man **Jim Morrison** drove his Shelby GT500 Mustang, dubbed "The Blue Lady," through Joshua Tree as the desert highway flashed by.

RANCHO DE LA LUNA

www.ranchodelaluna.com; closed to the public

The music scene is still alive and well. A smattering of recording studios, like the notable Rancho de la Luna in Joshua Tree, draw artists from all over the world, including Kurt Vile, Arctic Monkeys, The Duke Spirit, Mark Lanegan, Foo Fighters, and The Melvins. Drive through the national park and surrounding desert on any given day and you're likely to see a chicly clad poncho wearer posing photogenically against the iconic boulders, looking like they're shooting a music video. Pay attention—they probably are.

gallery, features the work of painters, photographers, jewelers, and sculptors. Exhibitions are by Southern California artists and rotate monthly.

World Famous Crochet Museum

61855 Hwy. 62; www.sharielf.com; 10am-6pm daily

Artist Shari Elf displays her quirky, life-affirming folk art collection at the World Famous Crochet Museum, more roadside attraction than art gallery. Look for the Art Queen sign just east of the Joshua Tree Saloon. The World Famous Crochet Museum is housed in a tiny green trailer in the back of which was once an old Fotomat drive-through film-developing kiosk.

La Matadora Gallery

61857 Hwy. 62; https://lamatadoragallery.org; 11am-5pm daily

La Matadora is a sponsored nonprofit art gallery in downtown Joshua Tree with regular installations and art openings. The gallery showcases postmodern art and local artists.

Simi Dabah Desert Sculpture Garden

5255 Sunfair Rd.; 760/501-1718; https://simidabahsculptures.com; usually 9am-4pm Sat., text to confirm

Simi Dabah Desert Sculpture Garden is the creation of artist and welder Simi Dabah. He created steel sculptures from scrap materials for more than 40 years from 1970 to

2018. On the property of his Joshua Tree studio, nearly 500 sculptures, some more than 20 ft (6 m) high, are scattered across 8 acres (3.2 ha), where they rust to a warm patina in the elements. You can visit the property most Saturdays, and you can also see the sculptures from the road.

High Desert Test Sights

62923 Sullivan Rd.; www.highdeserttestsites.com; studios and store 11am-4pm Tues. and Thurs., 12:30pm-4pm Sat., permanent exhibits dawn-dusk daily; free, tours by advance booking $35

High Desert Test Sights is a nonprofit organization based in Joshua Tree that supports experimental artwork in the high desert. HDTS hosts residencies by local and visiting artists. It is based at **A-Z West,** a sustainable living compound set on 80 acres (32 ha) in the Mojave Desert east of Joshua Tree. It was created by Andrea Zittel, one of the HDTS founders. Tours ($35) are offered monthly except in summer by reservation. You can visit the studios and store without a reservation. It is also possible to visit a series of permanent art installations created on different parcels of land; check the website for info and maps. The black planes of one installation, *Planar Pavilions,* can be seen from Highway 62, evoking ruins or construction. They are connected to the main A-Z site and can be visited without a reservation. Two experimental living cabins on the property are also available for short private stays. Andrea Zittel's house can be booked through www.homesteadmodern. com. A guest cabin can be booked directly through HDTS or Airbnb.

Route 62 Open Studio Art Tours

www.hwy62arttours.org; 3 weekends in Oct.

Joshua Tree's reputation as a haven for creative types means that it has a robust visual arts scene. For three weekends every October, the arts community across the Morongo Basin is galvanized by the Route 62 Open Studio Art Tours, sponsored by the town of Yucca Valley and Visit 29 Palms as well as local businesses. Artists literally open their studio doors to an art-thirsty public, showcasing the vibrant pieces available in the desert communities adjacent to Joshua Tree National Park. As diverse and compelling as its desert backdrop, works feature painting, sculpture, metalwork, ceramics, assemblage, photography, textiles, illustration, conceptual art, jewelry, and more. Visitors and locals get the chance to view the art and meet the artists in their studios, where all the magic happens.

With over 100 participating artists and studios scattered up and down the Morongo Basin, you'll want to plan your art tour according to what speaks most to you. Highway 62 Open Studio Art Tours pamphlets and maps are available on the website and also free from local businesses. If you can't make the October exhibition, you can take in work by artists in the Morongo Basin at a few galleries open year-round or most of the year.

Festivals

Joshua Tree Music Festival

2601 Sunfair Rd., Joshua Tree; 760/366-1213; www. joshuatreemusicfestival.com; May and Oct.; $275-450 adults, $110 ages 11-17, $75 ages 5-10, free under age 5

"The Desert Is Freedom, Music Is Power, & Community Is Crucial" reads the tagline for the Joshua Tree Music Festival, a four-day outdoor, independently produced music festival held twice yearly at the Joshua Tree Lake RV and Campground (www.joshuatreelake.com). This musical carpet ride takes place in an intimate setting outside the national park with the open desert as backdrop to an eclectic mix of up-and-coming bands. There are two alternating stages, so you don't have to make any tough decisions. The spring festival in May features a groovier vibe with dance, world, electro-funk, and groove artists. The event in October gets rootsier, dipping into folkadelic, raw rock and roll, space rock, newgrass, and rootsicana realms. Communal festival tent camping is included with the price of a ticket. Cozy vintage trailers and limited RV spaces are also available. The all-ages festival is family friendly, with a designated Kidsville for entertainment and activities. Festival amenities include organic food and beverage vendors, yoga classes, a saloon, an espresso bar, a world market, restrooms, showers, and free drinking water.

SHOPPING

The main hub of Joshua Tree is at the intersection of Highway 62 and Park Boulevard, leading to the park's main West Entrance. Anchored by the Joshua Tree Saloon and one outdoor outfitter offering rock climbing, camping, and other outdoor gear, Joshua Tree's downtown also has an increasing selection of shopping for new and vintage clothing and gifts.

Ricochet Vintage Wears

61731 29 Palms Hwy.; 760/366-1898; 11am-4pm daily

Stop into Ricochet Vintage Wears for their selection of groovy American threads for men and women. They also offer boots, handbags, belts, jewelry, and more.

Coyote Corner

6535 Park Blvd.; 760/366-9683; www.jtcoyotecorner. com; 9am-6pm Mon.-Fri., 9am-7pm Sat.-Sun.

Coyote Corner is the place to go if you're looking for a souvenir, gift, or novelty item for yourself or the unlucky person who didn't get to come out to Joshua Tree. The store's eclectic inventory includes T-shirts, jewelry, vintage clothing, novelty items, books, and gifts. The store also stocks camping and rock climbing supplies.

JT Trading Post

61716 29 Palms Hwy.; call or text 442/359-0016; https://jttradingpost.com; noon-5pm Mon.-Fri., 9am-5pm Sat.-Sun.

Shop a curated collection of lifestyle goods from local vendors that includes art, vintage and new clothing, home decor, and tech and camera gear. The brick-and-mortar trading post is open daily; weekends bring an outdoor marketplace with additional vendors and shopping that skews toward jewelry, accessories, and vintage clothing. The Tiny Pony supplies a pop-up with food and adult beverages,

making this bustling corner of Joshua Tree a fun destination.

The Station

61943 29 Palms Hwy.; 760/974-9050; www. thestationjoshuatree.com; 10am-5pm Thurs.-Mon.

Housed in an old gas station, The Station offers an eclectic blend of gifts, including T-shirts and Mexican blankets. You can also pick up vintage and new housewares, including pottery and objets d'art.

FOOD
Crossroads Café

61715 29 Palms Hwy.; 760/366-5414; www. crossroadscafejtree.com; 7am-9pm daily; $11-18

Crossroads Café is a Joshua Tree institution, offering reimagined diner fare with a Southwest hippie bent and lots of vegetarian options. Knotty pine walls and reclaimed wood touches bring warmth to the small contemporary diner space, which bustles with hungry hikers as well as locals. Breakfast and lunch are the most popular times, but they have a simple dinner menu as well. Beer and wine are served.

Sam's Indian Food & Pizza

61380 29 Palms Hwy.; 760/366-9511; www. samsindianfood.com; 11am-3pm and 4:30pm-9pm Mon.-Sat., 3pm-8pm Sun.; $11-20

While Sam's Indian Restaurant primarily serves heaping plates of authentic Indian classics, it ingeniously appropriates some of its fluffy naan into pizza and subs, making for a diverse menu that totally makes sense once you think about it. Situated in a strip mall, the casual, cozy space serves satisfying food and beer that hits the spot after a day in the park. The menu is also available for takeout.

★ Joshua Tree Saloon

61835 29 Palms Hwy.; 760/366-2250; www. thejoshuatreesaloon.com; 10am-11pm Sun.-Thurs., 10am-midnight Fri.-Sat., kitchen until 10pm; $12-20

The burgers are hot and the beers are cold at the Joshua Tree Saloon. As the go-to place in a small town with limited options, the Joshua

Tree Saloon does a surprisingly good job of obliging a steady stream of hungry travelers and locals with consistently good food and service amid weathered Wild West decor. The bar and grill are open daily, dishing out well-executed burgers, salads, sandwiches, and solid veggie options as well as a full bar. The Yard, their outdoor patio, is open for tacos, cocktails, and live music. Pets are allowed, and it's a good spot for kids. The inside saloon and outdoor patio are all-ages.

JT Country Kitchen

61768 29 Palms Hwy.; 760/366-8988; 7am-3pm daily; $12-20

JT Country Kitchen is a down-home café serving tasty American diner-style breakfast and lunch. They also serve a few original Cambodian dishes created by previous chef-owner and Mareine Yu, who ran the diner 1989-2016 and amped up the American greasy spoon menu with a flavorful hot salsa, her own secret recipe. The new owners got rid of some of the interior bric-a-brac, but the space and menu remain true to form, right down to the salsa. Try the sausage breakfast burrito or pancakes.

Sky High Pie

61740 29 Palms Hwy.; 760/974-1050; noon-8pm Sun.-Mon. and Wed.-Thurs., noon-9pm Fri.-Sat., hours vary seasonally

Having delicious pizza is a no-brainer after a day spent hiking or exploring the park. Sky High Pie bakes fresh crispy pizzas with sourdough crust, San Marzano tomatoes, and mozzarella as well as signature pies and vegan options. The menu adds some salads and appetizers for good measure. Enjoy your freshly baked pie on a shaded patio with cold beer and wine. A bakery window opens at 9am and serves quiche, pastries, and cookies some mornings, which you can enjoy on the same shared patio with a cup of Joshua Tree Coffee Company Coffee.

Joshua Tree Coffee Company

61738 29 Palms Hwy.; 760/974-9272; www.jtcoffeeco.com; 7am-3pm Fri.-Mon., 7am-1pm Tues.-Thurs.

The Joshua Tree Coffee Company may be exaggerating slightly when it claims to serve the best-tasting coffee available, but it is pretty good. This is organic locally roasted coffee made by people who are super into coffee in a small industrial space tucked behind the yoga studio and Sky High Pie. Grab some pastries from the Sky High Pie takeout window and enjoy your coffee on their outdoor patio.

The Dez

61705 29 Palms Hwy.; 760/794-9747; https://thedezfinefood.com; 7am-5pm daily

One of several fancy additions to Joshua Tree's tiny downtown, The Dez offers espresso, charcuterie, sandwiches, pastries, takeout, and catering. A well-stocked deli case and boxed lunches means that you can grab picnic items for a day in the park, capping it off with a coffee to go.

Bottle Shop

61707 29 Palms Hwy.; 760/465-0001; www.joshuatreebottleshop.com; 11am-7pm Mon.-Thurs., 11am-8pm Fri., 9am-8pm Sat., 10am-6pm Sun.

Bottle Shop offers a curated selection of wine, beer, spirits, and sake for your desert weekend.

BARS AND NIGHTLIFE

Más o Menos

66031 29 Palms Hwy.; call or text 442/370-2266; https://masomenosjt.com; 7am-5pm Mon., 7am-10pm Tues.-Thurs., 7am-midnight Fri., 8am-midnight Sat., 8am-8pm Sun.

Coffee shop by morning, cocktail spot as sun heads back toward the mountains, Más o Menos offers a full coffee and cocktail menu as well as light bites. The vibe is chill at this adobe outpost 5 mi (8.1 km) east of Joshua Tree with an airy tile-floored indoor space dotted with local art along with a shaded patio. Sip a latte, boozy breakfast

1: JT Trading Post **2:** Joshua Tree Saloon **3:** cocktail at Más o Menos **4:** Joshua Tree Coffee Company

cocktail, mezcal margarita, natural wine, draft beer, or one of their refreshing mocktails. Sometimes they have live music as well as pop-up shopping and food. The bar is 21-and-over, but with children it is possible to order coffee from their coffee window and sit at one of a few tables in the non-bar zone.

ACCOMMODATIONS

The area around Joshua Tree is known for its unique lodging with distinctive high desert modern style available on sites like Airbnb or the highly curated Homestead Modern (www.homesteadmodern.com). Lodging ranges from rustic-chic tiny homesteads to design-centric architectural gems with swimming pools. A few motels, inns, and compounds provide additional options to these private stays.

Safari Motor Inn

61959 29 Palms Hwy.; 760/366-1113; www.joshuatreemotel.com; $89-108

For the price, the Safari Motor Inn is a fine enough base camp for exploring Joshua Tree. This basic budget motel has drive-up motel rooms with single king, single queen, or two queen beds, coffeemakers, minifridges, and a swimming pool on the property. It's the closest motel to the park's West Entrance and walking distance to food and drinks.

★ Joshua Tree Inn

61259 29 Palms Hwy.; 760/366-1188; www.joshuatreeinn.com; office 3pm-8pm daily; from $151

The 1950s hacienda-style Joshua Tree Inn offers funky courtyard rooms and rock and roll history. With eclectic furniture, Spanish tile floors, and outdoor patios in its 11 rooms, as well as a huge seasonal pool, landscaped courtyard, and fire pit, it has tapped into a formula that keeps a dedicated following coming back. Speaking of dedicated followings, room 8 is where country rocker Gram Parsons spent his last days, going from rock star to cult legend. Pay your respects at a small shrine in the landscaped desert courtyard.

★ Mojave Sands

62121 29 Palms Hwy.; 760/550-8063; www.mojavesandsatjoshuatree.com; $249-349

There's no way to tell from the unassuming outside of this 1950s desert hideaway that the Mojave Sands is an impeccably renovated, eco-chic desert-modern retreat, with emphasis on the *treat*. Its five rooms and suites faced with glass and steel beams look over common grounds brought to life with a reflecting pool, reclaimed wood, and metal. The rooms feature polished concrete floors, open showers, locally made bath products, vintage turntables, and mini record collections. The two suites add kitchens and living areas. Suite 5 has an outdoor claw-foot tub and shower. They're tapped into some deep feng shui here; do yourself a favor.

The Bungalows by Homestead Modern

59700 29 Palms Hwy.; 760/299-5010; www.homesteadmodern.com; from $400

The 14 suites of The Bungalows are situated on the historic 152-acre (62-ha) Joshua Tree Retreat Center. The Michelin-rated bungalows are in four mid-century post-and-beam buildings originally constructed in 1960 for the center's teachers. They feature the original wood exteriors with architecturally restored interiors. The organic architectural style blends with the surrounding desert; floor-to-ceiling glass opens to private patios and the Joshua tree-filled desert beyond. Inside, the one-bedroom suites feature earth tones and jute rugs. Suites come equipped with full kitchens. Property amenities includes access to the retreat center's swimming pool and vegetarian café. The property is restricted to guests age 18 and over.

Auto Camp Joshua Tree

62209 Verbena Rd.; 844/366-9715; https://autocamp.com; from $431

Auto Camp Joshua Tree offers glamping with a swimming pool in downtown Joshua Tree walking distance to shops and restaurants.

Classic and premium Airstreams come with a bedroom, a sitting room, a private bath, and a grill fire pit. Classic and premium cabins add a kitchen with stovetop and a living area. Central amenities include a general store, a kitchen with prepared foods, a lodge, and a swimming pool. Additional on-site offerings like prepared grill kits and happy hour ensure you are in no way roughing it.

CAMPING

⭐ Joshua Tree Lake RV and Campground

2601 Sunfair Rd.; 760/366-1213; www.joshuatreelake. com; reservations recommended, first come, first served available; $15 pp tent sites, $5 ages 2-12, $30-55 RV sites

The well-maintained property offers tent and RV camping in open desert. The sites include picnic tables and fire pits, and the campground has a small fishing lake, a camp store with firewood and basic supplies, RV hookups, hot showers, flush toilets, and a playground. The campground is 5 mi (8.1 km) north of the town of Joshua Tree. From the intersection of Highway 62 and Sunfair Road in Joshua Tree, head north for 5 mi (8.1 km).

GETTING THERE AND AROUND

The town of **Joshua Tree** is 7 mi (11.3 km) east of Yucca Valley along Highway 62. To enter the park through the West Entrance, follow Quail Springs Road as it heads south, becoming Park Boulevard at the park boundary. The sights of Hidden Valley in Joshua Tree National Park can be reached in 14 mi (22.5 km).

The **Morongo Basin Transit Authority** (760/366-2395; www.mbtabus.com; $1.25-2.50 exact fare only, or download the mobile Token Transit app) operates bus service in Joshua Tree and surrounding areas.

Taxi and Rideshare

Roadrunner Car Service (760/660-9115; https://roadrunnercarservice.com; noon-midnight daily) is based in Yucca Valley and serves the communities of Yucca Valley, Pioneertown, Joshua Tree, Twentynine Palms, and Morongo Valley. Call to make a reservation or book online. **Desert Sun Cab** (760/475-2310; www.desertsuncab.com) serves Twentynine Palms, Joshua Tree, and Yucca Valley. Cell service is limited, and wait times for a taxi can be long, so plan to book ahead and consider pre-booking your return trip.

Twentynine Palms

SIGHTS

Sky's the Limit Observatory and Nature Center

9697 Utah Tr.; www.skysthelimit29.org; campus free, night sky programs $20 per vehicle

Joshua Tree is just far enough from light-filled Los Angeles to be a world away when it comes to clear dark skies. Of course, you can kick back at your campsite or cabin and admire the stars. For more guided stargazing, the Sky's the Limit Observatory and Nature Center, just outside the North Entrance to Joshua Tree National Park, offers reservation-only viewing parties one Saturday per month, closest to the new moon, when the sky is darkest.

For these Night Sky Programs, astronomers set up telescopes trained on different celestial objects in the night sky and answer questions about them. Some astronomers use laser pointers to identify constellations. Hours are typically from half an hour after sunset and last for two hours. Check the website calendar for a schedule and to reserve a spot. There is usually a docent at Sky's the Limit on Saturday mornings, when visitors can explore the orrery (scale model of the solar system) and nature garden. The campus is always open.

Wonder Valley

Locals from Joshua Tree and other

communities farther west joke that the wonder of Wonder Valley is that anyone would live there at all. But don't tell that to the artists, desert dreamers, and others who call this austere desert valley home. The region took hold with passage of the Small Tract Act in 1938; would-be homesteaders flocked here in the 1940s to build tiny "jackrabbit" homesteads and eke out a living. Today you can still see the old homesteads scattered across the desert scrub—tiny wooden dwellings, some inhabited, some in disrepair. Artists seeking both refuge and inspiration have made a small arts community in this neck of the desert. Wonder Valley is also home to the dusty **Palms** roadhouse and venue. Wonder Valley is about 13 mi (20.9 km) east of Twentynine Palms, along Highway 62.

ART GALLERIES

Not to be overshadowed by Joshua Tree to the west, the town of Twentynine Palms has its own arts scene, ranging from outsider installations to snowbird workshops.

29 Palms Art Gallery and Artist Guild

74055 Cottonwood Dr.; 760/367-7819; https://29palmsartgallery.com; 11am-3pm Fri.-Sun., check the calendar for extended hours and events

Since 1963, the 29 Palms Art Gallery has been a nexus for Hi-Desert art. The well-established historic adobe gallery at the Oasis of Mara near the North Entrance to Joshua Tree National Park features ongoing exhibitions as well as opening receptions and events, and art classes for youth and adults.

FOOD

Outpost 29

71845 29 Palms Hwy.; https://outpost29.com; 8am-2pm Sun.-Mon. and Wed., 8am-2pm and 6pm-10pm Thurs.-Sat.

Coffee. Kitchen. Bar. Music Venue. Laundry. Water-refills. Outpost 29 caters to hungry and thirsty visitors to the growing downtown. They serve pour-over coffee and breakfast burritos in the morning, adding burgers and drinks later in the day. The space is a sturdy and functional with a shaded poured concrete patio and picnic tables.

Grnd Sqrl

73471 29 Palms Hwy.; 760/800-1275; www.grndsqrl29p.com; noon-9pm Mon., 4pm-9pm Tues., 4pm-10pm Thurs., noon-10pm Wed. and Fri.-Sat.

Grnd Sqrl is a gastropub on a prime corner of downtown Twentynine Palms. The sleek-casual space features a central bar pouring craft beers, a wall of merch, and a shaded front patio. Their small but mighty menu includes hearty salads, sandwiches, burgers, and veggie options. They also offer a Lil' Sqrls menu for kids age 10 and under.

★ Kitchen in the Desert

6427 Mesquite Ave.; 760/865-0245; www.kitcheninthedesert.com; 5pm-11pm daily; $10-25

Kitchen in the Desert serves up high-quality New American cuisine with Caribbean undertones in an unlikely rural desert location. The restaurant is on the historical site of Tintown, a 1947 roadside attraction evoking the area's mining history with equipment and murals, and there are still enough rusty artifacts sitting around to create a Wild West meets artsy outpost vibe. Kitchen in the Desert offers full-service dining and cocktails on a patio alternately shaded or heated.

29 Palms Inn

73950 Inn Ave.; 760/367-3505; www.29palmsinn.com; call for dinner reservations; 2pm-4pm and 5pm-8pm Wed.-Sun.; $22-37

The 29 Palms Inn is the charming center of the desert inn's 70-acre (28-ha) universe, offering dining room and poolside dining for late lunch and dinner daily. The eclectic menu pulls off classic steaks, seafood, and pastas with a fresh touch. They bake their own sourdough bread and source fresh veggies and herbs from the inn's garden when they can.

1: Twentynine Palms Visitors Center **2:** Wonder Valley Hot Springs carved entrance **3:** Twentynine Palms downtown main street

BARS AND NIGHTLIFE
Out There Bar
73839 29 Palms Hwy.; 760/800-1222; @outtherebar; 5pm-midnight Wed. and Sun., 5pm-2am Thurs.-Sat.

New owners took a Marine bar and painted it pink, turning it into a psychedelic desert roadhouse a step above a dive but with all the character and characters. A mural on the side proclaims: "Last cold beer on Hwy. 62," good information if you are continuing into the remote desert regions to the east or north.

The Palms Restaurant
83131 Amboy Rd., Wonder Valley; 760/361-2810; 3pm-9:30pm Fri.-Sat., 9am-noon Sun.

You're never sure what you're going to get at the weather-beaten roadhouse that is The Palms Restaurant, but it won't be boring. Whether you're sipping icy cold dirt-cheap PBR (think $2 drafts) with the locals on a laid-back Sunday or there for a weekend festival held out back on the rickety stage in the scrubby open desert, there's a certain charm to this dusty outpost with the out-of-tune piano. Live music is on the weekends, but music and events are sporadic; check the Facebook page or call if seeing music is your main goal. Be advised: They're not afraid of the experimental, and music that tends toward the neo-psychedelic and the out-there. The limited menu features bar food with veggie options; it's better than it has any right to be, considering this place looks like the patron saint of abandoned homesteads.

ACCOMMODATIONS
Harmony Motel
71161 29 Palms Hwy.; 760/367-3351; www.harmonymotel.com; $105-120

The Harmony Motel's claim to fame is that the band U2 stayed here when making their iconic album *The Joshua Tree*. The colorful 1950s motel is set on a hilltop above Twentynine Palms, 6 mi (9.7 km) from the park's North Entrance. The grounds have a pool, a hot tub, and nice views of the Little San Bernardino Mountains. The hotel offers seven cheerful homey rooms and one cabin. Some rooms have kitchenettes, and a common dining room with coffee is available to guests. This place is a great value.

Ramsey 29 Motel
73842 29 Palms Hwy.; 323/828-3658; www.ramsey29.com; from $120

Ramsey 29 Motel is a nine-room 1940s motor court located near the North Entrance to the park. The rooms have been stylishly reimagined. A big perk is its proximity to the on-site restaurant **Kitchen in the Desert,** offering vibrant New American cuisine.

★ 29 Palms Inn
73950 Inn Ave.; 760/367-3505; www.29palmsinn.com; from $170

The 29 Palms Inn is so great that I once stayed there for a weekend and never left the premises, not even to visit Joshua Tree National Park just a few minutes away. Drive onto the grounds and you'll be greeted by a glass-lined art-filled lobby and funky wooden signs that direct you around the inn's 70 palm-dotted acres (28 ha). The eclectic lodging includes nine 1930s adobe bungalows with tile floors, fireplaces, and private sun patios; eight wood-frame cabins with private decks; and seven two-bedroom guesthouses. Stroll the grounds past the Oasis of Mara, a 9,000-year-old palm oasis used as a settlement by the Serrano and Chemehuevi Indians into the 1900s. The on-site **29 Palms Inn Restaurant** serves up lunch, dinner, and daily specials and draws inn guests as well as other visitors and locals to its dining room and bar. A charming swimming pool allows for poolside dining and great lounging.

Wonder Valley Hot Springs
4715 Wilson Rd.; www.wondervalleyhotsprings.com; by reservation only; $252-300 cabins, $50-80 pp day-use

A small collection of houses and cabins accompanied by outdoor soaking tubs makes up the Wonder Valley Hot Springs. Each of the short-term rentals includes a private alfresco granite soaking tub. Rentals range from a four-bedroom house to studio cabins. Day soaking is also possible for groups of 1-4 people; a few granite tubs are scattered across the property with wide views of the desert and mountains.

INFORMATION AND SERVICES

Twentynine Palms Visitors Center

73484 29 Palms Hwy.; 760/367-6197; https://visit29. org; 11am-3pm daily

Located in downtown Twentynine Palms, just two blocks west of the Joshua Tree National Park Visitor Center, Twentynine Palms Visitors Center offers local books, maps, and visitor information for the 24 local murals and nearly 40 public art installations across the city.

GETTING THERE AND AROUND

Car

The town of **Twentynine Palms** is 15 mi (24 km) east of Joshua Tree along Highway 62 in a remote section of the basin. The Joshua Tree National Park Visitor Center is in downtown Twentynine Palms. The North Entrance to the park is accessed by heading south on Utah Trail, which becomes Park Boulevard in about 4 mi (6.4 km).

Public Transit

The **Morongo Basin Transit Authority** (760/366-2395; www.mbtabus.com; $1.25-2.50 exact fare only, or download the mobile Token Transit app) runs bus service in and around Twentynine Palms.

Taxi and Rideshare

Roadrunner Car Service (760/660-9115; https://roadrunnercarservice.com; noon-midnight daily) is based in Yucca Valley and serves the communities of Yucca Valley, Pioneertown, Joshua Tree, Twentynine Palms, and Morongo Valley. Call to make a reservation or book online. **Desert Sun Cab** (760/475-2310; www.desertsuncab.com) serves Twentynine Palms, Joshua Tree, and Yucca Valley. Cell service is limited, and wait times for a taxi can be long, so plan to book ahead and consider pre-booking your return trip.

Sand to Snow National Monument

The dramatic topography of California means that the sand, cacti, and palm trees of the Mojave and Sonoran Deserts are in range of the pine forests and snowcapped peaks of the lofty San Bernardino Mountains. Sand to Snow National Monument (www.fs.fed. us), established in 2016, knits together desert preserves, national forest, and mountain wilderness to create a 154,000-acre (62,320-ha) monument that extends from Sonoran low desert to the soaring, forested mountains of the San Gorgonio Wilderness and the San Bernardino National Forest, which continues north and west beyond the monument boundaries.

Orientation

The heart of the monument is the San Bernardino Mountains, home to snow-capped San Gorgonio Peak at 11,503 ft (3,510 m). Parcels of protected desert land include Whitewater Preserve, Mission Creek Preserve, and Big Morongo Canyon Preserve. The monument also protects sacred Native American archaeological and cultural sites, including petroglyphs and village sites. Some of these are located in the Black Lava Butte and Flat Top Mesa desert areas north of Yucca Valley and Pioneertown. These locations have not been developed for hiking or visitation.

Planning Your Time

Visiting Sand to Snow National Monument can be done as a day trip or overnight add-on from either Palm Springs or Joshua Tree. From Palm Springs, a good destination is the Barton Flats Visitor Center, about 1.5 hours from Palm Springs via Highway 111, I-10, and Highway 38. The drive is highly scenic, and you will have opportunities to hike. From Joshua Tree, the Barton Flats Visitor Center is about 1.5 hours via Highway 62, I-10, and Highway 38. From Joshua Tree it is also possible to do a scenic loop by continuing north toward Big Bear Lake and then returning to Joshua Tree via Highway 247 (Old Woman Springs Rd.). Be prepared for a long day in the car if you choose to do this, or stay in one of Big Bear's many lodgings. Staying overnight in Sand to Snow will give you the chance for a longer hike or to kick back under the trees and enjoy the cooler temperatures. If you choose to make a night of it, you will want to make reservations.

EXPLORING SAND TO SNOW NATIONAL MONUMENT

Visitor Centers

Whitewater Preserve Visitor Center

9160 Whitewater Canyon Rd., Whitewater; 760/325-7222; www.wildlandsconservancy.org; 8am-5pm daily

A combined visitor center and ranger station, Whitewater Preserve Visitor Center is located in the Whitewater Trout Farm's historic building, graced by a picturesque trout pond and wading pool. The visitor center has exhibits and hiking maps of the region. Permits are available for camping at the preserve. Permits are also available both in person and by phone for backcountry trip parking or after-hours hiking. It is located off I-10, 16 mi (26 km) northwest of Palm Springs and 35 mi (56 km) southwest of Joshua Tree National Park's West Entrance visitor center.

Mill Creek Visitor Center

34701 Mill Creek Rd., Mentone; 909/382-2882 or 800/735-2922; www.fs.usda.gov; 9am-4:30pm daily

Mill Creek Visitor Center is a combined visitor center and ranger station, offering a range of passes and permits, including San Gorgonio Wilderness permits and Forest Adventure Passes. Call ahead for availability, especially for wilderness permits, which are subject to a quota. They also offer forest maps, gifts, and bear-resistant canisters for sale and rental. Mill Creek Visitor Center is on the corner of Bryant Street and Highway 38 in Mentone, 45 mi (72 km) northwest of Palm Springs and 65 mi (105 km) west of Joshua Tree National Park's West Entrance visitor center.

Barton Flats Visitor Center

Hwy. 38, Angelus Oaks; 909/794-4861 or 800/735-2922; www.fs.usda.gov; 9am-4pm Sat.-Sun. Memorial Day-Labor Day

Barton Flats Visitor Center is the main hub for campgrounds in the area and visitors to the San Bernardino National Forest and San Gorgonio Wilderness. The center is staffed and operated by the San Gorgonio Wilderness Association and provides San Gorgonio Wilderness permits. Other permits are available at the Mill Creek Visitor Center. The center also offers maps, books, and gifts. Staffers at the center are helpful and can provide trail conditions and sightseeing tips. The visitor centers also has picnic tables and very well-maintained restrooms. A 3-mi (4.8-km) round-trip trail to Jenks Lake leaves from the visitor center parking area. The Barton Flats Visitor Center is off of Highway 38, about 7 mi (11.3 km) east of the hamlet of Angelus Oaks. It is 63 mi (101 km) northwest of Palm Springs and 84 mi (135 km) west of Joshua Tree National Park's West Entrance visitor center.

Permits and Passes

All visitors to San Bernardino National Forest that park in developed parking areas (restrooms, picnic tables, trailheads) must display an Adventure Pass ($5 per day, $30 annually, 2nd car pass $5). This means that all mountain visitors to Sand to Snow

Sand to Snow National Monument

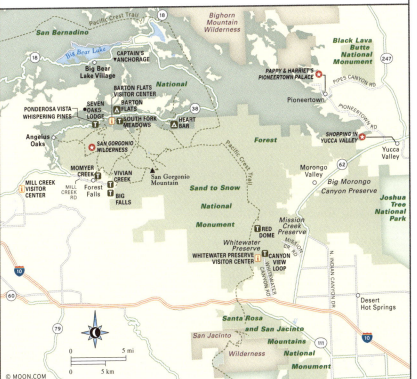

(excluding Whitewater Preserve and Big Morongo Canyon Preserve) need a pass for any stops. Adventure Passes are available at visitor centers, ranger stations, and some local businesses, including convenience stores and outdoors outfitters. Information about specific outlets where you can buy a pass and when they are required is available on the US Forest Service website (www.fs.usda.gov). Passes are also good for the Angeles National Forest and Los Padres National Forest.

Free permits are required for all day hikes and overnight hikes in the San Gorgonio Wilderness and Cucamonga Wilderness. They are available in person at the Mill Creek Visitor Center, Barton Flats Visitor Center (summer only), or online through the San Gorgonio Wilderness Association website (www.sgwa.org/permits).

SIGHTS
★ San Gorgonio Wilderness

The San Gorgonio Wilderness forms the largest and most dramatic segment of the national monument. Spanning nearly 95,000 acres (38,450 ha), the topography shifts from low foothills to rugged canyons to lofty mountains, wildly vacillating 2,300-11,500 ft (700-3,500 m) in elevation. The crown jewel of Sand to Snow National Monument is lofty **San Gorgonio Mountain.** At 11,503 ft (3,506 m), it is the highest peak in Southern California. The summit is only accessible on foot via one of the long difficult trails.

A vast network of hiking trails crisscrosses the wilderness region, making it a rich zone for day hiking and backpacking. Forest fires in 2018 closed sections of the San Gorgonio Wilderness and damaged trees. Check for current conditions at the Barton Flats Visitor Center or online with the San Gorgonio Wilderness Association (www.sgwa.org) or US Forest Service (www.fs.usda.gov).

Big Falls

Big Falls is a popular a destination within the San Gorgonio Wilderness. Big Fall Creek plunges into Mill Creek Canyon over a series of narrow cascades. The sight is best seen from a viewing platform 200 yards (183 m) below the falls during spring, when snowmelt feeds the cascading waters. A short 0.7-mi (1.1-km) round-trip trail leads to the falls. People also lounge and splash in the creek along the trail below the falls. The trail, falls, and picnic area are popular day-use spots.

Big Falls is accessed at the end of Valley of the Falls Drive. From its junction with Highway 38, turn right toward the village of Forest Falls. Continue 4.3 mi (6.9 km) through the village until the roads end at a parking and picnic area and the signed trailhead to Big Falls.

Whitewater Preserve

9160 Whitewater Canyon Rd., Whitewater; 760/325-7222; www.wildlandsconservancy.org; 8am-5pm daily; donation

The scenic riparian corridor at the Whitewater Preserve features 2,851 acres (1,154 ha) surrounded by the San Gorgonio Wilderness, tucked behind the arid hills north of I-10. The preserve is named for the Whitewater River, a wild year-round river winding through scenic Whitewater Canyon. Once used for cattle grazing, the river's crystal-clear waters have since been restored.

A combined visitor center and ranger station is located in the Whitewater Trout Farm's historic building, graced by a picturesque trout pond and wading pool. If you plan to hike, pick up a trail map at the ranger station or online. All day hikers are required to register at the ranger station or sign in at the trailhead. Other facilities include individual and group picnic areas, camping spots, and seasonal activities such as bird walks (registration required; free). Check the preserve's online program calendar.

Getting There

Whitewater Preserve is north of Palm Springs off I-10. From I-10, take exit 114 and follow

Whitewater Preserve

Tipton Road to Whitewater Canyon Road. Drive 5 mi (8.1 km) north on Whitewater Canyon Road to the preserve entrance. The preserve gates are open for hiking (7am-6pm daily Sept.-Nov. 1, 7am-5pm daily Nov. 2-Mar. 9, 7am-6pm daily Mar. 10-May). Visitors must park and then walk in outside of visitor center hours. The gates are closed June-August.

Big Morongo Canyon Preserve

11055 East Dr., Morongo Valley; 760/792-1843; www.bigmorongo.org; 7:30am-sunset daily; donation

The Big Morongo Canyon Preserve is a desert oasis in the San Bernardino Mountains, with interpretive trails, world-class bird-watching, and a chance to experience a desert riparian habitat. An interpretive kiosk has pamphlets describing the landscape. The diversity of native flora is what makes this space so special. Palm trees, aspen groves, mesquite, cottonwood, and willow blend together in this transition zone between the Mojave and Colorado Deserts, while distant views of dramatic snowcapped Mount San Jacinto bring home the sand-to-snow aspect of the monument. The preserve spans 31,000 acres (12,500 ha), with elevations ranging from 600 ft (180 m) on the canyon floor to 3,000 ft (915 m) on ridgelines. Just over 3 mi (4.8 km) of interpretive trails wind through the habitat, including wheelchair-accessible boardwalks across marsh and stream terrain. A longer 8.3-mi (13.4-km) round-trip Canyon Trail leaves from the preserve and descends from the cooler Mojave Desert into the lower-elevation Colorado Desert and then returns the same way. The preserve is open year-round, but the best times of the year to visit are fall, winter, and spring due to summer heat. It makes a good stop on your way into or out of Joshua Tree National Park.

Getting There

The preserve is located in Morongo Valley, one block south of Highway 62. From I-10, take Highway 62 (29 Palms Hwy.) to Morongo Valley. Turn right into the signed preserve.

Valley of the Falls

The picturesque mountain hamlet of **Forest Falls** (www.forestfalls.com) is nestled in Mill Creek Canyon at the base of the steep, mountainous San Gorgonio Wilderness. It is pitched in a pine forest at 5,700 ft (1,740 m) elevation, making it a good place to escape the Southern California heat in summer or to play in the snow in winter. The scenic 4-mi (6.4-km) stretch of road from the Highway 38 turnoff to the road's end gives access to the network of San Gorgonio Wilderness trails, including the Momyer Trail and trail camps. The road ends at a large parking and picnic area, where visitors can take the 0.7-mi (1.1-km) round-trip stroll to Big Falls, hike some or part of the Vivian Creek trail (ultimately leading to San Gorgonio Peak), or picnic in the fresh mountain air.

Getting There

From I-10 east, take exit 80 for University Street in Redlands. Turn left onto North University Street and follow it for 1 mi (1.6 km). Turn right onto Highway 38 (E. Lugonia Ave.). Follow Highway 38 for 13 mi (20.9 km) to a signed junction. Continue right, toward Forest Falls, to reach the village in 4 mi (6.4 km).

HIKING

Hiking in the Sand to Snow National Monument is spectacular and is the reason many visitors trek to the region. Hundreds of miles of trail network allow for plentiful day hikes as well as backpacking opportunities to established trail camps. Hikes range from interpretive low desert strolls to demanding sky-scratching summits reaching over 10,000 ft (3,050 m). The most impressive of these is the hike-able 11,503-ft (3,506-m) San Gorgonio Mountain, which rises steeply from the Sonoran Desert floor. It keeps company with 10 other peaks over 10,000 ft (3,050 m) in the southeast San Bernardino Mountains.

San Gorgonio Wilderness

A vast network of hiking trails crisscrosses

the San Gorgonio wilderness region, making it a rich zone for day hiking and backpacking. Forest fires in 2018 and 2024 closed sections of the San Gorgonio Wilderness and damaged trees. Check for current conditions at the Barton Flats Visitor Center or online with the San Gorgonio Wilderness Association (www.sgwa.org) or US Forest Service (www.fs.usda.gov). There are hiking access points along the Valley of the Falls Drive/Falls Road, at Angelus Oaks, and at Barton Flats Visitor Center/Jenks Lake. For any overnight hikes in the San Gorgonio Wilderness, you must obtain a free wilderness permit. These are available at the Mill Creek Visitor Center, Barton Flats Visitor Center (summer only) or online through the San Gorgonio Wilderness Association website (www.sgwa.org/permits).

Vivian Creek Trail

Distance: *17 mi (27 km) round-trip*
Duration: *9 hours*
Elevation gain: *5,500 ft (1,673 m)*
Effort: *Strenuous*
Trailhead: *Parking area for Big Falls*
Information and Maps: *www.fs.usda.gov*
Directions: *From the village of Forest Falls, head east on Valley of the Falls Drive for 1.9 mi (3.1 km), passing the Falls picnic area. Park at the trailhead parking past the picnic area.*

There are several routes to the summit of San Gorgonio Mountain; however, the classic is the Vivian Creek Trail, clocking in at 17 mi (27 km) round-trip. The trail was built in 1893 with the creation of the San Bernardino Forest Reserve. Although there are many other routes up the mountain, this is the shortest, steepest, and preferred route for some hikers. It is possible to do it as a strenuous day hike or two-day backpacking trip. Trail camps offer possibilities to break up the hike: Vivian Creek Trail Camp at 1.5 mi (2.4 km), Halfway Camp at 3.2 mi (5.2 km), and High Creek Trail Camp at 5.2 mi (8.4 km). They also make shorter day-hiking turnaround points. None of the camps have a huge payoff, but they set a manageable goal as you delve into the wilderness. The Vivian Creek Trail begins at the parking area for Big Falls. It crosses Mill Creek before switchbacking up the flank of the mountain, offering views of the canyon. You will cross into the San Gorgonio Wilderness after approximately 1 mi (1.6 km). Vivian Creek is a shaded scenic glade for a pleasant stop.

Other routes to the summit include the San Gorgonio via Dollar Lake Saddle (20 mi/32 km round-trip) and Mine Shaft Saddle (22 mi/35 km round-trip). Both begin from Jenks Lake Road at the South Fork Trailhead.

Momyer Creek Trail

Distance: *7.2 mi (11.6 km) or 11.5 mi (18.5 km) round-trip*
Duration: *4-6 hours*
Elevation gain: *2,100 ft (640 m) or 2,800 ft (853 m)*
Effort: *Moderate*
Trailhead: *Valley of the Falls Drive*
Information and Maps: *San Gorgonio Wilderness Association (www.sgwa.org)*
Directions: *From the junction of Valley of the Falls Drive and Highway 38, turn on Valley of the Falls Drive toward Forest Falls. After 3 mi (4.8 km), park in the lot on the left, just before the fire station.*

The Momyer Creek Trail offers views of Mill Creek Canyon and Yucaipa, scenic creeks, and two shaded trail camps. It is one of the more underused trails in the San Gorgonio Wilderness section of Sand to Snow and makes good day-hiking or overnight backpacking. From the trailhead, cross the wide wash of Mill Creek. (Do not attempt this if water is rushing in the creek, which can happen during the spring snowmelt.) Check the San Gorgonio Wilderness Association website for trail conditions. On the other side, the trail switchbacks through chaparral and oaks and eventually Jeffrey pines as it navigates the divide between Momyer Creek and Alger Creek. The cedar-shaded Alger Creek Camp (7,100 ft/2,164 m elevation) is located above Alger Creek, 3.7 mi (6 km) from the Mill Creek wash. Continue for another 2 mi (3.2 km) to Dobbs Camp, with the log foundation remains of the cabin of John W. Dobbs, who built a section of the trail in 1898.

The trailhead is accessed on Valley of the Falls Drive. From its junction with Highway 38, turn right (east) toward the village of Forest Falls. Continue toward Forest Falls for 3 mi (4.8 km) to a large parking area on your left, 100 yards (91 m) before the fire station.

Whitewater Preserve

The famous **Pacific Crest Trail** (PCT), the continuous trail system that runs 2,650 mi (4,267 km) from Mexico to Canada, crosses 30 scenic mi (48 km) of Sand to Snow. Starting at the southernmost end of the monument near the Whitewater Preserve and Mission Creek Preserve, the trail climbs to the Mission Creek drainage south of Big Bear in a section known as the **Nine Peaks Challenge,** featuring more than 8,300 ft (2,530 m) of elevation change. The PCT hike here offers a striking cross section of Sand to Snow's diverse landscape. It passes through the exposed fanglomerate cliffs of the desert Whitewater Canyon cut by the snaking Whitewater River to end in the high pines. For an in-depth description of the Sand to Snow section of the PCT, check out *Hiking the Pacific Crest Trail, Southern California* by hiking expert Shawnté Salabert.

From the Whitewater Preserve parking, the PCT is accessed via the Canyon Loop Trail in 0.5 mi (0.8 km). From the Mission Creek Preserve, access to the PCT is 4 mi (6.4 km) beyond the locked gate near the parking area. To get to the preserve from Palm Springs, take I-10 west to Highway 62 toward Joshua Tree. Continue 5.5 mi (8.9 km) to Mission Creek Road, on the left, marked with a small green sign. Turn left onto Mission Creek Road and park at a parking area and locked gate. By prior arrangement, using an online request form, you can also request access to a second parking area located 1.5 mi (2.4 km) beyond the access gate. From here, access to the PCT is 2.5 mi (4 km) along preserve trails.

Canyon View Loop Trail

Distance: *3.5 mi (5.6 km) round-trip*
Duration: *2-3 hours*
Elevation gain: *790 ft (240 m)*

Effort: *Moderate*
Trailhead: *Whitewater Ranger Station*
Information and Maps: *https:// wildlandsconservancy.org/preserves/whitewater*
Directions: *From I-10, take exit 114 and follow Tipton Road to Whitewater Canyon Road. Drive 5 mi (8.1 km) north on Whitewater Canyon Road to the preserve entrance.*

To experience a tiny section of the PCT, check out the moderate and family-friendly Canyon View Loop Trail, a rewarding hike that gives you great canyon and mountain views as well as passage along the Whitewater River. It leaves the Whitewater Ranger Station to follow a section of the PCT heading south across the river on a small wooden footbridge. In addition to the PCT section, a series of hikes varying in length and difficulty start from the Whitewater Preserve visitor center. They offer great views of the surrounding mountains and canyons, and passage along the Whitewater River basin.

Red Dome

Distance: *4 mi (6.4 km) round-trip*
Duration: *2-3 hours*
Elevation gain: *413 ft (126 m)*
Effort: *Easy to moderate*
Trailhead: *Whitewater Ranger Station*
Information and Maps: *https:// wildlandsconservancy.org/preserves/whitewater*
Directions: *From I-10, take exit 114 and follow Tipton Road to Whitewater Canyon Road. Drive 5 mi (8.1 km) north on Whitewater Canyon Road to the preserve entrance.*

The hike to the colorful red-rock outcropping known as Red Dome begins near the ranger station to cross the canyon's river basin. The family-friendly trail continues on the west bank of the canyon, connecting with the PCT to reach the destination to the left of the trail—a large colorful rock outcropping.

San Bernardino National Forest

In the area around the Barton Flats Visitor Center and Jenks Lake, there are several easy family-friendly hikes that make for nice outings in a day of mountain sightseeing.

The **Ponderosa Vista Nature Trail** offers a 0.7-mi (1.1-km) loop walk around a hillside through varied forest flora marked by interpretive signs. You can hear cars on the rural highway below, so this is not a secluded spot, but it does prompt visitors to stop and take in the mountain air. Across the road, another interpretive trial, the 0.7-mi (1.1-km) **Whispering Pines Nature Trail** climbs to a vista point with far-reaching mountain views. Both trails can be reached from Highway 38, just 0.1 mi (0.2 km) south from the turnoff to Jenks Lake (Jenks Lake Rd. W.). The trails are 1.5 mi (2.4 km) southwest of the Barton Flats Visitor Center.

South Fork Meadows

Distance: *9 mi (14.5 km) round-trip*
Duration: *4 hours*
Elevation gain: *1,400 ft (427 m)*
Effort: *Moderate*
Trailhead: *Jenks Lake Rd., 2.5 mi (4 km) from Highway 38*
Information and Maps:
Directions: *From the junction of Highway 38 and Jenks Lake Road, turn right (southeast) and head 2.5 mi (4 km) to a large paved parking area. The trail starts on the opposite side of the road.*

The hike to South Fork Meadows follows a well-marked graded trail through stands of Jeffrey pine and white fir to a shaded glen where several streams converge. At 2.2 mi (3.5 km) into the hike, there is a short side trail up Poopout Hill offering outstanding views of San Gorgonio. From Redlands, follow Highway 38 east to Jenks Lake Road. Turn right and follow Jenks Lake Road 2.5 mi (4 km) to the signed South Fork Trailhead.

FOOD

There are no food options within the national monument, but the small towns of Forest Falls and Angelus Oaks, both jumping-off points for hikes in the San Gorgonio Wilderness, offer a few options.

The Elkhorn General Store

40987 Valley of the Falls Dr., Forest Falls; 909/794-1212; 7am-8pm Mon.-Fri., 8am-8pm Sat.-Sun.

The Elkhorn General Store stocks basic groceries, beer, and wine as well as other sundries and supplies.

El Mexicano Restaurant

40977 Valley of the Falls Dr., Forest Falls; 909/794-3186; 11am-7pm Mon.-Thurs., 11am-8pm Fri., 9am-7pm Sat., 9am-6:30pm Sun.; $7-20

El Mexicano Restaurant is a rustic café with a cozy interior and open-air patio for Mexican standards and cold drinks.

The Oaks Restaurant

37676 Hwy. 38, Angelus Oaks; 909/794-2777; 7:30am-close daily; $9-16

The Oaks Restaurant is a family restaurant serving American diner standards, including breakfast, burgers, and sandwiches as well as pasta and pizza. They are reliably open for breakfast and early lunch, but call for closing times.

ACCOMMODATIONS AND CAMPING

Rustic cabins, developed campgrounds, and hike-in trail camps make up the overnight lodging in the Sand to Snow region. The village of Angelus Oaks offers a couple of lodging options. Limited supplies are available at the general store in Forest Falls. Big Bear to the north and Yucaipa to the south are full-service towns with gas, groceries, and other supplies. For an overnight visit, pack in everything you will need. Most campgrounds offer potable water.

Lodges

The Lodge at Angelus Oaks

37825 Hwy. 38, Angelus Oaks; 909/794-9523; www.lodgeatangelusoaks.com; $140

Located just 7 mi (11.3 km) south of the Barton Flats Visitor Center and near popular trailheads in the San Gorgonio Wilderness, The Lodge at Angelus Oaks was once a stagecoach stop on the route from Redlands to Big

Bear. Now the lodge is under special permit from the San Bernardino National Forest, with eight rustic cabins dating from the 1930s for rent. Cabins accommodate 2-6 people and have baths, fully equipped kitchens, and front porches. Owners Sunny and Charlie are welcoming and hospitable, brightening an already lovely spot. The primary activities here are nearby hiking and biking trails, or you may opt for my favorite: porch sitting. There are no TVs, cell phones don't work, and the simplicity becomes the best feature under the trees and stars. Sitting on said porch, you can hear the occasional car go by on Highway 38, just enough reminder of civilization to make you glad you're sitting it out for a moment.

Seven Oaks Lodge
39950 Seven Oaks Rd., Angelus Oaks; 909/794-2917; restaurant 11am-6pm Sat., 11am-4pm Sun.; $8-13

Five mi (8.1 km) to the north, Seven Oaks Mountain Resort is home to a historic lodge still in operation that serves basic bar food and sandwiches and offers campsites along the banks of the Santa Ana River. Seven Oaks began as a sheep ranch but grew into a large cabin resort by the 1890s as the wagon road from Redlands ended here and travelers continued to Big Bear Lake via burro train. William H. Glass bought and expanded the resort in 1902, and the Glass family continued to run it until the 1960s. Another small group of cabins 1 mi (1.6 km) to the east was constructed in the 1920s to provide additional resort lodging. These still stand but are privately owned and separate from the resort. Today, the resort has seen better days. The original cabins are intriguing and picturesque but are now mostly privately owned, and the resort area is pushed into overused campsites on the banks of the Santa Ana River. However, if you are nosy about history, it is worth a stop.

Campgrounds
★ Heart Bar Campground
www.recreation.gov; May-Oct.; $29-56

Heart Bar Campground features 89 spacious sites under pine forest at an elevation of 6,880 ft (2,097 m). Of the sites, 63 are reservable and 26 are first-come, first-served, with single, double, tent, and RV sites (no hookups; dump station with potable water nearby). Reservations are advised and can be made up to six months in advance through www.recreation.gov. July-August sees the heaviest use. Amenities include campfire rings, picnic tables, bear boxes, potable water, vault toilets, and firewood sales. A camp host is on-site.

The Lodge at Angelus Oaks

The turnoff from Highway 38 to the campground is 6.3 mi (10.1 km) east of the Barton Flats Visitor Center, and the campground is another 0.3 mi (0.5 km), on the right. If you are prepared for dispersed camping, continue down this road to find other US Forest Service campsites.

Barton Flats Campground

www.recreation.gov; late Mar.-early Nov.; $36-71

Barton Flats Campground is a popular family campground offering single and double campsites for tent, trailer, and RV camping. Located at 6,360 ft (1,938 m) elevation, the level campsites are tucked into pine and oak forest. The campground has 51 reservable sites with picnic tables, fire rings, flush toilets, and drinking water. The campground is on Highway 38, about 0.8 mi (1.3 km) east of the Barton Flats Visitor Center. The campground is very popular and can fully book on weekends spring-fall. Reservations are advised and can be made up to six months in advance through www.recreation.gov.

GETTING THERE

Sand to Snow National Monument can be reached from the south via I-10 and Highway 38 at Redlands. From the north, the area is accessed by Highways 18 and 38 from Big Bear. From Palm Springs, count on a 1-1.5-hour drive via I-10 and Highway 38 from the south. From the town of Joshua Tree, the monument can be accessed from the north via Highway 247 (Old Woman Springs Rd.), Highway 18, and Highway 38, or from the south. Either way, count on approximately 1.5 hours of driving.

From the town of Joshua Tree, the trip to Forest Falls is 71 mi (11.4 km) and takes approximately 1.5 hours. Take Highway 62 southwest for 27 mi (43 km) to I-10 west. Travel west for 27.5 mi (44 km). Take exit 89, then take Singleton Road, Bryant Street, and Highway 38 for 16 mi (26 km) to Forest Falls.

From the town of Joshua Tree, the village of Angelus Oaks is 74 mi (119 km) west and takes 1.5-2 hours. Take Highway 62 southwest for 27 mi (43 km) to I-10 west. Travel west for 27.5 mi (44 km). Take exit 89, then take Singleton Road, Bryant Street, and Highway 38 for 28 mi (45 km) to Angelus Oaks.

BIG BEAR LAKE

Big Bear Lake is a charming mountain resort town in the San Bernardino Mountains. In winter, skiers and snowboarders flock to the slopes. In summer, visitors come to enjoy Big Bear Lake, rent a cabin, hike, camp, and explore the village's shops, restaurants, and bars. The adjacent Big Bear City has grocery stores, gas stations, chain stores, a hospital, and all the trappings of civilization. Big Bear is surrounded by the San Bernardino National Forest. It makes an excellent day or weekend visit and is also handy if you forget something major on your weekend camping trip to the Sand to Snow.

Being a tourist town, Big Bear Lake has an array of restaurants that give the people what they want on vacation: stick-to-your-ribs breakfast, good Mexican, upscale American with a patio, and sandwiches great for taking on a picnic.

Big Bear Lake and Big Bear City offer every type of accommodation, from rustic lodges to hotels to cabin rentals. Hundreds of cabins are available through third-party booking platforms like Airbnb and Vrbo as well as local property management companies like www.bigbearcoolcabins.com and https://bigbearcabins.com. Cabins range from small rustic getaways to luxury lodging for groups with hot tubs and game rooms.

Food

The Old German Deli

40645 Village Dr., Big Bear Lake; 909/878-0515; 10am-6pm Wed.-Mon.; $11-18

The Old German Deli is operated by German-trained chef Karl Winkelmann and his wife, Carol. They opened this spare German deli and butcher shop in 2016. The meat case showcases an arsenal of German sausages served as a lunch specialty with homemade sauerkraut and potato salad. The menu also includes heaping cold-cut sandwiches served on crusty bread with pickles and German potato salad. Other offerings include pastries and German beers. It's a great spot to pick up a picnic lunch, or there's a tiny patio for dining on-site.

★ Teddy Bear Restaurant

583 Pine Knot Ave.; 909/866-5415; https:// teddybearrestaurant.com; 7am-9pm daily; $10-21, cash only

The popular Teddy Bear Café has been serving giant portions of homespun American classics since 1944. The bracing mountain air up here can make you hungry for their gutbuster of a menu, including biscuits and gravy, omelets, pastrami, burgers, sandwiches, and signature pies. For a Mexican angle, try the machaca breakfast burrito or tacos. The casual spot offers breakfast served all day, lunch, dinner, and takeout.

Azteca Grill

40199 Big Bear Blvd.; 909/866-2350; www. aztecabigbear.com; 10am-9pm Mon.-Thurs., 10am-10pm Fri.-Sat., 9am-9pm Sun.; $13-23

Azteca Grill serves up satisfying Mexican standards, better-than-average salsa, and a full drink menu (including good skinny margaritas) in a casual space. The vibe is unfussy, and they have a large patio, good for groups and kids. The game might be on in the bar. It is conveniently located near the cabin resorts on the west side of town before entering Big Bear Village.

Peppercorn Grille

553 Pine Knot Ave.; 909/866-5405; https:// peppercorngrille.com; 11am-9pm Sun.-Thurs., 11am-10pm Fri.-Sat.; lunch $18-38, dinner $18-65

Peppercorn Grille offers upscale New American cuisine in the heart of the village. The extensive menu includes excellently executed salads, wood-fired pizza, pastas, sandwiches, seafood, chicken, and steak. Dinner specialties include lobster ravioli and a peppercorn-mushroom New York strip steak.

The restaurant is bustling; make a reservation. A small patio allows for good people-watching and is dog-friendly. It may be a good spot if you have kids also.

★ Captain's Anchorage

42148 Moonridge Way; 909/866-3997; https:// captainsanchorage.com; 4:30pm-9:30pm Sun.-Thurs., 4:30pm-10pm Fri.-Sat.; $29-64

The atmosphere is the shining star at the 1946 landmark Captain's Anchorage. This time capsule of a restaurant features lodge-style wood paneling, cozy booths, dim lighting, and a cocktail lounge, making this a perfect date night or special-occasion spot. Oh, and staff will tell you that the restaurant is haunted by a ghost named George. The food ranges from adequate to good with a menu that features seafood and steak house classics, including Alaskan king crab legs, scallops, chicken, prime rib, and steaks. Dinners come with a salad and a soup bar featuring a tasty clam chowder.

Accommodations

There are a range of accommodations in Big Bear, from luxury chain hotels to simple lakefront lodges. Many people rent private cabins year-round through booking platforms like Airbnb or Vrbo. Two other platforms, https://bigbearcabins.com and www. bigbearcoolcabins.com, offer online booking for cabins in the area.

Sessions Retreat and Hotel

41421 Big Bear Blvd.; 858/879-8805; https:// sessionsretreat.com; from $150

An artistically remodeled lodge in the center of Big Bear Village, the property is a good option for the budget- and style-conscious traveler. The 34-room hotel is on the main boulevard, so it is not a secluded property, but the price point and convenience recommend it. Queen, king, and double queen deluxe rooms and cabins can accommodate up to six guests. The property also offers a central gathering space with a full bar, a pool table, and games.

AROUND JOSHUA TREE
SAND TO SNOW NATIONAL MONUMENT

The Outpost

41421 Big Bear Blvd.; 858/879-8805; https:// sessionsretreat.com; from $219

The aptly named The Outpost refers to a collection of five cabins situated in the quiet historic village of Fawnskin on the north side of Big Bear Lake. The restored 1931 cabins offer lake views, wood-burning stone fireplaces, record players, charcoal grills, and full kitchens and can accommodate 2-4 guests. From the quiet side of the lake, guests can enjoy the quiet of the San Bernardino Mountains while still close enough (15 minutes' drive) to access Big Bear's restaurants, shopping, and ski resorts.

Getting There

Big Bear is located near the confluence of mountain Highways 18 and 38 on the northern edge of Sand to Snow National Monument and San Gorgonio Wilderness. It is approximately 45 minutes from the Barton Flats Visitor Center and surrounding campgrounds, and 1 hour from Angelus Oaks. From the town of Joshua Tree, the trip to Big Bear Lake is 68 mi (109 km) and takes 1.5 hours. Head west on Highway 62 for 6 mi (9.7 km) to Yucca Valley and the intersection of Highway 247 (Old Woman Springs Rd.). Take Highway 247 (Old Woman Springs Rd.) for 45.5 mi (73 km) to Camp Rock Road in Lucerne Valley. Turn left on Camp Rock Road for 5 mi (8.1 km). Continue on Highway 18 for 17 mi (27 km) to Big Bear Lake.

Palm Springs and the Coachella Valley

When considering its 300 days of annual sun, well-watered canyons, and natural hot springs, it's hard to imagine what could make Palm Springs more charmed—until you see its impeccable mid-century architecture preserved like a time capsule.

After the town's initial heyday for the Hollywood set from the 1920s through the 1960s, it was somehow left alone in its former glory. Lucky for us. Today you can stay in a retro boutique hotel, lounge by a gleaming pool, shop the design district, and live like you're on permanent vacation in this timeless hot spot.

Sights	116
Sports and Recreation	125
Entertainment and Events	136
Shopping	142
Food	146
Bars and Nightlife	151
Accommodations	153
Transportation	158
Information and Services	160
The Coachella Valley	160
Mount San Jacinto State Park and Wilderness	173

Highlights

Look for ★ to find recommended sights, activities, dining, and lodging.

★ **Palm Springs Aerial Tramway:** This dizzying feat of engineering whisks you nearly 6,000 ft (1,830 m) from the desert floor to the San Jacinto Mountains (page 116).

★ **Palm Springs Art Museum:** This highly acclaimed art museum houses contemporary and Western American art in its sleek lofty space (page 119).

★ **Indian Canyons:** Hike through the world's largest fan palm oasis and explore miles of trails through sacred land, scenic streams, and dramatic canyons (page 128).

★ **Mount San Jacinto State Park:** Escape the heat of the desert at this 14,000-acre (5,670-ha) state park in the San Jacinto Mountains (page 131).

★ **Pool-Hopping:** Choose between lively party scenes and quiet oases—poolside is the place to be (page 140).

★ **Vintage Shopping:** The walkable and chic Uptown Design District, bustling downtown, and resort-filled south end offer vintage couture clothing, pristine mid-century antiques, and reproduction housewares and furnishings (pages 142 and 145).

★ **Cabot's Pueblo Museum:** This Hopi-inspired pueblo is an artistic masterpiece (page 160).

★ **Coachella Valley Music and Arts Festival:** This annual music festival draws big names and huge numbers of people to the desert valley south of Palm Springs (page 162).

★ **Thousand Palms Oasis Preserve:** Short hiking trails lead to shaded fan palm oases set against the rocky landscape along the San Andreas Fault (page 163).

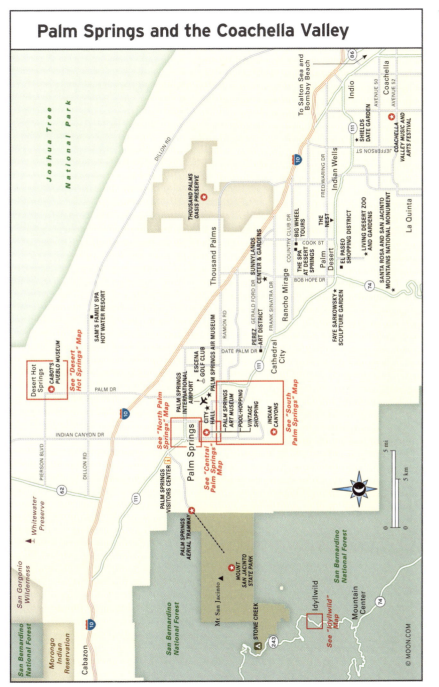

ORIENTATION

Palm Springs may be on the small side, but the town sprawls widely across the valley floor. The **North Palm Springs** and **Uptown Design District** runs along North Palm Canyon Drive from East Vista Chino (north) to Alejo Road (south). The **Central Palm Springs** and **Downtown** neighborhood encompasses the blocks south of Alejo Road all the way to Ramon Road. A bit farther off the beaten path, Ramon Road forms the northern boundary of **South Palm Springs,** which stretches south to Indian Canyons and east past the "curve."

The western border to this desert oasis, the **San Jacinto Mountains,** offer a quick place to cool off from the valley heat. The charming mountain town of Idyllwild provides a good jumping-off point for camping and hiking.

The **Coachella Valley** sprawls eastward, stretching all the way to the barren Salton Sea and encompassing the mostly residential towns of Desert Hot Springs, Palm Desert, and Coachella. Today, it's best known as the home of the popular Coachella Valley Music and Arts Festival.

PLANNING YOUR TIME

Los Angeles residents have a special relationship with Palm Springs; being so close, it's easy for them to pop out here for a **weekend** or enjoy a couples spa getaway.

January-April is high season in Palm Springs, with spring break and big events like Modernism Week and the Coachella Valley Music and Arts Festival packing in the crowds (and raising the prices). Advance hotel reservations during these peak times are always a good idea. Weather is beautiful October-May, so planning a trip during the fall shoulder season (September-December) will give visitors an experience with fewer crowds and pleasant weather. In **summer,** temperatures rise, tourism slows, and room rates drop significantly.

Sights

Palm Springs is a vibrant resort city that is continually reinventing itself. New businesses are constantly being added as old ones are refreshed and made contemporary. Call to confirm operating hours in advance of planning a trip.

UPTOWN DESIGN DISTRICT AND NORTH PALM SPRINGS

★ Palm Springs Aerial Tramway

1 Tram Way; 888/515-8726; www.pstramway.com; every 30 minutes 10am-8pm Mon.-Fri., 8am-9pm Sat.-Sun. and holidays fall-spring, 10am-8pm Mon.-Thurs., 10am-9pm Fri., 8am-9pm Sat., 8am-8pm Sun. summer; $31 adults, $19 ages 3-10, $29 over age 64

One of the paradoxes of California's dramatic geography is that at times, stark desert and green alpine push up against each other as strange neighbors, separated only by a few thousand feet of rocky elevation. The Palm Springs Aerial Tramway allows you to marvel at just how startling this transition can be. The tramway consists of suspended cable cars that zip visitors from Valley Station on the desert floor (elevation 2,643 ft/806 m) to Mountain Station in the lofty San Jacinto Mountains (elevation 8,516 ft/2,596 m) over the course of a 2.5-mi (4-km), 10-minute ride traversing rugged Chino Canyon. As you dangle from the cable, the cars rotate, offering dizzying views of the rocky canyon below, salt-crusted desert, and pine-studded mountain peaks.

Frances Crocker, a young electrical

Previous: High Bar on the rooftop of the Kimpton Rowan; Thousand Palms Oasis Preserve; Trina Turk boutique.

North Palm Springs

PALM SPRINGS AND THE COACHELLA VALLEY

SIGHTS

engineer living in the heat-stoked town of Banning, dreamed up the project in 1935 as a way to get to the cooler temperatures that were within sight but out of reach. After a series of interruptions and political roadblocks, the project was finally completed in 1963.

When the sun is blazing in the desert, the tram provides swift relief as temperatures average about 40°F (20°C) cooler at the top. In summer, most visitors buy day passes

and spend the day picnicking and hiking the San Jacintos, which offer a range of options from easy interpretive trails like the 1.6 mi (2.6 km) round-trip Desert View Trail to the more difficult 12 mi (19.3 km) round-trip trek to San Jacinto Peak. Wilderness permits are required for day hikes and can be obtained at the Long Valley Ranger Station at the top of the tramway. Mountain Station also provides a jumping-off point for many

The Hollywood Rat Pack

Copley's

In the 1930s, the arrival of Hollywood celebrities put Palm Springs on the map. By the 1950s and 1960s, the scene was in full swing. Hollywood A-listers fled from Los Angeles to "winter" in Palm Springs, kicking off with a party at the now-gone Racquet Club, presided over by Frank Sinatra, Sammy Davis Jr., Bing Crosby, and Bob Hope.

Sinatra and Hope settled in Palm Springs permanently, while celebrities like Elvis Presley, Dean Martin, Dinah Shore, and Lucille Ball continued to winter here. Today, you can still experience the nostalgia of the Rat Pack era in a few of the old hangouts and homes.

- **Twin Palms Frank Sinatra Estate:** Designed by E. Stewart Williams, Sinatra's former Palm Springs estate set the standard for Hollywood glamour post-World War II (page 119).

- **House of Tomorrow:** Tour the site of Elvis and Priscilla Presley's May 1, 1967, honeymoon, a home popularly known as the Elvis Honeymoon Hideaway (page 119).

- **Bob Hope Residence:** Hike the Araby Trail for views of the entertainment icon's former home, a massive orbital glass-and-concrete structure designed by John Lautner (page 128).

- **Copley's:** Experience a piece of Cary Grant's former 1940s estate (the guesthouse, to be specific), at this restaurant located in the historic Movie Colony neighborhood (page 146).

- **Melvyn's:** At this time capsule where Frank Sinatra once held court, you're likely to see long-time regulars swanning around in matching pantsuits alongside young hipsters yearning for a glimpse of the old days (page 152).

- **Colony Palms Hotel** (572 N. Indian Canyon Dr.): In the late 1950s, this former underground casino, speakeasy, and brothel drew the glitterati (including Frank Sinatra, Zsa Zsa Gabor, Kirk Douglas, Howard Hughes, and Ronald Reagan), who reveled at its poolside supper club, featuring Las Vegas acts.

- **Purple Room** (1900 E. Palm Canyon Dr.): It's one of the last holdouts of the Rat Pack nightlife. The usual suspects—Frank Sinatra, Sammy Davis Jr., and Dean Martin—graced the place with their presence, and you can too.

- **The Willows** (412 W. Tahquitz Canyon Way): Throughout the 1930s, this glamorous mansion turned inn was the occasional home of superstar lawyer Samuel Untermyer, who entertained luminaries like Hollywood child star Shirley Temple and scientist Albert Einstein.

well-established backpacking routes. The mountains are often crusted with snow in winter months, when visitors enjoy snowshoeing, cross-country skiing, snow camping, or just good, old-fashioned snow frolicking. A Winter Adventure Center is open seasonally and rents snowshoe and ski equipment.

For guests with disabilities, Valley Station has designated parking, and the tramcars are accessible. Mountain Station has accessible dining and a viewing platform.

Twin Palms Frank Sinatra Estate

1148 E. Alejo Rd.; 888/451-0156; https://sinatrahouse.com

Located in the historic Movie Colony district, Twin Palms, the original Palm Springs estate owned by Frank Sinatra, was designed by E. Stewart Williams in 1947 as Sinatra's weekend house. It was Williams's first residential commission. Sinatra originally wanted a Georgian-style mansion with columns and a brick facade, but Williams was able to lure him into a more desert-appropriate modernist style. The 4,500-sq-ft (418-sq-m) residence features four bedrooms, seven baths, and a piano-shaped swimming pool. The house is now available for private events.

House of Tomorrow

1350 Ladera Circle

Originally christened the House of Tomorrow for its iconic shape (three stories of four concentric circles), this estate was built by well-known Palm Springs developer Robert Alexander for his family. It was leased for Elvis and Priscilla Presley in 1966, and they retreated here for their honeymoon on May 1, 1967. The home popularly known as the Elvis Honeymoon Hideaway is privately owned but opens its doors to tours during modernism week.

CENTRAL PALM SPRINGS AND DOWNTOWN

★ Palm Springs Art Museum

101 N. Museum Dr.; 760/322-4800; www.psmuseum.org; 10am-5pm Fri.-Mon., noon-8pm Thurs.; $16 adults, $14 seniors, free under age 19 and active-duty military

With its three lofty floors kept at a cool 75°F (24°C), the sophisticated Palm Springs Art Museum is a refreshing oasis of art. Spread across 28 galleries and two outdoor sculpture gardens, the museum showcases collections of international modern and contemporary painting and sculpture, architecture and design, Native American and Western art,

the Palm Springs Art Museum

Central Palm Springs

photography, and glass. The midsize collection approaches those of metropolitan museums with works by such well-known artists as Marc Chagall, Ansel Adams, Roy Lichtenstein, Pablo Picasso, and Andy Warhol. The museum was originally established in 1938 as the Palm Springs Desert Museum, specializing in Native American artifacts and the natural history of the Coachella Valley. The newest exhibit is the iconic Aluminaire House. Designed by A Lawrence Kocher and Albert Frey in 1931, the first metal prefab house designed and built in the United States has found a permanent home on the museum grounds. The current museum, designed by architect E. Stewart Williams in 1974, has expanded as a cultural center with an Architecture and Design Center and the Annenberg Theater. The museum also houses a café and a museum store.

Admission is free every Thursday evening 5pm-8pm.

Frey House II

686 Palisades Dr.; 760/904-0904; www.moderntour. com; tour $275-375 pp

Up the road from the Palm Springs Art Museum, the 1963 Frey House II sits tucked on a hillside 220 ft (67 m) above the desert floor. The tiny rectangular glass box is the second home of famed architect Albert Frey, with an interior that comes in at less than 1,000 sq ft (93 sq m)—much of that being taken up by the giant boulder that the house was built around. Frey House II is owned and managed by the Palm Springs Art Museum Architecture and Design Center. Tours can be arranged through the museum's official tour operator, The Modern Tour, as part of the Insider's tour. The 2.5-hour tour features a selection of celebrity homes, famous residences, and the work of notable Palm Springs architects.

Architecture and Design Center, Edwards Harris Pavilion

300 S. Palm Canyon Dr.; 760/423-5260; www. psmuseum.org; noon-8pm Thurs., 10am-5pm Fri.-Mon.; $10 adults, free under age 19 and active-duty military

The Palm Springs Art Museum Architecture and Design Center is the hub of the Palm Springs Art Museum's growing collection of architecture and design holdings, which include drawings, photography, and models. The center is intended as a space for architects, scholars as well as the general public. Free docent-guided tours of current exhibitions are available several times per week with a rotating schedule.

Palm Springs Historical Society

PSHS; 221 S. Palm Canyon Dr.; 760/323-8297, tickets online or 760/844-2242; www.psmuseum.org; $40 pp walking, $85 pp biking, reservations required

The Palm Springs Historical Society keeps the history of Palm Springs alive through seasonal walking and biking tours of Palm Springs's historic neighborhoods. A wide range of docent-led walking tours give visitors a chance to see Palm Springs's charming neighborhoods through the lens of architecture, celebrity, and pioneering efforts. Tours run 1-2.5 hours and must be reserved ahead of time.

In addition to tours, the Palm Springs Historical Society runs the Palm Springs Historical Research Library at the Welwood Murray Memorial Library (760/656-7394; call for hours) and operates two museums housed in the two oldest remaining buildings in Palm Springs, both open to the public and located in downtown Palm Springs.

McCallum Adobe

221 S. Palm Canyon Dr.; 760/323-8297; www. psmuseum.org; 10am-4pm Wed.-Mon.

The McCallum Adobe was built in 1884 as a home for Palm Springs's first pioneer family. It now houses varying exhibits focusing on Palm Springs history, architecture, and culture. In addition, the museum houses hundreds of photographs documenting Palm Springs's history from the 1880s to the 1980s.

Cornelia White House

221 S. Palm Canyon Dr.; 760/323-8297; www. psmuseum.org; call for hours

The Cornelia White House, built in 1893, is an example of a turn-of-the-last-century Palm Springs residence. The house was originally part of the Palm Springs Hotel, Palm Springs's first hotel, and is named for the pioneer Cornelia White, who later called the residence home.

Agua Caliente Cultural Museum

140 N. Indian Canyon Dr.; 760/778-1079; www. accmuseum.org; 10am-5pm Tues.-Sun.; $10 adults, $5 seniors, ages 6-17, and students, free under age 6, Native Americans with ID, military, and veterans

The Agua Caliente Cultural Museum is part of the impressively constructed Agua Caliente Cultural Plaza that anchors the corner of North Indian Canyon Drive and East Tahquitz Canyon Way in downtown Palm Springs. Native American ties to the Coachella Valley are strong. The ancestral lands of the Agua Caliente Band of Cahuilla Indians span the scenic water- and palm-filled Indian Canyons (open to visitors for hiking) at the base of the San Jacinto Mountains. The museum celebrates the tribe's past and present by featuring a rotating gallery designed to showcase both traditional and contemporary Native American art. An oasis trail is a permanent outdoor exhibit evocative of the Indian Canyons. The plaza also features Spa at Séc-he, a day spa fed by the ancient hot mineral springs for which the tribe is named.

Palm Springs Air Museum

745 N. Gene Autry Tr.; 760/778-6262; www. palmspringsairmuseum.org; 10am-5pm daily, café 10am-2pm daily; $23 adults, $21 ages 13-17 and over age 64, free active-duty military and family, retired military, and under age 13

The fact that most of the aircraft are still flyable at the Palm Springs Air Museum makes the facility's larger-than-life exhibits even more impressive. This living history aviation museum features 40 flyable fixed-wing aircraft from World War II, the Korean War, and the Vietnam War as well as permanent and temporary exhibits and artwork across three climate-controlled hangars and an outside tarmac. Docents, many of whom are veterans, give added depth to the experience. A small café and gift shop are on-site.

SOUTH PALM SPRINGS
Moorten Botanical Garden

1701 S. Palm Canyon Dr.; 760/327-6555; www. moortenbotanicalgarden.com; 10am-4pm Thurs.-Tues.; $5 adults, $2 ages 5-16, free under age 5

Moorten Botanical Garden has been introducing visitors to the wonders of cacti and other desert plants since 1938. Chester "Cactus Slim" Moorten and his wife, Patricia, established the landmark on their own 1-acre (0.4-ha) property, and the gardens have remained in the family, operated today by their son, Clark Moorten. You'll glimpse the Moorten's Mediterranean-style home, "Cactus Castle," as you wander the sinewy pathways.

The private desert garden was established just two years after what is now Joshua Tree National Park became a national monument, when appreciation for desert life was less widespread. Seeing the homespun sign for Moorten Botanical Garden, it's easy to imagine motoring along a dusty road in a different

Moorten Botanical Garden

South Palm Springs

PALM SPRINGS AND THE COACHELLA VALLEY

SIGHTS

era to stop for this curious roadside attraction. The minimal entrance fee allows you to wander the wide trails among the jagged lattice formed by the more than 3,000 varieties of plants that make up this natural habitat. It's a peaceful place despite the rattling screech of desert insects that have made the habitat their home. The hushed green of the place quickly transports visitors from the street to a microcosm of desert trees, cacti, and plants from around the world. Hand-painted rocks provide labels for the myriad fuzzy, spiky, leafy, jaunty, and snaky plants. A small nursery offers desert plants and pottery for sale. It's a feel-good place—educational, relaxing, and filled with nature—and it offers a novel break from the dining, shopping, and pool lounging that make up much of the Palm Springs experience. The hotel pool will feel that much more refreshing when you return.

Cultural Oases: Exploring the Legacy of Indigenous Heritage

Named after the natural hot springs in the area, the Agua Caliente (hot water) Band of Cahuilla Indians still own the canyons on the south end of Palm Springs.

HISTORY

The first inhabitants came to Palm Springs 2,000 years ago, establishing complex communities in the well-watered canyons at the base of the San Jacinto Mountains. These people fished, trapped, and gathered as well as developed agricultural systems by diverting streams to irrigate crops.

WHERE TO GO

the Indian Canyons

- Native American art and artifacts, including baskets, pottery, textiles, kachinas, and jewelry can be viewed at the **Palm Springs Art Museum.** The permanent collection, Art of the West in the Americas, originated in 1938 and remains a collection and installation focus for the museum (page 119).

- The **Agua Caliente Cultural Museum** is dedicated to the history and culture of the Agua Caliente people, celebrating the tribe's past and present through art and history exhibitions (page 121).

- The **Spa at Séc-he** is a day spa fed by the ancient hot mineral springs for which the tribe is named, one of the most important cultural resources protected by the Agua Caliente Band of Cahuilla Indians (page 125).

- You can see evidence of the ancient village sites in the **Indian Canyons,** which are sacred to the Agua Caliente Band of Cahuilla Indians who own and manage the land (page 128).

Sunnylands Center and Gardens

37977 Bob Hope Dr., Rancho Mirage; www.sunnylands. org; 8:30am-4pm Wed.-Sun., café 8:30am-4pm Wed.-Sun.; gardens free, house $55

In its history as private residence and high-level retreat center, Sunnylands has seen a host of distinguished guests, including US presidents, British royalty, and Hollywood icons. The historic modernist estate now known as Sunnylands Center and Gardens was designed for media tycoon Walter Annenberg and his wife, Leonore, in the mid-1960s by Los Angeles-based architect A. Quincy Jones. The architect's signature style is apparent in the statement roof (a pink pyramid), overhangs that shield the sun, and glass walls for brightness.

Outside, 9 acres (3.6 ha) of sustainable landscape design create a serene setting designed to change with the seasons. When drought-mandated water restrictions put an end to the era of the estate's traditional green lawns, landscape architect James Burnett created a canvas of native and drought-resistant plants, with inspiration from the Annenbergs' large collection of impressionist and postimpressionist art (including Cézannes and Van Goghs). Garden paths wander through arid species and more than 53,000 individual plants. The center and gardens are open to the public with no reservation.

Tours of the historic house are available by online reservation only. The 90-minute guided house tour takes guests to key areas of the home and features information about the estate's history, architecture, and interior design. Tickets must be purchased two weeks in advance. They are released in blocks at 9am on the 15th of each month for the following month. They often sell out, so getting them the morning of release is advisable. No children under age 10 are allowed. Wheelchairs can be accommodated with advance notice.

The Sunnylands Center and Gardens offers a gift shop and café on-site. The café serves a variety of light lunch items, including salads, wraps, coffee, and tea.

Sports and Recreation

DAY SPAS

Many of Palm Springs's larger resort hotels offer spa services, including massage and skin and body treatments. A few have standout day spas with services such as deep-tissue massage, raw botanical treatments, or private pools. They cater to guests and nonguests, individuals and couples; a few are good for spa parties or groups. The town of Desert Hot Springs, 12 mi (19.3 km) north (a 20-minute drive), has a cluster of spa hotels with swimming pools and hot tubs that are fed by the natural hot mineral springs for which the town is named. The Coachella Valley to the south has luxurious destination spas located within several of the valley's major resorts.

Spa at Séc-he

200 E. Tahquitz Canyon Way; 866/777-3243; https:// thespaatseche.com; spa 8am-7pm daily, café 7am-6pm daily; day pass $145, $125 Mon.-Thurs.

The Agua Caliente band of Cahuilla Indians continue their tradition of stewardship of the area's natural hot springs on a grand scale with the Spa at Séc-he, opened in 2023. Tapping into the natural hot springs for which the tribe is named, the downtown day spa offers 22 private hot mineral baths, a eucalyptus steam room, a sauna, a fitness center, and a café. The common areas are linked by halotherapy salt caves. Set amid native landscaping, the pool deck features a waterfall pool, a whirlpool, and a mineral pool as well as cabanas and day beds. The spa is part of the Agua Caliente Cultural Plaza and requires reservations. The spa also features a range of treatments including massages, facials, body scrubs and wraps, nail and hair care, and IV and vitamin therapy. Spending $200 or more on services also gains access to the day spa amenities.

Estrella Spa

415 S. Belardo Rd.; 760/318-3000; www. avalonpalmsprings.com; 9am-4pm Thurs.-Sun.; day pass $50

Part of the classic Avalon Hotel, Estrella Spa is located in a garden hacienda with access to an outdoor hot tub with shaded day beds, a fitness center, and private courtyards. They offer a luxury boutique experience with six treatment rooms for customizable treatments including massage, body wraps, scrubs, and facials. Estrella Spa is good for small groups; they offer a group package complete with a bottle of bubbly and a fruit platter.

Feel Good Spa

701 E. Palm Canyon Dr.; 760/866-6188; www.acehotel. com; by appointment 10am-4:30pm Sun.-Thurs., 10am-6pm Fri.-Sat.; $190-372

The hip Ace Hotel features organic treatments with raw botanical products in its Feel Good Spa. Body treatments range from massage and facials to hair care and styling and can be booked for individuals and groups. The spa is located poolside with easy access to the popular swimming pool and open-air bar.

GOLF

Palm Springs's moderate winter temperatures and spectacular mountain views help make it a golfing destination. Within Palm Springs proper are a few standout courses for visitors. The Coachella Valley to the east and south is a golfing mecca, boasting more than 100 courses. Many of these are within hotel resorts, so you can enjoy the best of all worlds.

Most golf courses maintain online booking for tee times on their websites. Pricing is dynamic, reflecting real-time conditions, including weather, demand, and other market factors.

Booking Resources
Palm Springs Golf Reservations

760/350-4653; www.palmspringsgolfreservations.com
Palm Springs Golf Reservations is a golf concierge and tee-time service that consolidates course descriptions and pricing for golf courses in Coachella Valley communities, including Palm Springs, Cathedral City, Rancho Mirage, Palm Desert, Indian Wells, La Quinta, and Indio. You can request a desired tee time and course directly through the website.

Golf Now

www.golfnow.com
Golf Now offers an online tee time retail service for Palm Springs and other international golfing destinations.

Public Courses
Escena Golf Club

1100 Clubhouse View Dr.; 760/778-2737; www. escenagolf.com; bar and grill 7am-6pm Sun.-Mon., 7am-9pm Tues.-Sat.; $59-199
Escena Golf Club is as much about the setting as it is about golf. The dramatic mountain backdrop, palm trees, and native landscaping are what make this public 18-hole, par-72 championship golf course, spanning 172 acres (70 ha). Golf club rentals ($80 pp) are available along with an on-site bar and grill and a pro shop. Tee times can book quickly on weekends.

Indian Canyons Golf Resort

1097 E. Murray Canyon Dr.; 760/833-8724; www. indiancanyonsgolf.com; $113-135
The Indian Canyons Golf Resort maintains two distinct golf courses set on 550 acres (223 ha) of Native American tribal property; both are 18-hole championship courses. The classic par-72 North Course plays 6,943 yards set in the canyon district and is bordered on three sides by the San Jacinto Mountains. The course, designed by noted architect William F. Bell, dates to 1961 and winds through historic mid-century properties, including some originally owned by Walt Disney. The famous Walt Disney fountain acts as a water hazard and visual centerpiece, shooting water jets more than 100 ft (30 m) high.

The par-72 South Course was redesigned in 2004. The 6,582-yard championship course features four large lakes, five par-5 holes, rolling mounds, fairways, and hundreds of native palm trees important to the Agua Caliente tribe. There are on-site club rentals, a pro shop, and restaurant.

Tahquitz Creek Golf Resort

1885 Golf Club Dr.; 760/328-1005; www. tahquitzgolfresort.com; pro shop 6am-6pm daily, Traditions Café 6am-4pm daily; $95-149, club rentals $55 before twilight, $30 after twilight
Tahquitz Creek Golf Resort is a public course offering a pro shop, a bar and grill, and two courses. The Legend Course was designed in 1957 and offers a traditional country club-style golf experience. The 18-hole regulation golf course plays more than 6,800 yards and meanders through historic neighborhoods with undulating "push up" greens. The Resort Course is a par-36 regulation course designed in 1995. It features environmentally friendly design elements, including the use of drought-tolerant native landscaping, reclaimed irrigation, and reclaimed materials for mounding. The Resort plays more than 6,700 yards and offers tees for various handicaps to create a fair playing field. Rental clubs are available.

HIKING

Although it may be difficult to tear yourself away from the hotel swimming pool, Palm Springs offers some good hiking opportunities in its surrounding canyons and mountains. A few trails leave directly from near the Palm Springs Art Museum, climbing into the foothills and offering views of Palm Springs and the Coachella Valley. Locals treat these as workout trails, but in addition to the health benefits, they pay off with sweeping views.

Palm Springs

Trails in Palm Springs are exposed and are best hiked **October-March,** when temperatures are more moderate. If hiking other times of the year, start very early (plan to finish by 9am-10am during summer) and make sure you are off the trail before the heat of the day. Carry plenty of water, sunscreen, and a hat for shade.

Palm Springs Museum Trail

Distance: *2 mi (3.2 km) round-trip*
Duration: *1.5-2 hours*
Elevation gain: *1,000 ft (305 m)*
Effort: *Moderate*
Trailhead: *North parking lot of the Palm Springs Art Museum*
Directions: *From the Palm Springs Visitors Center, head south on North Palm Canyon Drive for 2.9 mi (4.7 km). Turn right on Tahquitz Canyon Drive. Drive one block, then turn right on North Museum Drive. Pass the Palm Springs Art Museum on your left and make a left into the north parking lot. The signed trailhead begins from the parking lot.*
Information and Maps: *www. visitgreaterpalmsprings.com*

Don't let the 2-mi (3.2-km) round-trip distance or the quaint trail name fool you. This is an intensely steep hike. The payoff is the bird's-eye view of downtown Palm Springs.

From the Palm Springs Art Museum (101 N. Museum Dr.), the trail starts with a bang in a series of tightly wound switchbacks that navigate the rocky hillside and never let up until the summit. (Stick to the main trail and avoid social trails that cut switchbacks and cause erosion.) The summit is marked by a picnic table where you can have a triumphant slug of water or a snack as you look out over the modernist lines of Palm Springs below. Just beyond the summit, the trail intersects with the 5-mi (8.1-km) **North Lykken Trail** that continues north and south above Palm Springs. The Museum Trail also links up with the Skyline Trail, the backbone of the infamous Cactus to Clouds Hike, a grueling 19-mi (31-km) trip that takes intrepid hikers up to 10,400 ft (3,170 m) in elevation from the desert floor to the peak of Mount San Jacinto in one day.

South Carl Lykken Trail

Distance: *6 mi (9.7 km) round-trip to Tahquitz Canyon overlook, out and back along the same route*
Duration: *2-3 hours*
Elevation gain: *1,000 ft (305 m)*
Effort: *Moderate*
Trailhead: *South Palm Canyon Drive*
Directions: *From the Palm Springs Visitors Center, take North Palm Canyon Drive south for 6.4 mi (10.3 km); continue straight when it turns into South Palm Canyon Drive. The signed trailhead is on the west (right) side of South Palm Canyon Drive just south of Canyon Heights Road.*
Information and Maps: *www. visitgreaterpalmsprings.com*

This exposed hike into the toothy hills outlining the west side of Palm Springs offers excellent views of Palm Springs with a bonus peek into Tahquitz Canyon. The trail is in a neighborhood and is used by locals during the early morning hours and cooler winter months. There is a good reason—rewarding climbs give way to expansive city views as the trail levels out and winds along a north- and east-facing ridge.

The trail begins at a signed trailhead near the road at 550 ft (168 m) elevation. It heads west before beginning a series of switchbacks up to a lookout point, checking in at 1,170 ft (357 m). From here the trail levels out, winding along the rocky hillside before climbing again to top out at 1,550 ft (472 m) above Tahquitz Canyon. This is a good turnaround point, marked by picnic tables, and you can return the way you came.

It is also possible to continue the trail down a steep drop to street level, where it intersects with a second trailhead at the end of West Mesquite Avenue. You can arrange for a car shuttle from here or, as one enterprising hiker suggested, call a cab or rideshare to get back to your hotel.

This trail is completely exposed. Carry enough water, and make sure you start early and are off the trail no later than mid-morning in summer months. The good news is that even if you are not able to make it to the final turnaround point, the continuous views mean that hiking almost any length of the trail will be a satisfying experience.

Araby Trail

Distance: 3 mi (4.8 km) round-trip
Duration: 2 hours
Elevation gain: 800 ft (244 m)
Effort: Moderate
Trailhead: South Palm Springs at Rim Road/ Southridge Road. Parking area is on the right, past the turnoff from Highway 111.
Information and Maps: www.visitgreaterpalmsprings.com

The Araby Trail reaches excellent heights above the city of Palm Springs, winding past celebrity homes and offering expansive views of the town and the windmills to the north. This is a popular neighborhood exercise trail, and it does provide a great workout while rewarding with interesting views and architecture.

From the parking area, the trail cuts switchbacks steeply up the rocky hillside to the south, passing famed architect John Lautner's dramatic Elrod House with its circular bladed rooftop. (This is where part of the 1971 James Bond thriller *Diamonds Are Forever* was filmed.) Next door is the groovy bachelor pad of actor Steve McQueen. Continue climbing the steep switchbacks and you'll pass the crowning rooflines of yet another celebrity house and architectural wonder: the **Bob Hope Residence,** a massive domed structure designed by John Lautner that sits perched on the hillside. It is the highest structure in Palm Springs. The trail winds to a ridge above the house, a good place to turn around.

★ Indian Canyons

760/323-6018; www.indian-canyons.com; 8am-5pm daily Oct.-July 4, 8am-5pm Fri.-Sun. July 5-Sept.; $12 adults, $7 over age 61 and students, $6 ages 6-12, free military

The Indian Canyons refer to the rugged, scenic canyons that burrow into the flanks of the San Jacinto Mountains in the southwest corner of Palm Springs. The steep, often snowcapped San Jacintos feed the seasonal streams that transform the rocky canyons in spring. Natural fan palm oases and groundwater feed perennial pools and streams year-round, making the canyons a haven from the surrounding arid landscape and a delight for hikers.

The Indian Canyons are sacred to the Agua Caliente Band of Cahuilla Indians who own and manage the land. Ancestors of the Agua Caliente Cahuilla settled Tahquitz, Andreas, Murray, Palm, and Chino Canyons, establishing villages and irrigating and planting crops. The Agua Caliente own 32,000 acres (12,950 ha) spread across desert and mountains in the Palm Springs area. Tahquitz and three other canyons are listed on the National Register of Historic Places, while Palm Canyon boasts the world's largest California fan palm oasis.

These trails are best hiked **October-March** due to soaring temperatures in other months. You have the best chance of encountering the seasonal snowmelt streams that feed these canyons in early spring. However, because the canyons offer short hikes with some shade, visiting the canyons at other times of the year is also worthwhile. When it is hot, start early; the canyons open at 8am daily year-round. Seasonal **ranger talks** are held Monday-Thursday at the Trading Post (10am) and at Andreas Canyon (1pm). Ranger-led **interpretive hikes** (10am-11:30am and 1pm-2:30pm Fri.-Sun. Oct.-June) are also available.

Getting There

A **Trading Post** and ranger station on South Palm Canyon Drive form the hub for exploring Andreas, Murray, and Palm Canyons. The Trading Post has hiking maps, drinks and snacks, books, and jewelry as well as Native American pottery, baskets, and weaving. Restrooms and parking are available. To get here from the Palm Springs Visitors Center (2901 N. Palm Canyon Dr.), head south on Palm Canyon Drive for 9 mi (14.5 km) until the road ends at the Trading Post and Palm Canyon overlook. Visitors pass through a toll gate to pay the entrance fee prior to reaching the Trading Post.

The entrance to **Tahquitz Canyon** (500 W. Mesquite Ave.; www.tahquitzcanyon.com) is from the Tahquitz Visitors Center, where water, maps, parking, and restrooms are available. From the Palm Springs Visitors Center (2901 N. Palm Canyon Dr.), head south on Palm Canyon Drive for 3.8 mi (6.1 km) and turn right on Mesquite Avenue. The road ends at the Tahquitz Canyon Visitors Center in 0.4 mi (0.6 km).

Tahquitz Canyon

Distance: 2 mi (3.2 km) round-trip
Duration: 1 hour
Elevation gain: 240 ft (73 m)
Effort: Easy
Trailhead: Tahquitz Canyon Visitors Center
Information and Maps: www.tahquitzcanyon.com/trail_maps

Tahquitz Canyon is the most popular trail in the Indian Canyons, and for good reason. This moderate 2-mi (3.2-km) loop winds through a scenic rocky canyon full of native vegetation across an ancient Cahuilla village site to end at Tahquitz Falls, a rare desert waterfall. At the visitor center, pay your fee and pick up a Tahquitz Canyon trail guide for interpretive descriptions of historic and scenic points along the trail. Water is also available for purchase.

The trail follows a seasonal creek dependent on snowmelt from the San Jacinto Mountains. The best time to hike is **February-April** for more moderate canyon temperatures and the best chance of water in the canyon. On the way back you'll have wide views of Palm Springs and the Coachella Valley to the east.

Lower Palm Canyon Trail

Distance: 2.2 mi (3.5 km) round-trip
Duration: 1 hour
Elevation gain: 100 ft (31 m)
Effort: Easy
Trailhead: Trading Post and scenic overlook for Palm Canyon
Directions: From the Palm Springs Visitors Center (2901 N. Palm Canyon Dr.), head south for 9 mi (14.5 km) until Palm Canyon Drive ends at the Trading Post and Palm Canyon overlook.
Information and Maps: www.indian-canyons.com/indian_canyons

You'll catch the views of the world's largest fan palm oasis, hundreds of green palms clustered improbably at the bottom of a rocky gorge, before strolling down to the canyon floor to be dwarfed by their primordial trunks. Fifteen mi (24 km) long, Palm Canyon marks the divide between the Santa Rosa and San Jacinto Mountains. It offers stunning contrasts—the lush proliferation of palms set against the craggy canyon walls and arid desert.

A graded trail winds down into the canyon from the **Palm Canyon overlook.** The trail wanders through mammoth palms offering shaggy seclusion and shade. Depending on the season and snowmelt, you'll come across hidden pools and intermittent streams studded with boulders. The canyon feels mysterious and Jurassic—it wouldn't seem out of place to catch a glimpse of a dinosaur strolling along. You'll follow a trail on the right side of the canyon above the level of the streambed for about 0.7 mi (1.1 km), continuing through spectacular palm groves. At 0.7 mi (1.1 km) the trail crosses to the left side of the canyon, an easy or more difficult task depending on water flow in the canyon. Soon, after 1 mi (1.6 km) total, the palms become less dense and the trail becomes exposed, forking with the **East Fork** and **Victor Trails.** This is a good turnaround point if your goal was to

PALM SPRINGS AND THE COACHELLA VALLEY
SPORTS AND RECREATION

experience the palm oasis; return the way you came. The full trail travels 15 mi (24 km) one-way. Seasonal **ranger-led hikes** (10am Fri.-Sun. Oct.-June) are also available.

Andreas Canyon Loop
Distance: *2 mi (3.2 km) round-trip*
Duration: *1 hour*
Elevation gain: *50 ft (15 m)*
Effort: *Easy*
Trailhead: *A picnic area and trailheads for Andreas and Murray Canyons*
Directions: *From the intersection of South Palm Canyon Drive and Highway 111, continue south for under 3 mi (4.8 km), following signs for Indian Canyons. After the toll booth, take the road to the right for 0.7 mi (1.1 km) until it ends. Start by hiking the right (north) side of the canyon to follow the creek.*
Information and Maps: *www.indian-canyons. com/trail_maps*

The trail through lovely Andreas Canyon follows a permanent creek through hundreds of native California fan palms. Secluded pools and striking rock formations make this well worth the small amount of effort the hike requires. Until the late 1800s, the Cahuilla people used the creek to irrigate crops of melons, corn, and pumpkins. The turnaround point for this scenic desert stroll is a fence blocking off land for the Andreas Canyon Club. The secretive and exclusive club was formed in 1923. Members bought land from the Southern Pacific Railroad and built a series of rock houses, 22 in all, into the craggy hills to blend in with the desert landscape. A clubhouse was built in 1925. Prior to procuring the land, members camped in the canyon's streambed in rock caches. The return route on the left side of the canyon follows a high ridge south of the stream. Seasonal **ranger-led hikes** (10am and 1pm Fri.-Sun. Oct.-June) are also available.

Murray Canyon
Distance: *4 mi (6.4 km) round-trip*

Duration: *2 hours*
Elevation gain: *500 ft (152 m)*
Effort: *Moderate*
Trailhead: *A picnic area and trailheads for Andreas and Murray Canyons*
Directions: *From the intersection of South Palm Canyon Drive and Highway 111, continue south for under 3 mi (4.8 km), following signs for Indian Canyons. After the toll booth, take the road to the right for 0.7 mi (1.1 km) until it ends.*
Information and Maps: *www.indian-canyons. com/trail_maps*

The winding trail through Murray Canyon offers a longer chance to explore a palm-filled canyon than its scenic neighbor Andreas.

The trail begins at the parking area for Andreas and Murray Canyons and heads south before entering Murray Canyon proper. It delves into the lower edges of the San Jacinto Mountains, providing views of its soaring cliffs as you meander through the palm-enclosed stream-crossed canyon. The second half of the trail requires hopping back and forth across a picturesque stream that varies in intensity depending on the season. California fan palms are abundant and mixed in with a scattering of cacti, desert willows, and cottonwoods. A series of gentle cascades, the **Seven Sisters Waterfall,** marks the end of the hike. Return the way you came.

★ Mount San Jacinto State Park
The granite peaks of the San Jacinto Mountains may be a world away from the sunbaked desert floor, but the miracle of engineering that is the Palm Springs Aerial Tramway was designed to allow visitors to reach the cool mountain air in about 10 minutes.

The tramway leaves from Valley Station on the desert floor (elevation 2,643 ft/806 m) and lifts visitors on a dizzying ride via suspended cable cars to traverse the length of rugged Chino Canyon, alighting in a crisp alpine climate at Mountain Station (elevation 8,516 ft/2,596 m) in Mount San Jacinto State Park (951/659-2607; www.parks.ca.gov). From

1: Murray Canyon **2:** Tahquitz Canyon **3:** hiker on the Araby Trail

Mountain Station, a network of trails totaling 54 mi (87 km) within the 14,000-acre (5,670-ha) wilderness leads to pine forests, meadows, and striking views.

Stop at the **Long Valley Ranger Station** (0.25 mi/0.4 km west of Mountain Station) for maps and info. All trails, except the Long Valley Discovery Trail and Desert View Trail, require that you check in and complete a **day-use permit,** available at the ranger station.

Because of the drastic change in elevation, the hiking season generally runs **April-November.** Keep in mind that temperatures may be very cold and trails may be impassable due to snow and ice. Expect a temperature difference of 30-40°F (15-20°C) from the valley floor.

Long Valley Discovery Trail

Distance: 0.6 mi (1 km) round-trip
Duration: 30 minutes
Elevation gain: Negligible
Effort: Easy
Trailhead: Upper Terminal Mountain Station via the Palm Springs Aerial Tramway
Information and Maps: www.visitgreaterpalmsprings.com

This easy, level nature trail lies outside the back entrance of Mountain Station, after a thrilling lift on the Palm Springs Aerial Tramway to the top of Mount San Jacinto State Park. The signed trail starts at the bottom of the walkway and follows a 0.6-mi (1-km) loop through pine forest and past a gorgeous meadow with interpretive signs providing an introduction to the park's plants and animals.

Desert View Trail

Distance: 1.6 mi (2.6 km) round-trip
Duration: 1 hour
Elevation gain: 160 ft (49 m)
Effort: Easy-moderate
Trailhead: Upper Terminal Mountain Station via the Palm Springs Aerial Tramway. Exit Mountain Station via the back entrance. The signed trail starts at the bottom of the walkway.
Information and Maps: www.visitgreaterpalmsprings.com

Slightly longer than the Long Valley Discovery Trail, this trail offers another option from the **Mountain Station** after your tram ride to the top. Enjoy the striking contrasts between this fresh alpine haven and the austere desert below via an easy to moderate loop trail that clocks in at less than 2 mi (3.2 km). The trail, which can be hiked clockwise or counterclockwise, undulates through rich pine forest, passing five rocky lookouts, called notches, that give way to sweeping views of the Coachella Valley below. Each notch gives a different panoramic perspective and up-close views of colorful rock outcroppings.

Round Valley Loop to Wellman Divide

Distance: 4.5-6.5 mi (7.2-10.5 km) round-trip
Duration: 3-4 hours
Elevation gain: 1,300 ft (396 m)
Effort: Moderate
Trailhead: Long Valley Ranger Station
Directions: Take the Palm Springs Aerial Tramway to the Upper Terminal Mountain Station. From Mountain Station, the ranger station is 0.25 mi (0.4 km) to the west. Check in and complete a day-use pass before beginning your hike.
Information and Maps: www.visitgreaterpalmsprings.com

Hike the Round Valley Loop with lovely Round Valley and its luxuriant meadow as your destination (4.5 mi/7.2 km round-trip) or tack on a steep addendum (6.5 mi/10.5 km round-trip) to see the spectacular views from Wellman Divide.

From the Long Valley Ranger Station, follow the well-marked trail (Low Trail on maps) southeast toward Round Valley. The trail climbs steadily through pine forests. In early summer you may be crossing or traveling alongside bubbling seasonal snowmelt streams. At 1.8 mi (2.9 km), the trail splits. Continue right toward Round Valley and the meadow. You reach Round Valley at 2.1 mi (3.4 km); it's a satisfying destination. Many people use it as an overnight spot, camping at the Round Valley backcountry campground or Tamarack Valley to the north.

Continuing from Round Valley, the trail gets real, climbing 660 ft (201 m) in elevation over 1 mi (1.6 km). The spectacular views from Wellman Divide make the short and steep trek worth it, casting a visual net toward venerable Tahquitz Peak and deeper over the Santa Rosa Mountains. From here it's only 2.7 mi (4.3 km) to San Jacinto Peak.

Assuming you've had enough for the day (continuing on to San Jacinto Peak will add an additional 5.4 mi/8.7 km round-trip), return 0.3 mi (0.5 km) to a trail junction past Round Valley. Mix it up by taking the right loop (High Trail on maps). This will add a mere 0.3 mi (0.5 km) to your hike but will vary your return scenery and give you unexpected views of Mountain Station as you descend the last 1 mi (1.6 km) to the ranger station.

San Jacinto Peak

Distance: 12 mi (19.3 km) round-trip
Duration: 6 hours
Elevation gain: 2,300 ft (700 m)
Effort: Strenuous
Trailhead: Long Valley Ranger Station
Directions: Take the Palm Springs Aerial Tramway to the Upper Terminal Mountain Station. From Mountain Station, the Ranger Station is 0.25 mi (0.4 km) to the west. Check in and complete a day-use pass before beginning your hike.
Information and Maps: www.parks.ca.gov

Naturalist John Muir proclaimed the view from San Jacinto Peak to be one of the most sublime on earth. Topographically, it makes sense. San Jacinto Peak is the highest peak in the San Jacinto Mountains and one of the most prominent peaks in the contiguous United States, its north escarpment rising 10,000 ft (3,050 m) in 7 mi (11.3 km) from the San Gorgonio Pass and its low desert wind farms. The peak towers over Palm Springs to the east and the mountain village of Idyllwild to the south. The vistas from the top are amazing, taking in the Coachella Valley, the Salton Sea, and looking north to the impressive San Bernardino Mountains and lofty San Gorgonio Mountain.

There are several routes to San Jacinto Peak, including from the town of Idyllwild. The most direct and shortest route begins from the top of the Palm Springs Aerial Tramway. From the Long Valley Ranger Station, follow the well-marked trail (Low Trail on maps) southeast toward Round Valley. The trail winds and ascends steadily through pine forests. In early summer, if there has been a good season of winter snowfall, you may come across lively seasonal streams. At 1.8 mi (2.9 km), the trail splits. Continue right toward Round Valley, reaching Round Valley at 2.1 mi (3.4 km). From here the trail begins to climb more seriously toward Wellman Divide, climbing 660 ft (201 m) over the course of 1 mi (1.6 km). Take in the spectacular views from Wellman Divide; Tahquitz Peak and the Santa Rosa Mountains are in your sights. From here it's only 2.7 mi (4.3 km) to San Jacinto Peak. Follow the trail north toward San Jacinto Peak as it switchbacks steeply and the views grow increasingly sweeping. Just below the peak (0.3 mi/0.5 km), the trail splits again. Follow the steep trail up to the giant granite massif that is San Jacinto Peak. Soak in the views from the steep and sometimes windy pinnacle.

Return the way you came. After Round Valley you reach a split with the Low and High Trails. Both return to the Long Valley Ranger Station. The High Trail (right split) adds a small amount of mileage (0.3 mi/0.5 km), but it takes you over ground you haven't covered. The good news: Either way, you're close to some well-earned food, drinks, and continued views (from the comfort of a chair) at Mountain Station.

BIKING

Scenic bike paths thread along the base of the rocky foothills and through Palm Springs's historic neighborhoods, past old Rat Pack-era haunts with architectural pedigree and storied histories.

Biking is best **October-May.** Summers can be way too hot. If you do bike in summer, start early and return no later than midmorning.

Bike Paths

For cruising around town, a network of paved bike paths traverses Palm Springs, extending from Indian Canyon Drive northeast of the Palm Springs Visitors Center south toward the Indian Canyons and Murray Canyon Drive and southeast to Golf Club Drive. There are several types of bike paths: Class 1 are road-separated trails with exclusive right-of-way for bicycles and pedestrians; Class 2 are striped lanes for one-way bike travel on city streets; and Class 3 are signed trails that share roads with motor vehicles and have no on-street striping.

Visitors can download a free map of bike routes and trails from the Palm Springs Visitors Center website (https://visitpalmsprings.com).

Citywide Tour
Palm Canyon Dr. and Tachevah Dr.; 13 mi (20.9 km)

For a great introduction to town, take the Citywide Tour. This ride brings you on a wide loop around Palm Springs, from residential neighborhoods to golf courses and country clubs to civic buildings. Start on the north end of town at Palm Canyon Drive and Tachevah Drive. The trail begins by heading west toward the mountains to explore historic residential neighborhoods, including Las Palmas. It then heads south, skirting the foothills of the San Jacinto Mountains and passing the Palm Springs Art Museum. The trail continues south to weave through the country clubs and golf course on the south end of town. On the return, the loop makes an arc through the eastern side of town paralleling Palm Springs International Airport and some of Palm Springs's civic buildings.

Downtown Tour
N. Palm Canyon Dr. and E. Alejo Rd.; 3 mi (4.8 km)

Cruise around downtown Palm Springs on the Downtown Tour, a quieter take on Palm Springs's bustling center. Begin at Palm Canyon Drive and Alejo Road. The first part of the loop runs along the foot of the mountains along Belardo Road. It parallels the main downtown thoroughfares of Palm Canyon Drive and Indian Canyon Drive and dips past the Palm Springs Art Museum. The route continues down to Ramon Road, where it begins its northward return path at the north-south Calle El Segundo.

Deepwell Tour
Mesquite Ave. and Sunrise Way; 3.5 mi (5.6 km)

For an easy and scenic trip, try the Deepwell

Many hotels offer complimentary bikes for exploring Palm Springs.

Tour. This route begins at Mesquite Avenue and Sunrise Way to follow Calle Palo Fiera and Camino Real south, with a quick eastward jog on East Palm Canyon Drive, to take you through the palm-lined residential streets of one of the city's older neighborhoods on the south end of town. The loop returns via La Verne Way and Sunrise Way to connect again with Mesquite Avenue.

Bike Rentals

Many hotels offer complimentary cruiser bikes for tooling around town. If your hotel does not have bikes or if you would like a mountain, road, tandem, or electric bike, they are available for rent at two locations.

BIKE Palm Springs Bike Rentals

194 S. Indian Canyon Dr.; 760/832-8912; 267 E. Tahquitz Canyon Way; 760/318-0010; www. bikepsrentals.com; 8am-5pm daily Oct.-May

BIKE Palm Springs Bike Rentals has two locations in downtown Palm Springs. They rent standard pedal bikes ($25 for 4 hours, $35 per day), premium road bikes ($70 for up to 4 hours, $90 per day), electric bikes ($60 for 4 hours, $85 per day), child bikes ($20 for 4 hours, $25 per day), child bike seats ($25 for 4 hours, $35 per day), and child carrier trailers ($25 for 4 hours, $25 per day). Rentals include free maps with touring routes, locks, and helmets.

Big Wheel Tours

1590 S. Palm Canyon Dr.; 760/548-0500, ext. 1; 74200 Hwy. 111, Palm Desert; 760/779-1837, ext. 2; www. bwbtours.com; tours 8am-1pm daily, summer hours vary; rentals by reservation, delivery available for $35

Big Wheel Tours features KHS and Benno brand bicycles for rent in the Palm Springs area. Cruisers, mountain bikes, hybrids, and road bikes are available for rent by the hour ($12-20), half day ($25-60), full day ($35-80), and week ($90-295). Big Wheel Tours has two locations: one in Palm Springs and one in Palm Desert, 15 mi (24 km) southeast of Palm Springs in the Coachella Valley.

Big Wheel Tours also offers bike tours (4

hours; 8am and 1pm daily Oct.-May; $129 pp). Its **Earthquake Canyon Express Tour** for beginner to intermediate riders travels the San Andreas Fault zone along the Colorado-Mojave Desert transition with views of the Salton Sea. The **Indian Canyon Bike and Hike** offers a 10-mi (16.1-km) round-trip excursion through some of Palm Springs's historic neighborhoods combined with a scenic nature walk in well-watered Andreas Canyon. A **Palm Springs Celebrity Bike Tour** is also available. The three-hour tour winds through beautiful Palm Springs neighborhoods past historic celebrity homes.

HORSEBACK RIDING
Smoke Tree Stables

2500 S. Toledo Ave.; 760/327-1372; www. smoketreestables.com; 9am, 11am, and 1pm Fri.-Tues. and holidays Oct.-May; $175 pp

Beyond its reputation as a sleek resort town, Palm Springs has a Wild West side. The last of the traditional ranch-style inns offering city slickers an escape to simpler times is the historic Smoke Tree Stables. Established in 1927, it offers guided horseback trail rides that allow you to experience the striking Palm Springs desert. Trips follow the nearby palm oasis-filled Indian Canyons.

Rides are offered Friday-Tuesday and some Thursdays during the season. For the most accurate availability, check the Smoke Tree Stables schedule online to confirm times, weather, and availability, and to book your trail ride. Advance reservations are required. Plan to arrive at least 30 minutes prior to departure. Trail rides lasting 1 hour 40 minutes follow Andreas and Murray Canyons, part of the well-watered Indian Canyons.

Murray Canyon Haul Rides

9am, 11am, and 1pm daily, other times by appointment; $175 pp

Murray Canyon Haul Rides follow the streams and palms of Andreas and Murray Canyons. Private guided trail rides (additional $250 per guide per hour) are available by advance reservation.

PALM SPRINGS AND THE COACHELLA VALLEY

SPORTS AND RECREATION

WINTER SPORTS
Mountain Station
Winter Adventure Center

https://pstramway.com; 10am-4pm Fri., 9am-4pm Sat.-Sun. and holidays

The Palm Springs Aerial Tramway Mountain Station offers cross-country ski packages and snowshoe packages for visitors looking to get immersed in mountain snow sports. The center is located at the bottom of the concrete path as you exit Mountain Station and is open seasonally with hours subject to change without notice. Check the website for weather conditions and rental availability.

PARKS

Palm Springs is nestled near such spectacular wilderness parks as Joshua Tree National Park and Mount San Jacinto State Park, and time adventuring outdoors is best spent in these destination spots; however, a skate park and a dog park near Palm Springs's downtown fill a niche.

Palm Springs Skate Park

Sunrise Plaza, 401 S. Pavilion Way; 760/656-0024; 1pm-9pm Mon.-Fri., 9am-9pm Sat.-Sun.

The Palm Springs Skate Park taps into Southern California's history of pool skating to offer bowls for smooth, fast skating with several feet of vertical walls, pool coping, and transitions. The skate park also features street skating elements like rails, pyramids, stairs, ramps, and quarter pipes. Actual skaters were consulted in the building of this park, with a fun and genuine result for board and in-line skaters of all skill levels.

Palm Springs Dog Park

N. Civic Dr., behind Palm Springs City Hall; 760/323-8117; www.palmspringsca.gov; 6am-10pm daily

The leash-free 1.6-acre (0.6-ha) Palm Springs Dog Park is behind city hall. Separate areas for large and small dogs offer your pets a place to run free. Park benches, shade canopies, and drinking fountains round out the amenities.

Entertainment and Events

THE ARTS
Annenberg Theater

101 N. Museum Dr.; 760/322-4800; www.psmuseum.org; box office 10:30am-4pm Fri.-Sun.; ticket around $110

The Annenberg Theater, housed within the Palm Springs Art Museum, hosts live professional performances in its 430-seat state-of-the-art theater. The Annenberg Theater combines the visual and performing arts to feature a yearly series showcasing theater, dance, music, and mixed-media works. Order tickets on the website or call the box office. Tickets sell out well in advance.

FESTIVALS AND EVENTS
Modernism Week

www.modernismweek.com; Feb. and Oct.; up to $150

Modernism Week is Palm Springs's signature annual event, celebrating mid-century modern architecture, design, and culture over two nonstop weekends every February. Modernism Week fosters appreciation for Palm Springs's shining modernist history while encouraging a fresh approach and thinking about design, art, fashion, and sustainable modern living. The festival features more than 250 events, including signature home tours with a chance to peek into some of Palm Springs's fabulous historic houses, a modernism show and sale, modern garden tours, architectural double-decker bus tours (including sunset tours of illuminated mid-century classic buildings), nightly parties (soiree at Frank Sinatra's estate, anyone?), walking and bike tours, lectures and cocktail hour discussions, fashion events, a vintage travel trailer exhibition, films, music, and more. Modernism Week hosts a mini event,

Modernism Week-October (4 days) to kick off Palm Springs's social and recreation season. Check online for highlights, recommendations, and ongoing news.

Tickets for Modernism Week (on sale Nov. 1) and the Modernism Week-October (on sale Aug. 1) are sold online for individual events. Tickets sell out quickly, especially for the popular house tours.

Splash House
www.splashhouse.com; 2 weekends in Aug.; from $170

The pool party to end all pool parties is the annual Splash House, a three-day electronic dance music and pool party held in Palm Springs two weekends in August. The host hotels (The Saguaro, 1800 E. Palm Canyon Dr., and the Renaissance, 888 E. Tahquitz Canyon Way) form ground zero for Splash House, with deejays and daytime events; shuttles run between the host hotels. A general admission wristband gets you access to the pools and events at the hotels as well as the shuttle. General admission tickets can be purchased separately or as a package with hotel rooms. Late-night parties are held off-site at unique Palm Springs locations, such as the Palm Springs Air Museum. Tickets for the off-site parties (from $65) are sold separately.

Palm Springs Cultural Center Film Festivals
Palm Springs International Film Festival
www.psfilmfest.org; Jan.; 5-day pass $397-607

The Palm Springs International Film Festival is a well-established destination film festival that draws more than 135,000 filmgoers every January. The festival features more than 200 films from 78 countries over 12 days of events and film screenings, including the prestigious Film Awards Gala.

Screenings are held at several theaters in Palm Springs and the Coachella Valley, including **Camelot Theatres,** part of the Palm Springs Cultural Center (2300 E. Baristo Rd.; 760/325-6565; www.

palmspringsculturalcenter.org), **The Annenberg Theater,** part of the Palm Springs Art Museum (101 N. Museum Dr.; 760/322-4800; www.psmuseum.org), **Palm Canyon Theatre** (538 N. Palm Canyon Dr.; 760/323-5123; https://palmcanyontheatre. net), and **Mary Pickford is D'Place** (36850 Pickfair St., Cathedral City; 760/328-7100).

Advance tickets go on sale in December and can be purchased online, by phone (800/898-7256 or 760/778-8979; 9am-5pm Mon.-Fri.), or in person at box office locations that include the Palm Springs Cultural Center and screening locations on days with screenings.

Palm Springs International ShortFest
www.psfilmfest.org; June; screenings $15, passes $250

The Palm Springs International Film Society also offers an International ShortFest every June. The festival screens hundreds of shorts from over 60 countries over 7 days of screenings, classes, and panels. Passes are available for advance purchase in April. Passes give unlimited access to programs throughout the festival and can be purchased online. Tickets for individual programs can be purchased at box office locations on the day of the program.

American Documentary and Animation Film Festival
www.americandocumentaryfilmfestival.com; Mar.; screenings $10, passes $50-169

American Documentary and Animation Film Festival showcases films from around the globe that focus on making an impact through real stories with real issues. First held in 2012, the nonprofit festival screens more than 100 documentaries during its five-day annual run. Tickets to individual screenings, many with Q&As, as well as tickets to the opening-night gala and festival passes are available online. Films are screened in venues in Palm Springs, Rancho Mirage, and Palm Desert.

LGBTQ+ Events
Palm Springs is a year-round LGBTQ+

TOP EXPERIENCE
Mid-Century Modernism

In the 1930s, celebrities streamed from Los Angeles to Palm Springs, acquiring second homes to hide in and party away the winter season. This laid-back desert lifestyle allowed architects the creative freedom to explore modernist materials, designing structures inspired by the clean lines of the desert. The 1950s and 1960s were the height of modernist design. Throughout the city are design examples from noted architects Albert Frey, E. Stewart Williams, William F. Cody, Donald Wexler, John Lautner, and Richard Neutra. A visit to Palm Springs is a trip back in time.

The Palm Springs Visitors Center sells a mid-century modern map ($5) highlighting civic buildings, inns and hotels, celebrity homes, and other exceptional residences. Interior tours of some gems are available during **Modernism Week** (www.modernismweek.com; Feb.).

Don't miss these Rat Pack-era abodes, whimsical desert structures, and modernist design examples from noted architects. The following are listed from north to south:

- **Tramway Gas Station** (2901 N. Palm Canyon Dr.): This 1965 gas station once serviced the Palm Springs Aerial Tramway. Now the **Palm Springs Visitors Center,** it features iconic lines and a soaring roofline designed by Albert Frey with Robson Chambers.

- **Alexander Steel Houses** (between E. Molino Rd. and N. Sunnyview Dr.): Designed by Donald Wexler and Richard Harrison and built in 1960-1962 by the George Alexander Construction company, these seven prefabricated homes use light-gauge steel to frame glass walls that afford striking mountain views.

- **Kaufmann House** (470 W. Vista Chino): Designed by Richard Neutra in 1946-1947 for Edgar Kaufmann Sr., who had also commissioned Frank Lloyd Wright to design the Fallingwater house in Pennsylvania, this private residence has been impeccably restored.

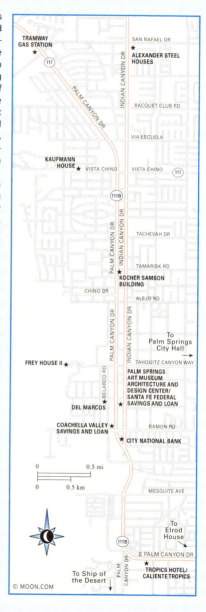

mid-century homes in South Palm Springs

- **Kocher Samson Building** (766 N. Palm Canyon Dr.): Albert Frey's first commercial structure, bringing Palm Springs into the international modernism movement, is located in what is now the Uptown Design District.

- **Frey House II** (686 Palisades Dr.): This 1963 rectangular glass box sits tucked on a hillside 220 ft (67 m) above the desert floor and was constructed around a giant boulder.

- **Del Marcos Hotel** (225 W. Baristo Rd.): Designed by William F. Cody in 1947, the Del Marcos was ahead of its time, featuring post-and-beam construction with organic, natural materials that include redwood and stone. The angular lines highlight interior garden rooms that form a U shape around the pool, all complete with mountain views.

- **Santa Fe Federal Savings and Loan** (300 S. Palm Canyon Dr.): Now the **Palm Springs Art Museum Architecture and Design Center,** this iconic 1961 structure has been impeccably restored. Note the elevated concrete foundation and aluminum solar screens.

- **Coachella Valley Savings and Loan** (499 S. Palm Canyon Dr.): Designed by architect E. Stewart Williams in 1960, the structure, now a Chase Bank, stands out with its arched facade and vertical bronze siding.

- **City National Bank** (588 S. Palm Canyon Dr.): Designed in 1959 by Rudi Baumfeld of Victor Gruen Associates, this current Bank of America branch is striking for its curved exterior and blue mosaic tile.

- **Ship of the Desert** (1995 S. Camino Monte): Designed in 1936 by Los Angeles architects Eric Webster and Adrian Wilson, this streamlined nautical house gets its name from the prow-front living room. Bedroom suites can only be accessed by an exterior redwood deck. The home is currently owned by fashion designer Trina Turk.

- **Tropics Hotel** (411 E. Palm Canyon Dr.): Now the **Caliente Tropics,** the 1964 Polynesian-themed resort still retains some of its fun and kitschy tiki elements.

- **Elrod House** (2175 Southridge Dr.): The 1968 residence of interior designer Arthur Elrod features bold concrete circles, movable walls, a fully retracting glass living room wall, and an infinity pool. Designed by architect John Lautner, it was featured in the 1971 James Bond thriller *Diamonds Are Forever.*

TOP EXPERIENCE

★ Pool-Hopping

For most people, a Palm Springs vacation means catching up on summer reading at the hotel pool. Of course, there are other things to do—golfing, shopping, day tripping. But at the end of the day (probably sometime after lunch), you will likely be relaxing at your hotel of choice. Choose your hotel wisely: Some pools are known for their serene atmosphere while others have a party vibe. Some are BYOB while others have a full-service bar. Some skew young while others... you get the picture.

The pool scene in Palm Springs tends to be relaxed compared to, say, Las Vegas. But a handful of hotels book deejays and sling poolside cocktails with events that are open to both hotel guests and the public. Check individual hotel websites for event information. The pool party season runs **March-September**.

vintage pool umbrella

- The chic uptown **Arrive** hotel (page 153) offers a scene-y pool hang with breakfast, lunch, snacks, and frosty cocktails. The hotel prides itself on being open to the neighborhood and typically allows in non-guests and neighborhood folks. During special events or when the pool is extra crowded, it may be limited to hotel guests. Poolside loungers (age 21 and over only; nonguests $25) are reserved with a patio room.

- **The Rowan** (page 154) claims the only rooftop pool in the desert. From seven stories up you will have the stunning mountain views visitors demand from their poolside loungers as well as

vacation destination with hotels and nightlife that cater exclusively to the LGBTQ+ community.

The Dinah

locations vary; www.thedinah.com; Sept.; individual events $40-300, packages $279-650

Established in 1991, The Dinah is the self-proclaimed largest queer, lesbian, and non-binary party and music festival in the world. This four-day, four-night annual getaway takes Palm Springs by storm every September. It kicks off with a massive opening party on Thursday night and continues its deluge of celebrity-studded events and parties throughout the weekend. The event features deejays, including celebrity guest deejays, dancers, daytime pool parties, live concerts, comedy, and nightclub parties throughout the weekend.

The festival is based in a few of the larger Palm Springs hotels, which are where the daytime pool parties take place. Stay at one of the featured hotel sponsors to make sure you are at the center of the action. Tickets are available on The Dinah website with weekend package deals or tickets to individual events.

The White Party

locations vary; https://whitepartyglobal.com; Mar.; individual events $40-250, passes from $499

The White Party is a massive LGBTQ+ music festival and dance party geared toward gay men. The three-day, three-night festival is held annually in March. It kicks off at noon Friday and goes strong until 7am Monday morning, with daytime pool parties, deejays, live performances, and themed nighttime events. The White Party festival's main event

panoramic views of Palm Springs. The aptly named open-air High Bar serves snacks and craft cocktails. Daytime cabanas ($200 plus $200 food and drink minimum) are available for hotel guests. Nonguests can rent an evening cabana ($150 plus $200 food and drink minimum).

- The central pool at the 1951 **Holiday House** (page 154) is surrounded by citrus trees and the clean lines of the hotel designed by Herbert H. Burns, one of the heavy hitters of Palm Springs's mid-century modern style. An open-air lobby bar and restaurant adds margaritas, sandwiches, and more reasons not to leave the property. Day passes (age 21 and over only; $50) are available through www.resortpass.com.

- With the reinstatement of a tiki bar on the premises, the **Caliente Tropics** hotel (page 155) regained its purpose in the world. Quirky Polynesian architecture, affordable motel rooms, a children-allowed policy, and a free-for-all vibe mean that the Caliente Tropics has always had a pool scene. However, The Reef brings some purpose to the mayhem. Tiki snacks and libations are available poolside at The Reef. Day passes to the pool (over age 10; $20) are available at the front desk.

- The stylish, sprawling **Ace Hotel & Swim Club** (page 156) is home to some of the biggest weekend pool parties in town, with poolside drink service, outdoor bar, and deejays. The enthusiastic crowds are carefree and cool (some might say "too cool for school"). The Feel Good Spa is available for massages, facials, and body and hair services.

- The trendy **Saguaro** has a lively pool scene. An outdoor pool with two hot tubs, lounge seating, and an outdoor bar offers a great place to relax and party against the Technicolor hotel backdrop. The hotel also hosts pool parties during Coachella weekend (Apr.) and **Splash House** (Aug.; page 137), with international deejays and high-profile art, music, and fashion influencers catering to a young dance-loving crowd. The hotel pool is open to anyone, which means it can get crazy. Day passes ($40) are available through www.resortpass.com.

happens on Saturday night—a 10-hour dance party with multiple levels, dancers, special effects, and huge sound system. The White Party Ferris wheel and fireworks display choreographed to a deejay music remix add even more spark to the event.

White Party is centered on several host hotels in Palm Springs. Weekend passes are available on the White Party website, or you can buy tickets to individual events.

Cinema Diverse

www.palmspringsculturalcenter.org; Sept.; screenings $13.25, passes $179

Started in 2008, Cinema Diverse is a Palm Springs gay and lesbian film festival held annually in September. The festival showcases feature films, short films, and new media as well as a series of after parties in popular Palm Springs bars and restaurants. Tickets are available online.

Pride Weekend

https://apps.pspride.org; Nov.

Pride Weekend happens annually on one weekend in November to celebrate lesbian, gay, bisexual, and transgender diversity. There are host hotels for centralized gathering and party zones, but the entire town of Palm Springs fills up for a celebratory weekend. Festivities include a block party and a parade.

Shopping

Palm Springs is known for its mid-century antiquing and stylish desert home furnishings.

UPTOWN DESIGN DISTRICT AND NORTH PALM SPRINGS

The sleek Uptown Design District has the highest concentration of mid-mod shopping in Palm Springs. Stroll colorful North Palm Canyon Drive between Vista Chino (north end) and Alejo (south end) to find vintage and new-retro home furnishings, art, gifts, clothing, and fashion accessories.

TOP EXPERIENCE

★ Vintage

For vintage clothing shopping, check out the string of shops clustered along Highway 111 north and south of the intersection with West Racquet Club Road for denim, tropical, and designer fashion.

Bustown Modern

2235 N. Palm Canyon Dr.; 760/285-3168; 11am-4pm Thurs. and Mon., 11am-5pm Fri.-Sat., noon-5pm Sun.

A standout is Bustown Modern. Owner Anessa Woods has had a few incarnations of her vintage shops in LA and the high and low deserts, and her taste is unerring across them. Her Palm Springs store offers luscious racks of 20th-century vintage and designer fashion. Its location on the north end of town on the way into Palm Springs means you can arrive in style.

The Shops at Thirteen Forty-Five

1345 N. Palm Canyon Dr.; 760/464-0480; www. theshopsat1345.com; 11am-5pm Thurs.-Mon.

The elegant building that now houses The Shops at Thirteen Forty-Five is a historic mid-century building designed by iconic architect E. Stewart Williams in 1955. Inside, a collective of 13 unique shops feature vintage and new furniture, home accessories, and art.

Iconic Atomic

1103 N. Palm Canyon Dr.; 760/322-0777; www. iconicatomic.com; 10am-6pm Fri.-Sun.

Iconic Atomic is a cheerful shop specializing in vintage clothing and accessories as well as bonus housewares from the 1960s and 1970s. You might find party dresses, sport coats, tiki ware, vintage magazines, or furniture.

A La MOD

886 N. Palm Canyon Dr.; 760/327-0707; www. alamodps.com; 11am-5pm Mon. and Wed.-Sat., by appointment only noon-3pm Sun.

After visiting A La MOD, with its room after groovy room of impeccable vintage furnishings, you might just wish you could move in here instead of trying to update your own place to be this stylish. Couches, lamps, tables, chairs, bookends—one of each, please.

Christopher Anthony Ltd.

803 N. Palm Canyon Dr.; 760/322-0600; www. christopheranthonyltd.com; 10am-5pm Mon. and Wed.-Sat., noon-5pm Sun.

The large glass front of Christopher Anthony Ltd. encourages window-shopping with its eye-catching collection of high-end mid-century home collectibles and an original line of retro-inspired lighting and furnishings. From sleek 1960s lounge chairs to abstract paintings, it's everything you need to seriously step up your household game.

Bon Vivant

766 N. Palm Canyon Dr.; 760/534-3197; www.gmcb. com; 10:30am-4pm Thurs.-Mon.

Vintage cuff links? Check. Chunky necklaces? Check. Animal curios, curvy lamps, and massive multicolored glassware collection? Check, check, and check. Find it all at Bon Vivant, on the street level in the original Albert Frey-designed Kocher-Samson building.

Modernway

2500 N. Palm Canyon Dr.; 760/320-5455; www.psmodernway.com; noon-5pm Thurs.-Mon.

Just north of Vista Chino, Modernway is a well-established and well-regarded Palm Springs vintage retail outlet specializing in mid-century modern furnishings from the 1950s, 1960s, and 1970s, including vintage hi-fi and stereo pieces.

The Frippery

664 N. Palm Canyon Dr.; 760/699-5365; www.thefrippery.com; 11am-5pm daily

Should you find yourself in a fashion emergency while on vacation, The Frippery has vintage finery for many different desert scenarios, from resort lounging in Palm Springs to boulder gazing in Joshua Tree. Their collection ranges from mod to bohemian with accessories to complete your look.

Boutique
Trina Turk

891 and 895-897 N. Palm Canyon Dr.; 760/416-2856; www.trinaturk.com; 10am-6pm Mon.-Sat., 11am-5pm Sun.

Local fashion design star Trina Turk has come to be synonymous with California chic. Her flagship store, Trina Turk, occupies a luxurious glass-walled corner space originally designed by Albert Frey. The revamped modernist bohemian location features women's apparel, accessories, and Mr. Turk menswear.

Elizabeth and Prince

800 N. Palm Canyon Dr., Suite A; 760/992-5800; www.elizabethandprince.com; 11am-5pm daily

Elizabeth and Prince is an elegant boutique offering a curated collection of chic modern clothing brands and accessories. New York transplants and co-owners Analisa and Shawn have expanded their stylish empire from their original location in La Quinta to boutiques in Palm Desert and Palm Springs.

Their hand-selected collection includes designers like Ulla Johnson, Black Crane, and Raquel Allegra.

Gift and Home
Phylum

901 N. Palm Canyon Dr., Suite 101; 760/424-2110; www.shopphylum.com; 11am-5pm Sun.-Mon., 10am-6pm Thurs.-Sat.

Phylum offers a tempting array of vibrantly colored home and fashion accessories, including place and table mats, linen robes, textiles, and ceramics. It's a good place to stock up on gifts for yourself and others.

Just Fabulous

515 N. Palm Canyon Dr.; 760/864-1300; www.bjustfabulous.com; 9am-5:30pm Mon.-Thurs., 9am-6pm Fri.-Sun.

Just Fabulous taps into Palm Springs's sunny vibes and culture to stock everything from accents to apparel to art. Elevate your space with a scented spa candle, Jeff Koons-inspired balloon dog, or Taschen design book. Snag a pool float or sunglasses to up your weekend game.

CENTRAL PALM SPRINGS AND DOWNTOWN

The main downtown drag, which runs along Palm Canyon Drive from Alejo Road to Ramon Road, tends to be much more touristy than the Design District. Since 2015, downtown Palm Springs has seen a lot of corporate development: the seven-story Kimpton Rowan Hotel, a giant fancy Starbucks, Tommy Bahama Restaurant and Bar, West Elm, and H&M now mingle with small mom-and-pop shops. While downtown doesn't constitute a shopping destination, some of the stores are fun to browse, and you can find gifts, ice cream, bathing suits, fast fashion, and skin products that may also come in handy for your vacation predicament. Filtering down from the Design District, a few shops showcase contemporary home decor and vintage finds.

Markets
Villagefest

www.villagefest.org; 6pm-10pm Thurs. Oct.-May, 7pm-10pm Thurs. June-Sept.

Every Thursday, the downtown blocks of Palm Canyon Drive close to vehicles and open to Villagefest. Over 180 vendors display art, sell handcrafted items, and set up food booths, and many shops, galleries, and restaurants stay open late.

★ Vintage
Palm Canyon Galleria

457 N. Palm Canyon Dr.; 760/323-4576; 11am-5pm daily

Palm Canyon Galleria is an arcade of shops that feature 20th-century home furnishings, ceramics, metal craft, art, and international design.

Accessories
Sunglasses of Palm Springs

152 N. Palm Canyon Dr.; 760/322-1344; 10am-3pm Mon.-Wed. and Fri., 6pm-9pm Thurs., 10am-9pm Sat., 10am-5pm Sun.

When my sunglasses broke on the first day of my Palm Springs vacation, I squinted up and down Palm Springs's downtown until I stumbled upon Sunglasses of Palm Springs. In Palm Springs, where the sun blazes 300 days of the year, a good pair of sunglasses can make or break your vacation. Whether you want to refresh your style or save yourself with this desert necessity, they have a great selection of styles and price points, from Ray-Ban to Prada.

Boutique
Mojave Flea

383 N. Indian Canyon Dr.; https://mojaveflea.com; 11am-5pm daily

Mojave Flea is a brand collective featuring dreamy styles inspired by both the high and low desert. The 10,000-sq-ft (930-sq-m) department store offers a venue for the makers and merchants of clothes, jewelry, housewares, gifts and other style necessities from Joshua Tree, the Coachella Valley, and beyond.

Gift and Home
Destination PSP

170 N. Palm Canyon Dr.; 760/354-9154; www.destinationpsp.com; 10am-6pm Sun.-Wed., 9am-8pm Thurs.-Sat.

Destination PSP offers a colorful and wide-ranging array of originally designed merchandise for the Palm Springs lifestyle, including swim apparel, towels, and housewares such as serving trays and coasters, decor, and gifts. This is a great place to pick up souvenirs and contemporary mid-century-inspired pieces for gift giving and living.

SOUTH PALM SPRINGS
★ Vintage
Market Market

1555 S. Palm Canyon Dr.; 760/248-8557; www.shopmarketmarket.com; 11am-5pm Sun.-Thurs., 11am-6pm Fri.-Sat.

In a part of town not traditionally known for shopping, Market Market came in strong. The destination-worthy emporium features vintage clothing, furniture, housewares, art and design as well as repurposed goods and clothing. The space is the size of an airplane hangar, and the loftiness coupled with the impeccable curation of the booths makes the experience feel less like shopping and more like visiting a museum to style. Perfect lamp specimens flank a pristine couch from the second half of the last century. Designer tunics hang temptingly near the vintage denim of your dreams. Your find here will have already been found and priced appropriately.

1: shopping in the Uptown Design District
2: downtown Palm Springs

Food

UPTOWN DESIGN DISTRICT AND NORTH PALM SPRINGS
Breakfast and Brunch
★ Cheeky's
622 N. Palm Canyon Dr.; 760/327-7595; www.cheekysps.com; 8am-2pm daily; $13-19

Brave the sidewalk line and start your day at Cheeky's for one of the most popular brunches in town. The sunny spot with a patio offers a seasonal, locally sourced menu that changes weekly, plus classics like Blondie's eggs Benedict with bacon, arugula, and a cheddar scone; Cheeky's BLT with jalapeño bacon and pesto fries; signature house-made cinnamon rolls; and a bacon flight. Their array of breakfast drinks includes spicy Bloody Marys, fresh-pressed green juice, and pomegranate mimosas.

Boozehounds
2080 N. Palm Canyon Dr.; 760/656-0067; https://boozehoundsps.com; 5pm-10pm Mon.-Thurs., 10am-11pm Fri.-Sat., 10am-10pm Sun.; brunch $15-28, dinner $18-32

This massive, stylish space can accommodate everyone in your weekend getaway crew plus their furry friends. A four-sided bar anchors the airy central space, and an atrium and patio give options for dog-owners as well as cozy nooks for dining and sipping. The menu brings a fresh pan-Asian twist to California cuisine with dishes like avocado poke toast for brunch and garlic noodles with galbi short rib for dinner. Highly recommend for their festive brunch, but a solid happy hour and late-night menu makes this spot a good choice for any time of the day.

California Cuisine
★ Eight4Nine Restaurant and Lounge
849 N. Palm Canyon Dr.; 760/325-8490; www.eight4nine.com; 11am-9pm Mon.-Thurs., 11am-10pm Fri., 10am-10pm Sat., 10am-9pm Sun.; brunch and lunch $15-37, dinner $23-48

Chic and swanky Eight4Nine Restaurant and Lounge offers a striking white decor set in the former 1954 post office. Now, the contemporary space is accented with colorful art and jewel tones while an upbeat patio provides mountain views. The restaurant offers fresh California nouveau classics with sea, land, and farm mains, featuring salads, sandwiches, and entrées ranging from a poblano chili relleno to miso-marinated sea bass. The lounge stays open all day, offering happy-hour bar and menu items every day.

Copley's
621 N. Palm Canyon Dr.; 760/327-9555; www.copleyspalmsprings.com; 5:30pm-close daily Sept.-mid-July, closed mid-July-Aug.; $29-56

Part of the former Cary Grant estate, Copley's offers New American fine dining in a romantic setting. The candlelit patio has the choicest seating and a stone fireplace. Entrées are geared toward the meat eater, with perfectly executed steaks, duck, fish, and lamb, with seafood and vegetarian options as well.

American
★ The Heyday
1550 N. Palm Canyon Dr.; 760/297-6937; www.theheydaypalmsprings.com; noon-9pm Sun.-Thurs., noon-10pm Fri.-Sat.; $10-20

This low-key burger spot fills a niche in the elevated high-design world of Palm Springs dining. Cute red booths and limited patio seating set the stage for perfectly executed smash burgers and favorite cocktail standards. The straightforward menu adds wings, crispy crinkle fries, and fresh-baked chocolate-chip cookies to round out your meal. They also do a vegan burger that stands

---

1: Pinocchio in the Desert **2:** Boozehounds
3: Eight4Nine Restaurant and Lounge

up to its counterparts. Try the martini and burger special.

★ Paul Bar

3700 E. Vista Chino; 760/656-4082; www. thepaulbarps.com; kitchen 4pm-10pm Wed.-Sun., drinks 4pm-11pm Wed.-Thurs., 4pm-midnight Fri.-Sat., 4pm-10pm Sun.; $16-24

Open a nondescript door in a shabby strip mall to another dimension where diners sip classic cocktails in a dimly lit, speakeasy-style space. One long bar plus a few small booths are where all the magic happens. Diners start lining up ahead of the 4pm open time for this singular experience. The whole place turns over again around 5:30 if you miss the opening, still in time to make the daily happy hour (4pm-7:15pm). A pared-down bistro-style menu features classics like steak frites and salmon as well as small plates.

1501 Gastropub

1501 N. Palm Canyon Dr.; 760/320-1501; www.1501uptown.com; happy hour 3pm-5pm daily, brunch 10am-3pm Sat.-Sun., lunch 11am-3pm Mon.-Fri., dinner 5pm-9pm Sun.-Thurs., 5pm-10pm Fri.-Sat.; happy hour $10-26, brunch $17-34, lunch $18-38, dinner $19-39

Situated in a handsome space designed by architect Chris Pardo, 1501 Gastropub is as classy as a pub can get. Sleek glass architecture with roll-up garage doors to take advantage of the weather and stylish vinyl booths meld with cold smoked salmon and trout, burgers, and comfort entrées like shepherd's pie.

Mexican
El Mirasol

266 E. Via Altamira; 760/459-3136; 9am-9pm Wed.-Sun.; $16-23

It's Palm Springs. Chances are you've spent a hard day at the pool or enjoying some festive event. El Mirasol, located in Los Arboles Hotel, offers the type of Mexican comfort food that can easily hit the spot. The signature smoky Doña Diabla sauce accompanies every meal in quart bottles. Strong margaritas and a charming patio make this an easy choice.

Sushi
Sandfish

1556 N. Palm Canyon Dr.; 760/537-1022; www. sandfishsushiwhiskey.com; 4:30pm-10pm Sun.-Thurs., 4:30pm-11pm Fri.-Sat.; $10-34

Reservations are advised for dinner at Sandfish. Chef-owner Engin Onural has drawn from around the globe to create a buzzy spot with Japanese sushi and seafood uniquely paired with an extensive whiskey list. The menu is served against a stylishly spare Scandinavian interior.

CENTRAL PALM SPRINGS AND DOWNTOWN
Breakfast, Brunch, and Coffee
Farm

6 La Plaza, La Plaza Shopping Center; 760/322-2724; 8am-2pm Wed.-Thurs., 8am-2pm and 5:30pm-9:30pm Fri.-Tues.; $12-22

Once you manage to find the French-inspired Farm tucked down a walkway and nestled past a wedding chapel, it oozes charm. Farmhouse-style wooden tables are scattered under a shady canopy. Brunch-goers enjoy a New American and Provençal-inspired menu with French-press coffee, mimosas, sweet and savory crepes, omelets, sandwiches, salads, and other brunch specialties. Farm prides itself on its menu. Translation: It does not allow substitutions, and the food can take a while. Be prepared to choose something and relax. Friday-Tuesday adds dinner with a five-course chef's-choice prix-fixe ($69) that varies daily.

Pinocchio in the Desert

134 E. Tahquitz Canyon Way; 760/322-3776; www. pinocchiops.com; 7:30am-10pm daily; $13-24

Pinocchio in the Desert is a full-on party. By sometime around noon, the eggs and hash browns are flying onto packed tables in the kitschy setting, and the cheap bottomless mimosas are flowing. The patio gets cranked up to a fever pitch, fanned by the pink-fringed umbrellas, speedy service, and drink specials. Dinner adds European specialties like chicken parmesan, halibut, and pastas while the drink specials keep going.

Wilma and Frieda
155 S. Palm Canyon Dr., Suite A21-A27; 760/992-5080; https://wilmafrieda.com; 8am-2pm daily; $12-25

Wilma and Frieda offers brunch classics in its second location in Palm Springs, including the post-brunch-coma-inducing banana caramel French toast and griddled meatloaf and eggs. Look for the original Palm Desert spot (73575 El Paseo, Suite 2310, Palm Desert; 760/773-2807; https://wilmafrieda.com; 8am-2pm daily; $12-31) on the 2nd floor in the El Paseo shopping district.

California Cuisine
★ The Tropicale Restaurant and Coral Seas Lounge
330 E. Amado Rd.; 760/866-1952; www.thetropicale. com; 4pm-10pm Mon.-Tues., 11am-10pm Wed.-Thurs. and Sun., 11am-11pm Fri.-Sat.; $19-52

Maybe only in Palm Springs does an upscale, retro, tropical-themed restaurant with mood lighting and a neon color scheme not only make sense but also seem like a great idea. The Tropicale Restaurant and Coral Seas Lounge serves a very eclectic menu with a focus on Pacific Rim plates. Pizzas and sandwiches are thrown in for good measure. Deep banquette booths, chandeliers, and a buzzing tropical patio and bar are throwbacks to the dinner clubs and themed cocktail bars Palm Springs does so well.

European
Johanne's
196 S. Indian Canyon Dr.; 760/778-0017; https:// johannespalmsprings.com; 5pm-9pm Wed.-Thurs. and Sun., 5pm-9:30pm Fri.-Sat.; $24-48

A sleek, modern spot tucked into an unassuming corner location in downtown, Johanne's offers a fresh continental menu in an airy upscale setting. The Austrian chef-run kitchen puts out sophisticated versions of Austrian and Pacific Rim specialties, including schnitzel and seared salmon. The menu can be pricey, but there is also a bar menu

that includes several of the signature schnitzels served in a bright bar that offers a view into the street and good downtown people-watching. No children under age 5.

Italian and Pizza
Johnny Costa's
440 S. Palm Canyon Dr.; 760/325-4556; www. johnnycostaspalmsprings.com; 5pm-9:30pm Tues.-Thurs., 5pm-10pm Fri.-Sat.; $27-49

The family-owned Johnny Costa's has been serving classic Italian specialties since 1976. Sink into a deep booth amid the dinner lighting at this low-key spot with an old-school feel. They offer a large and satisfying menu with a wide range of dishes—steak, veal, chicken, seafood, and pastas. Try the Steak Sinatra (the restaurant founder cooked for Sinatra at his estate) or comforting choices like linguine with clams and baked eggplant parmigiana.

Mexican
Crudo
515 N. Palm Canyon Dr., Suite B8; 442/268-9389; www.crudopalmsprings.com; 11am-9pm Mon.-Sat.; $16-26

Crudo Cervecheria is fresh, bright space on downtown's main drag with food and drinks to match. Colorful fresh ceviche or small plates like ahi nachos are good for sharing alongside inventive margaritas like pistachio lime and spicy pomegranate or one of the large selection of beers. The menu builds in substance, adding tacos, sandwiches that include a calamari steak and plates like crab enchiladas as well as a few non-seafood options, including a cheeseburger and flat-iron steak.

Clandestino
415 N. Palm Canyon Dr.; 760/417-4471; https://tacquila. com; noon-9pm Mon.-Thurs., 11am-10pm Fri.-Sun.; $11-32

The name suggests an off-the-beaten-path secret, but the restaurant is on the radar for its nicely curated menu of Latin American dishes, including street tacos, ceviches, and enchiladas. Hearty but not heavy dishes range from the simple red burrito filled with beef stew and red rice to more complex crab enchiladas in guajillo adobe over artichoke sauce with oyster mushrooms. Dining is mainly on the patio with views of the Palm Springs Arts Museum and San Jacinto Mountains. Try the margarita flight. The inside vibe is upscale cantina, offering bar seating and moody art. Try the margarita flight.

Tac/Quila
415 N. Palm Canyon Dr.; 760/417-4471; https://tacquila.com; noon-9pm Mon.-Thurs., 11am-10pm Fri.-Sun.; $15-34

Tac/Quila brings on the sensory overload (in a good way) with its high-design space-meets-high-design menu. Street taco plates, ceviche, and margarita flights are served against a backdrop of 1970s-reminiscent swank garnished with Moroccan-style pendant lighting, tiled floors, and mirrors galore.

SOUTH PALM SPRINGS
California Cuisine
★ Bar Cecil
1555 S. Palm Canyon Dr.; 442/332-3800; https://barcecil.com; 5pm-10pm Wed.-Sun.; $26-48

Posh bistro Bar Cecil is the most buzzed-about restaurant in Palm Springs, a fact to take into consideration when making a reservation. Reservations open one month out to the day and are a necessity, although it is possible to slip into a first-come, first-served spot at the bar. Decor strikes a charming and bold balance with a wood and marble bar and vibrant wallpaper; dinner does the same with a contemporary spin on classics like roasted chicken and grilled artichokes in a California-meets-continental menu. Hoteliers of the stylish Sparrows Lodge and Holiday House opened the eatery in 2021 and serve up the same excellent experience across their properties.

Crepes
Gabino's Creperie
170 E. Palm Canyon Dr., Suite 4; 760/808-8150; www.gabinos-creperie.com; 11am-3pm Tues.-Sun.; $14-18

Hearty crepes are served from a take-out window tucked into an alley near the curve of South Palm Canyon Drive. The crepes, featured on Guy Fieri's *Diners, Drive-ins and Dives* TV series, feature American sports-bar staples like buffalo chicken, barbecue chicken, and ranch dressing. The secret ingredient, cheese, is laced into the batter, creating a crunchy flavorful wrap. Diners consume the freshly made crepes at a few outdoor tables.

American
King's Highway
701 E. Palm Canyon Dr.; 760/969-5789; www.acehotel.com; 7am-10pm daily; brunch $14-24, dinner $15-28

Located inside the Ace Hotel, King's Highway offers reimagined locally sourced nouveau American classics in an airy mid-century space with Naugahyde booths and original terrazzo floors. This roadside diner, formerly a Denny's, has a breakfast and lunch menu that features simple plates like avocado toast and a breakfast burrito with crunchy tater tots alongside fresh salads and sandwiches, while dinner adds entrées like roasted salmon and fried chicken.

★ Mr. Lyon's
233 E. Palm Canyon Dr.; 760/327-1551; www.mrlyonsps.com; 5pm-10pm Wed.-Sun.; $19-65

The newest owners of Mr. Lyon's breathed new life into an old establishment, Lyons English Grille, opened in 1945, creating a sleekly designed upscale steak house with a modern twist. Dry-aged beef and prime rib are house specialties, with seafood and veggie options available. The dark bar is always buzzing thanks to its classic cocktails and a lounge menu featuring signatures like steak frites and the Mr. Lyons burgers.

European
Del Rey
1620 S. Indian Tr.; 760/327-2314; https://villaroyale.com/del-rey; 5pm-10pm Thurs.-Tues.; $12-32

The swanky restaurant tucked inside the Villa Royale Hotel features Spanish small plates served in a candlelit oak and marble bar. Tinned fish and tapas make for a romantic meal where you can run the gamut on the curated menu to fill your table with spicy tuna pâté, chicken croquettes, patatas bravas, and short-rib empanadas punctuated by signature cocktails and Spanish wines.

Italian and Pizza
Guiseppe's Pizza and Pasta
Smoke Tree Village Shopping Center, 1775 E. Palm Canyon Dr.; 760/537-1890; www.giuseppesps.com; 4pm-9pm Sun.-Thurs., 4pm-9:30pm Fri.-Sat.; $15-35

The Chicago-inspired Guiseppe's Pizza and Pasta is a fresher version of a generations-old comfortable neighborhood joint. The sleek-casual space has a relaxed dining room, a cozy bar, and a small patio. It's good for families while still feeling like a nice night out. It also does a brisk take-out and delivery business. Try the deep dish or hand-tossed pizzas

as well as pastas (mushroom ravioli, shrimp scampi linguine) and entrée classics like eggplant parmigiana and chicken piccata.

Vegetarian
★ Chef Tanya's Kitchen
706 S. Eugene Rd.; 760/832-9007; https:// cheftanyaskitchen.com; 11am-8pm daily; $8-16

The chef-owner of the popular Native Foods plant-based chain branched out with Chef Tanya's Kitchen, billing itself as a Cuban vegan deli. You're right to wonder how this can be, but they pull it off. Sandwiches like the signature slow-roasted citrus and garlic seitan El Cubano or Chupacabra chicken defy the imagination. The deli-style eatery features sandwiches, salads, and sides and is good for a casual lunch or takeout. Chef Tanya's Kitchen has a second location in Palm Desert (72695 Hwy. 111, Suite A6, Palm Desert; 760/636-0863).

Bars and Nightlife

Despite being a resort and party destination, Palm Springs has only a moderate number of bars. They range from well-styled watering holes to Rat Pack-era piano lounges to themed tiki bars. Depending on the type of scene you're looking for, you might want to get creative and check out some of Palm Springs's restaurants, which also have a festive (and early) cocktail scene.

BARS AND COCKTAILS
Uptown Design District and North Palm Springs
Tailor Shop
140 W. Via Lola; 760/537-7227; www.tailorshopps.com; 6pm-12:30am Mon.-Thurs., 5pm-12:30am Fri.-Sun.

A sophisticated addition to Palm Springs's cocktail bar scene, Tailor Shop serves distinctive cocktails in a moody interior with a marble bar and velvet booths. It's a good spot for a pre- or post-dinner libation—the menu includes classics as well as original creations.

Try the Spifflicated Butterfly with gin, green chartreuse, and rosemary. They serve a tiny menu of bright sushi-adjacent small plates like scallop crudo and salmon tartare as well as more traditional accompaniments including a cheese plate and olives. Make a reservation. Age 21 and over only.

Bootlegger Tiki
1101 N. Palm Canyon Dr.; 760/318-4154; www. bootleggertiki.com; 3pm-11pm Sun.-Thurs., 3pm-1am Fri.-Sat.

Bootlegger Tiki took on the legacy of tiki bar royalty when it opened on the site of the original Don the Beachcomber, Palm Springs, established in 1953. Velvet paintings, flocked wallpaper, red lighting, and guarded secret recipes impress with dramatic style, and the layered drinks earn their place in tiki history. Grab a friend and grab a booth. Pro tip: If you're not up for a heavily laced rum drink, the rotating menu typically includes

PALM SPRINGS AND THE COACHELLA VALLEY
BARS AND NIGHTLIFE

an herbaceous and refreshing gin-based cocktail. Reservations are strongly recommended for a 1-2-hour time slot. Age 21 and over only.

Central Palm Springs and Downtown

★ Las Palmas

461 N. Palm Canyon Dr.; 760/992-5082; www.laspalmasbrewing.com; noon-9pm Sun.-Mon., noon-10pm Tues.-Wed., noon-midnight Thurs.-Sat.

Las Palmas brewery and natural wine bar added its hip and understated hang to the Old Las Palmas neighborhood of downtown. The draft beers and wines tend toward the tropical and drinkable, perfect for sharing on the low-key back patio with ambient lighting and music. Las Palmas does not serve food, but you're welcome to bring your own. Age 21 and over only.

High Bar

100 W. Tahquitz Canyon Way; 760/904-5015

The aptly named High Bar is located poolside on the rooftop of downtown's chic seven-story Kimpton Rowan. The bar offers an open luxe setting with mountain views, fresh cocktails, and California-coastal Mexican-inspired snacks. Kids are allowed, and there are a few kid-friendly items on the menu. The bar is open for hotel guests 10am-10pm daily and opens to nonguests at 4pm. It makes a great spot to watch the sunset. All ages are welcome.

South Palm Springs

★ Melvyn's

Ingleside Inn, 200 W. Ramon Rd.; 760/325-2323; www.inglesideinn.com; 11am-10pm daily

Melvyn's, the iconic Palm Springs lounge, is still going as strong as its popular Rat Pack days. Nestled in the elegant Spanish Revival-style Ingleside Inn, it sports an old Hollywood Regency decor, chandeliers, and decadently upholstered booths. The lounge underwent an update in 2017, bringing it gracefully into this era while saving everything you like about the old. The lounge gets going most nights, fueled by live piano music and martinis that often inspire dancing on the tiny dance floor. Order a gimlet and enjoy the people-watching. The bar is age 21 and over; the restaurant is all ages.

PS Air Bar & Lounge

611 S. Palm Canyon Dr., Suite 22; 760/327-7701; https://psairbar.com; Mon.-Sat., check website for hours

Enjoy the perks of air travel without the TSA security line at PS Air, an airline-themed speakeasy located inside Bouschet wine and liquor store. It offers hosted brunch festivities some Sundays (by reservation only) as well as weeknight happy hours, karaoke, and live performances. Age 21 and over only.

★ Seymour's

233 E. Palm Canyon Dr.; 760/892-9000; 6pm-10pm Wed. and Sat.-Sun., 6pm-11:30pm Thurs., 6pm-2pm Fri.

As a culture, while on vacation in Palm Springs, we demand craft cocktails. Many bars promise but few deliver well enough to justify the hefty price tag. Seymour's is an exception. They may even have the best cocktails in town. Located behind the curtain at Mr. Lyon's Steakhouse, the intimate space has barstools you will want to take home and enthusiastic and knowledgeable bartenders. They show us the difference between a drink and a libation. Age 21 and over only.

LGBTQ+

All bars and nightlife venues in Palm Springs are gay-friendly; however, there are a range of bars geared specifically toward a gay clientele. Venues tend to be lively—think dance clubs, cafés with drag brunches, and karaoke nights.

Central Palm Springs and Downtown/Arenas Road

Arenas Road is known as for its gay bar-hopping scene. In this area just east of Indian Canyon Drive, several bars are clustered within walking distance, with more a few blocks north.

The Evening Citizen

220 E. Arenas Rd.; www.theeveningcitizen.com; 5pm-11pm Sun.-Wed., 5pm-1am Thurs.-Sat.

This Prohibition-era speakeasy is not strictly a gay bar, but it is a stylish, sedate addition to the Arenas district, known for its often rowdy scene. Once you're admitted beyond the nondescript outside, the space is glamorous, with dim lighting and a polished marble bar. Cocktails are impeccable. Make a reservation to receive the address. Age 21 and over only.

QuadZ

200 S. Indian Canyon Dr.; www.spurline.com; 2pm-2am Wed.-Mon.

QuadZ Video Bar is a popular neighborhood sing-along spot with strong drinks and a commitment to show tunes. On Friday, Saturday, and Monday, veejays play musical theater clips while the audience participates. Other nights bring trivia or karaoke. The inclusive bar draws a wide-ranging crowd, from young LA visitors to Palm Springs retirees. Age 21 and over only.

Blackbook Bar

315 E. Arenas Rd.; 760/832-8497; bar noon-1am Mon.-Sat., noon-11pm Sun., kitchen noon-midnight Mon.-Sat., noon-10pm Sun.

Blackbook Bar is a restaurant and cocktail bar in an industrial-chic space with a street-front patio. If you've been out making the rounds, it has a solid food menu. People rave about the Nashville fried chicken sandwich. Age 21 and over only.

Accommodations

HOTELS

October-May is when lodging rates are at their highest, and hotels can book weeks in advance. Prices dip in January, when temperatures are colder. Rates especially skyrocket in **March-April,** when thousands of revelers flock to Palm Springs and the Coachella Valley for a number of large-scale events and festivals. Hotels can be booked *months* in advance—although with the sheer number of hotels in the area, last-minute reservations will likely be available at a few places.

Summer is the low season due to soaring desert temperatures. But if your main goal is to lounge in a pool, there are great hotel rates to be had **June-September.**

Rates vacillate widely based on market pricing. The same room at one hotel could vary by hundreds of dollars depending on the weekend or time of year. In addition, midweek rates can drop by more than half. If your timing is flexible, many hotels are within pricing reach.

Uptown Design District and North Palm Springs
Arrive

1551 N. Palm Canyon Dr.; 760/507-1650; https://arrivehotels.com; from $427

A butterfly roofline lifts the hotel into Palm Springs's mid-century architectural pedigree, while rusted steel and natural elements anchor the hotel in the 21st century. Lots of sunlight and flow between inside and outside create a seamless backdrop for the modern boutique property with a buzzy social scene fueled by on-site coffee, ice cream, cocktails, and food. Most of the action revolves around the poolside restaurant and bar, after several iterations currently Palm Canyon Swim & Social (kitchen 8am-3pm Mon.-Fri., 8am-5pm Sat.-Sun., bar 8am-10pm daily), serving poolside cocktails, an all-day brunch, and weekly happenings. Cartel Coffee Lab (7am-6pm daily) offers espresso, filter drip, tea, and pastries. Ice Cream & Shop(pe) (noon-10pm daily) is a combination ice cream parlor with gourmet flavors, including vegan ones, and fun gifts. The 32 hotel rooms come in two forms: king studio or king patio, worth it for the private outdoor space and private fireplace. The hotel allows dogs; only adults 21 and over are permitted.

Central Palm Springs and Downtown
The Rowan
100 W. Tahquitz Canyon Way; 760/904-5015; from $350

At seven stories, The Rowan is a stylish anchor for Palm Springs's downtown strip. The open lobby soars with high ceilings and two-story windows, giving views of the San Jacinto Mountains. You have the same striking mountain views from room balconies and the hotel's signature rooftop pool (the only one in Palm Springs). The multiple stories defy traditional low-slung Palm Springs architecture (locals complain that it steals the views from everyone else), but the hotel's sleekly elegant design acknowledges its location in a mid-century mecca. A daily complimentary happy hour in the lobby provides some low-key mingling for a clientele that includes Palm Springs weekenders, families, and business travelers. The hotel property offers 153 rooms and suites plus a rooftop pool, a pool bar, pickleball courts, an exercise room, and the on-site restaurant **Juniper Table** (7am-4pm daily) for coffee, breakfast, café fare, and cocktails. The hotel allows children and pets.

Korakia Pensione
257 S. Patencio Rd.; 760/864-6411; www.korakia.com; from $433

The Korakia Pensione was built as a Moroccan-inspired artists retreat in 1924 and continues in this spirit in its incarnation as a stylish bed-and-breakfast resort. The 28 suites, studios, and bungalows are in two restored villas set amid fountains on 1.5 acres (0.6 ha). Many have private balconies or patios. Enter through the keyhole-shaped grand entrance flanked by ornately carved Moorish wooden doors. Moroccan fountains, a stone waterfall, and a stone courtyard complete the outside vibe, while the wood-beamed ceilings and antiques in the rooms ooze good taste. Guests under age 13 are not permitted.

★ Holiday House
200 W. Arenas Rd.; 760/320-8866; https:// holidayhouseps.com; from $434

Holiday House has made its tour in the best-of lists for good reason: A 1951 Palm Springs classic was reinvigorated into a fun, high-design, 28-room boutique hotel with a fresh blue-and-white theme and easygoing hospitality. It originally opened in 1951 as a sleek luxury hotel designed by Herbert H. Burns, one of the definers of Palm Springs's mid-century modern style. After many incarnations, the team behind the rustic-chic Sparrows Lodge made it shine, revealing clear lines and a livable style. Check-in is in the open lobby-bar, hung with original artwork by Roy Lichtenstein and Mr. Brainwash, among others, convenient for your welcome glass of rosé. The bright rooms have custom blue-and-white textiles, oversize showers, and an impeccable minibar. A fire pit, citrus trees, polka-dot cruiser bikes for loan, and the central swimming pool ensure you won't want to leave the grounds. Continental breakfast is included, and there is on-site dining at **The Pantry,** sharing the bar space, with an Americana-style menu of salads and sandwiches (11am-4pm daily), dinner (5pm-9pm daily), and weekend brunch (11am-3pm Sat.-Sun.). A bar stays open until 11pm. Only adults age 21 and over are permitted. Pets are allowed.

Del Marcos Hotel
225 W. Baristo Rd.; 760/325-6902; www. delmarcoshotel.com; $400-600

The stone and redwood Del Marcos Hotel welcomes guests through its boldly angled entrance to a bright lobby with white terrazzo floors and floor-to-ceiling glass looking out to the saltwater pool. Designed in 1947 by William F. Cody, the hotel received a historic designation for its post-World War II modern resort design. The Del Marcos's 17 suites are impeccably styled with individual charm from the Eames Poolside Suite with terrazzo floors and Eames furnishings to the Nat Reed Room and its redwood patio, claw-foot soaking tub, and fire pit. Beach cruisers are available for tooling around town. A daily complimentary continental breakfast is a nice touch. Ages 21 and over only.

La Serena Villas

339 S. Belardo Rd.; 760/832-8044; from $695

If you've dreamed about traveling the world in luxury, a version of La Serena Villas might have figured in your imagination. The Spanish hacienda-style property has 18 private bungalows set on 1 acre (0.4 ha) of landscaped grounds, walking distance to downtown shops and restaurants. Originally built in 1933, the property was redeveloped as a boho-chic luxury hotel in 2016. Rooms and suites have private patios with fire pits, claw-foot tubs, and built-in benches. The on-site restaurant, **Azucar,** is itself a destination, offering a rooftop lounge, poolside dining, and a contemporary California menu—think croquettes, beef tenderloin, and Dungeness crab-stuffed poblano—for brunch (7:30am-4pm daily; $17-27) and dinner (5pm-close daily; $27-45). Only adults 21 and over are permitted. Pets are allowed.

South Palm Springs
Caliente Tropics

411 E. Palm Canyon Dr.; 760/327-1391; www. calientetropics.com; from $269

Caliente Tropics was once one of the hippest games in town with its A-frame entrance, tiki swank style, Congo Room Steak House, and Rat Pack clientele. Times have changed, but the bones of the place are still there. Manage your expectations and this Polynesian-styled hotel may pleasantly surprise you. It offers 91 basic budget rooms with king beds or double queens as well as suites. Service can be unpolished, but the large pool, manicured grounds dotted with tikis, and affordable rooms make it worth the stay. Afternoon weekends at the pool can be a zoo; mornings and evenings are

more mellow. Nighttime brings out the lit tiki torches. The crowds are a downside, but on the plus, the hotel is family-friendly and the pool is large. An on-site tiki bar rounds out the experience: **The Reef** (bar noon-midnight daily, kitchen noon-9pm Sun.-Thurs., noon-10pm Fri.-Sat.) pours tropical cocktails with a satisfying bar food menu. The hotel allows children.

Ingleside Inn

200 W. Ramon Rd.; 760/325-0046; https://inglesideinn. com; from $275

Visiting the restored Ingleside Inn is like weekending at your sophisticated friend's swimming pool estate—which is exactly how the property was designed. Built in 1925 as a private home for the Birge family of the Pierce Arrow Motor Car Company, the home was opened as an elite hotel in 1939 by Ruth Hardy, Palm Springs's first councilwoman. New York businessman Melvyn Haber took over in 1975 and made Melvyn's Restaurant and Lounge the elegantly upbeat nighttime scene with serious Hollywood Rat Pack cred that continues to draw a crowd. The hotel has since been restored to highlight its Spanish Colonial Revival bones, giving Melvyn's dining room and lounge a skillful facelift that still evokes old Palm Springs glamour. Some of the 30 guest rooms offer sitting areas, private patios, and gas fireplaces. In theory, you could leave the grounds to drink, dine, swim, or relax elsewhere, but you know the saying, "Just because you can do something doesn't mean you should." The hotel is ages 21 and over only and allows pets.

Life House

1700 S. Palm Canyon Dr.; 833/938-2822; https:// lifehousehotels.com; from $305

In keeping with its name, Life House breathed new life into an overlooked hotel to create a stylish retreat that blends mid-century modern's clean lines with warm desert hues. Japanese design elements accent the comfortable and practical guest suites, some with private patios. On-site Minerva's restaurant and bar (named after Minerva Hoyt, who worked to protect California desert areas in the early 20th century) offers a well-executed plant-forward menu in a restrained space with hints of Hollywood glamour. A lovely outdoor bar completes the pool scene. The two-story layout and lack of a fully staffed front desk can be awkward, as opposed to Palm Springs's luxury courtyard hideaways, where the outside world becomes a distant memory, but its style, price point, and amenities recommend Life House. They also allow children.

Ace Hotel

701 E. Palm Canyon Dr.; 760/325-9900; www.acehotel. com; from $355

The Ace Hotel has a pitch-perfect hipness with its mid-century vintage-inspired style moored by polished terrazzo floors and textile art. This 179-room renovated hotel, spa, and resort, formerly a Westward Ho with a Denny's, offers two pools and a hot tub. The Ace Swim Club Pool has one of the major pool scenes in Palm Springs, with regular deejays and events. The quieter Commune Pool has a mellower family-oriented vibe. The on-site Amigo Room bar serves poolside drinks amid a late-night atmosphere. The Kings Highway Diner offers a poolside menu and a day and evening menu in its roadside diner setting. The on-site Feel Good Spa offers a full menu of services. Standard double and king rooms, suites, and patio rooms feature clean stylish design and flat-screen TVs. Some rooms offer vintage furniture, record players, or outdoor fireplaces. The Ace is recommended as the best stylish place to take children. Pets are also allowed for a fee.

Dive

1586 E. Palm Canyon Dr.; 760/323-2231; www. divepalmsprings.com; age 21 and over only; from $400

In a land of high-design boutique hotels, Dive is set apart with its 1960s French Riveria style. The charming 11-room resort offers a dreamy hideaway with freshly styled rooms that open onto a garden-like property dotted with palms and citrus trees, hammocks and fountains.

Breakfast is included, and a small kitchen and bar provide lunch and drinks, ensuring you can remain lounging on your black and white striped chaise and fully decompress.

Villa Royale

1620 S. Indian Tr.; 760/327-2314; https://villaroyale. com; from $475

Villa Royale offers a vibrant 38-villa hideaway with lush foliage, three swimming pools, and an intimate on-site bar and restaurant. Originally constructed in 1947, the California ranch-style hotel for the Hollywood set is a redesigned study in well-balanced contrasts. Spanish tile and warm wood are offset by striking splashes of pop art in guest rooms. A romantic wood and marble bar offers bright cocktails. Lush foliage contrasts with the stark mountain views. Guest rooms are poolside, with mountain views and fully stocked in-room dry bars. Suites are one or two bedrooms with a separate living area, some with a private patio, fireplace, or cocktail bar. Del Rey, the intimate on-site bar and restaurant, offers craft cocktails and Mediterranean-inspired small plates. The hotel is ages 21 and over only and is pet-friendly.

★ The Parker Palm Springs

4200 E. Palm Canyon Dr.; 760/770-5000; www. theparkerpalmsprings.com; from $524

The Jonathan Adler-redesigned The Parker Palm Springs began life in 1959 as California's first Holiday Inn. It's hard to make that mental leap as you wander the sumptuous 13 garden acres (5.3 ha) with two pools, a poolside bar, a fire pit, tennis courts, a croquet lawn, and retro-luxury suites. In the lobby, chandeliers merge with Moroccan-inspired antiques for a richly eccentric boho chic. Patio, suite, and estate rooms are available. Hefty resort fees ($50-150 per booking) cover valet parking and bellhop service at this upscale property.

★ Sparrows Lodge

1330 E. Palm Canyon Dr.; 760/327-2300; https:// sparrowslodge.com; from $539

The Sparrows Lodge is rustic-chic retreat.

Originally constructed in 1952 as the Red Barn, a hangout for the Hollywood elite, the lodge has been impeccably restored. Concrete and pebble-inlaid floors, exposed wood-beamed ceilings, open showers, horse trough bathtubs, and private patios grace the 20 poolside rooms and garden cottages. Imagine rustic mountain lodge meets mid-century ranch with a page from spare, traditional Japanese design. The vibe is understated. It manages to exceed expectations and blend in with the landscape. A central pool and hot tub make for a simple and relaxing scene. The barn-style communal area serves beer, wine, and cocktails, including a refreshing house-made sangria. The continental breakfast of muffins, yogurt, granola, fruit, and French-press coffee is as well thought out as everything else. The **Barn Kitchen** is open for lunch (11am-4pm daily) and dinner (5pm-9pm daily). Rooms are double occupancy and are restricted to ages 21 and over only. Pets are allowed for a fee.

LGBTQ+ HOTELS

All hotels in Palm Springs, from small boutique inns to large resorts, are gay-friendly. In addition, there are several that cater exclusively to gay male clientele, with accommodations that range from clothing-optional resorts to secluded retreats. There are no women-only resorts.

Uptown Design District
Descanso
288 E. Camino Monte Vista; 760/320-1928; https:// descansoresort.com; from $291

Descanso's serene garden style flows between inside and outside, with the property's native California landscaping and palm trees inspiring the fresh, restrained guest rooms. Think natural-fiber rugs and jade hues. Choose between balcony or poolside rooms and suites. The hotel is the newest addition to a trio of Palm Springs men's resorts known for thoughtful hospitality and sophisticated design. The property includes a heated saltwater pool and spa, poolside sun beds, and a communal fire pit. The many perks ensure you will have difficulty leaving the gravitational pull of the resort: complimentary continental breakfast, poolside lunch, a cantina with drinks and snacks, and weekend happy hour. If you manage to escape, do so on one of their city bicycles.

Trixie Motel
210 W. Stevens Rd.; 760/808-0014; https://trixiemotel. com; from $550

The Trixie Motel made a big pink splash with its debut in the Uptown Design District. Drag star and TV personality Trixie Mattel, along with her partner, film producer David Silver, bought the vintage Coral Sands Inn, kept the coral, and added a whole lot more. The result is a themed motel that retains its 1953 charm with a sparkling makeover documented on a Discovery+ show about transforming the property. Each of the seven rooms has its own distinct character with a design style that blends retro, high design, and camp. Stay in the Queen of Hearts, Atomic Bombshell, Malibu Barbara, Pink Flamingo, Flower Power, Yeehaw Cowgirl, or Oh Honeymoon. The on-site Barbara Bar (noon-8pm Sun.-Thurs., noon-10pm Fri.-Sat.) offers snacks and cocktails in a plush space that evokes 1980s Barbie. Reservations available for hotel guests and nonguests.

South Palm Springs/Warm Sands Neighborhood

The Warm Sands neighborhood is the mecca for gay resorts and hotels. Strictly defined, the neighborhood is located east of Palm Canyon Drive and bounded by Ramon Road to the north and East Sunny Dunes Road to the south. However, other gay resorts in the area extend south down to East Mesquite Avenue. More generally, the area is located south of downtown and before the curve where South Palm Canyon Drive becomes East Palm Canyon Drive. The hotels tend to offer privacy and welcoming atmospheres, situated on tropical landscaped grounds with lots of amenities, including large hot tubs and poolside lunches. Palm Springs's visitor website (www.

visitpalmsprings.com) offers a good list that describes the basic amenities and vibe to help visitors choose the best fit. A few hotels stand out for their blend of hospitality and design.

Twin Palms

1930 S. Camino Real; 760/841-1455; https://twinpalmsresort.com; from $275

The hoteliers behind the Descanso and Santiago resorts transformed the iconic mid-century Twin Palms Resort into a destination resort for gay men. The reimagined retreat pays homage to its mid-century pedigree with atomic style furniture and terrazzo floors while bringing it into this century with deluxe suites featuring spa baths, many with private patios. The impeccable grounds are anchored by a central pool and a 12-man spa, all with stunning views of the San Jacinto Mountains. The resort also boasts the hotel group's signature amenities, including complimentary breakfast, poolside lunch, and complimentary snacks and drinks.

Santiago

650 E. San Lorenzo Rd.; 760/322-1300; www.santiagoresort.com; from $337

The stylish Santiago is a male-only swimsuit-optional resort featuring chic modern rooms and landscaped grounds. The resort is warmly styled: The 23 suites have Spanish tile floors, king beds, and woven rugs. Hammocks, a fire pit, and a courtyard fountain complement the native landscaping. A pool and lounging area complete the tranquil atmosphere.

VACATION RENTALS

In addition to its many hotel options, Palm Springs has some stunning vacation rentals available through third-party booking sites like Airbnb and Vrbo. Additional sites like Oranj Palm Vacation Homes (www.palmspringsrentals.com) and Acme House Company (www.acmehouseco.com) feature curated portfolios of homes in Palm Springs and the Coachella Valley. The city has strict rules limiting vacation rentals, so they have not proliferated and taken over the hotel scene. Instead, they tend to be special lodging options with a historic pedigree—homes, estates, or small historic boutique hotels turned into single-party rentals. Some are small and intimate, while others are good for larger festive gatherings involving you and 16 of your closest friends.

Transportation

GETTING THERE

The two major airports closest to Palm Springs are in Los Angeles to the west and San Diego to the southwest; however, Palm Springs International Airport, located 2 mi (3.2 km) east of downtown Palm Springs, is worth looking into to eliminate the intense traffic slog from LA or San Diego.

Air

The tiny **Palm Springs International Airport** (PSP; 3400 E. Tahquitz Canyon Way; 760/318-3800; https://flypsp.com) is served by 12 airlines with connections from cities worldwide via nonstop flights to several major airline hubs. If you are flying into the Palm Springs airport, several hotels offer airport shuttle service. Contact the hotel directly prior to your flight to make a reservation. Major car rental carriers are located here, including Enterprise, Hertz, Dollar, and Alamo. Uber and Lyft rideshares are also available for airport pickup.

Los Angeles International Airport (LAX; 1 World Way, Los Angeles; 855/463-5252; www.flylax.com) has its advantages and disadvantages. Advantages: it's a major international airport with many carriers and flight options. All the major rental car companies are nearby, with regular shuttles from the airport. Disadvantage: LAX can be very congested.

San Diego International Airport (SAN; 3225 N. Harbor Dr., San Diego; 619/400-2404; www.san.org) is a busy single-runway airport 3 mi (4.8 km) northwest of downtown San Diego. Its major carriers include Southwest, American, United, Alaska, and Delta. A consolidated rental car center on the north side of the airport serves many major car rental companies and makes it easy to rent a car from the airport.

Ontario Airport (ONT; Ontario; 833/435-9668; www.flyontario.com) is a medium-hub, full-service airport located 70 mi (113 km) west of Palm Springs. Ontario Airport has all the major rental car companies on-site. It's big enough to have affordable flights with good time options and small enough to make it easy to navigate. From Ontario Airport, the drive to Palm Springs is slightly over an hour east via I-10. You can avoid the congestion of the major urban airports altogether and cut your drive time in half.

Car

Without heavy traffic, the drive from Los Angeles can take under two hours via I-10. Getting out of LA can be a slog, though, so you may need to factor in extra time (up to 5 hours) if driving from LA. **From Los Angeles,** take I-10 east for approximately 100 mi (161 km). The I-210 and 60 freeways can sometimes provide good eastbound alternatives if I-10 is jammed. They eventually join up with I-10 before Palm Springs. After approximately 100 mi (161 km), exit I-10 onto Highway 111 south toward Palm Springs. Highway 111B continues south to reach the Palm Springs city limits in just over 10 mi (16.1 km), turning into North Palm Canyon Drive, the main road through Palm Springs.

If traffic cooperates, the drive from San Diego takes just over two hours. **From San Diego,** take I-15 north (the same freeway that goes to Las Vegas) for about 50 mi (81 km). When I-15 splits with I-215, follow I-215

north and signs for Riverside/San Bernardino. Follow I-215 for 30 mi (48 km) until it intersects with Highway 60. Take the exit for Highway 60 and head east for 18 mi (29 km). Merge onto I-10 east and continue for another 18 mi (29 km) to the Highway 111 exit toward Palm Springs. Highway 111B continues south to reach the Palm Springs city limit in just over 10 mi (16.1 km), turning into North Palm Canyon Drive, the main road through Palm Springs.

Public Transit

The enterprising **Flixbus** (www.flixbus.com; from $26) is a Germany-based transportation start-up with no-frills, affordable bus service connecting major international cities. Direct bus routes run daily between downtown Los Angeles and Palm Springs. Provided all goes well (your bus shows up on time), this is the best option for public transportation.

There are no direct train routes to Palm Springs. There are no Greyhound stations in Palm Springs.

GETTING AROUND

Central Palm Springs is extremely easy to get around in. The main concentration of hotels and businesses spans a 4.5-mi (7.2-km) stretch. It's easy to plan much of your vacation to be walkable. In addition, many hotels provide free cruiser-style bicycles to guests, and Palm Springs has wide streets as well as bike lanes. Most hotels require bikes to be back before dark.

Rideshares and Taxis

Palm Springs is swarming with **Uber** (www. uber.com) and **Lyft** (www.lyft.com) rideshares, making this the best way to get from one end of town to the other. There are also a few taxi services that serve Palm Springs and the Coachella Valley. **Yellow Cab of the Desert** (760/340-8294; www. yellowcabofthedesert.com) is based in Palm Desert and serves Palm Springs, Cathedral City, Rancho Mirage, La Quinta, Indio, and Indian Wells.

PALM SPRINGS AND THE COACHELLA VALLEY
TRANSPORTATION

Information and Services

The official Palm Springs tourism website (www.visitpalmsprings.com) is helpful for planning. For a gay tourism perspective, check out www.visitgaypalmsprings.com for recommendations on lodging, dining, and activities.

Palm Springs Visitors Center

2901 N. Palm Canyon Dr.; 760/778-8418; www. visitpalmsprings.com; 10am-5pm daily

The first building you pass on entering Palm Springs is the Palm Springs Visitors Center. The iconic structure was designed in 1965 by renowned architect Albert Frey as a gas station for the Palm Springs Aerial Tramway. The fully staffed visitor center has a wealth of books and maps about the historic city.

The Coachella Valley

The Coachella Valley is recommended for its natural mineral waters, high-end shopping, and resorts. The spas and hot mineral springs of the town of Desert Hot Springs offer a low-key and affordable option to Palm Springs luxury lodging. On the other end of the spectrum, the Coachella Valley offers large resorts with lazy rivers, golf courses, tennis courts, casinos, spas, and restaurants. The El Paseo shopping district offers an upscale shopping, dining, and art destination.

Orientation

The Coachella Valley sprawls southeast from Palm Springs. This suburban desert is flanked by the San Jacinto Mountains on its southwest side, and Joshua Tree National Park and the San Bernardino Mountains bound the northwest edge. It's primarily residential, a checkerboard of gated communities and golf courses. It trends northwest to southeast all the way to the Salton Sea, and while not a destination, there are a few stops worth making. In the middle of it all is the surprising Thousand Palms Oasis Preserve, a literal oasis with shining palms and shaded pools set against a heat-baked landscape.

Planning Your Time

The sights in the Coachella Valley are

day-trip options or short drives from Palm Springs for sightseeing, recreation, dining, and resort accommodations. Towns and cities include **Desert Hot Springs** (a small mid-century resort community with hotel and spa opportunities), **Thousand Palms, Palm Desert,** and **Indio,** most of which can be accessed from I-10.

SIGHTS
Desert Hot Springs
★ Cabot's Pueblo Museum

67616 E. Desert View Ave., Desert Hot Springs; 760/329-7610; www.cabotsmuseum.org; 9am-3pm Tues.-Sun. Oct.-May, 9am-1pm Tues.-Sun. June-Sept.; grounds $5, free under age 6, tours $16, $14 seniors, active military, and ages 6-12, free under age 6

Cabot Yerxa is the man responsible for this fascinating Hopi-inspired 35-room pueblo, an artistic masterpiece he built entirely out of found materials between 1941 and 1950. Cabot's Pueblo Museum offers guided and self-guided tours of the home's interior, but you don't have to take the tour to visit the trading post and grounds, which include beautifully weathered outbuildings, a meditation garden, a well house, and *Waokiya*, a

---

1: Cabot's Pueblo Museum **2:** Living Desert Zoo and Gardens

43-ft-tall (13.1-m) Native American sculpture carved from a fallen cedar. Tickets are available online and in person up to one hour before tour start times.

Palm Desert
Living Desert Zoo and Gardens
47900 Portola Ave., Palm Desert; 760/346-5694; www. livingdesert.org; 8am-5pm daily Oct.-May, 7am-1:30pm daily June-Sept.; $40 adults, $30 ages 3-17

The Living Desert Zoo and Gardens is a desert botanical garden and zoo with an amusement park feel. Paved paths wind through exhibits representing major desert regions. The place is a huge draw for families and can be very crowded on weekends and holidays.

Faye Sarkowsky Sculpture Garden
72567 Hwy. 111, Palm Desert; 760/346-5600; www. psmuseum.org; sunrise-sunset daily; free

The Faye Sarkowsky Sculpture Garden is a branch of the acclaimed Palm Springs Art Museum. It is set on 4 acres (1.6 ha) with 14 outdoor sculptures amid landscaped gardens, water features, native plants, and walkways.

Indio
Shields Date Garden
80225 Hwy. 111, Indio; 760/347-0996; www. shieldsdategarden.com; 9am-5pm daily, café 8am-2pm daily; $11-21

In the 1920s, Highway 111 was lined with date farms, all vying for motoring tourists' patronage. Shields Date Garden is the last one standing. This family-friendly roadside attraction features a gift shop with free date samples, packaged dates, date milk shakes, and other gifts. A film, *The Romance and Sex Life of the Date,* chronicles the history of the date farm and, well, how these delicious dates come to be. Visitors can wander through the date gardens and oasis, which has strangely been reenvisioned as a biblical sculpture garden complete with famous biblical scenes.

There is also the on-site **Café at Shields** offering breakfast, lunch, beer, wine, and cocktails.

FESTIVALS AND EVENTS
★ Coachella Valley Music and Arts Festival
www.coachella.com; Apr.

The Coachella Valley Music and Arts Festival, known simply as Coachella (as in "Dude, are you going to Coachella this year? The lineup looks rad!") is an annual music festival held every April on the Empire Polo Club fields in the Coachella Valley. With folk rock, power pop, hip-hop, and electronic music, the festival draws big names and huge numbers of fans. Past headliners have included cultural icons like the Beastie Boys, Radiohead, Björk, the Black Keys, Red Hot Chili Peppers, Outkast, and Jack White. People come from far and wide to attend. The festival is so popular that it offers the same lineup two weekends back to back. Tickets are highly competitive to get and have been known to sell out within hours of going on sale in January. The crowd skews youngish, but it can be a fun time for anyone due to the predictably excellent band lineup. They don't shy away from the "art" aspect of the festival either, featuring a few choice Burning Man-level technology and sculpture installations. On-site camping is available. Outside the festival, local hotels as far as Palm Springs, 25 mi (40 km) away, book quickly. For transportation to and from the festival, if you're not camping on the grounds, prepaid and reserved shuttles are available at pickup points throughout the Coachella Valley and Palm Springs.

Stagecoach Festival
www.stagecoachfestival.com; end of Apr.

The Stagecoach Festival takes the Coachella Festival's place on those same polo fields to throw a massive outdoor country music festival at the end of April. Acts range from mainstream to outlaw country, old-timers to new blood, with some big names gracing the festival's three stages. Since its beginning in 2007, the festival has been on the rise. Past Stagecoach lineups have featured Merle Haggard, Emmylou Harris, Dwight Yoakam, and Hank Williams Jr. The three-day Friday-Sunday lineup is all-ages and draws thousands of festivalgoers. Accommodations are tight and should be booked well in advance. There is limited on-site RV camping that fills up months ahead of time as well as glamping-style tents and yurts. Beyond this, visitors rely on campgrounds and hotels in the area outside the festival grounds. Shuttles (with prepaid weekend shuttle passes) transport festivalgoers from designated hotel shuttle stops in the Coachella Valley and Palm Springs.

Desert X

https://desertx.org; early Mar.-early Apr.

Desert X is a series of site-specific contemporary art installations in the Coachella Valley. Acclaimed artists from around the world create and present art that engages with the desert environment. The exhibits change every year and generally remain open for viewing early March-early May. One of the best-known pieces from 2021 was the "Indian Land" sign placed in open desert next to the Palm Springs Visitors Center. Titled *Never Forget,* the piece was created by Tlingit and Unangax̂ artist Nicholas Galanin to reference Southern California's movie past and its romanticized white lens of the West. It was also a call to action for the land-back movement for local Indigenous communities. The Desert X website offers a visitors guide, map, and the ability to book guided tours.

SPORTS AND RECREATION
★ Thousand Palms Oasis Preserve

29200 Thousand Palms Canyon Rd., Thousand Palms; 760/343-1234; www.cnlm.org; check website for hours

The 20,114-acre (8,140-ha) Thousand Palms Oasis Preserve is hidden unexpectedly in the middle of the suburban Coachella Valley, protecting a fragile and diversely beautiful desert habitat in an area otherwise overrun by suburban sprawl. Shaped by the San Andreas Fault zone, the landscape features both rocky barren ridges and lush oases. Across the preserve,

clusters of native California fan palms flash in the glaring sun, protecting hidden pools. The preserve is closed to all pets and bikes. The parking area cannot accommodate large vehicles like RVs. The preserve closes periodically for restoration efforts; check the website for updates.

McCallum Trail

Distance: *2 mi (3.2 km) round-trip*
Duration: *1 hour*
Elevation gain: *none; 220 ft (67 m) with 0.5-mi (0.8-km) addition of the vista point*
Effort: *Moderate*
Trailhead: *The trail begins just past the welcome center at a well-marked trailhead between two large palm trees.*
Directions: *The preserve is located east of Palm Springs and north of I-10. From Palm Springs, follow Ramon Road east to Thousand Palms Canyon Road. Turn left (north) and continue along Thousand Palms Canyon Road to the preserve turnoff, a short dirt road that leads to the visitor center parking lot. Services here are limited.*
Information and Maps: *https://hikingguy.com/ hiking-trails/palm-springs-hiking-trails/mccallum-trail-hike-guide*

The preserve is a peaceful and striking destination, good for a picnic or a hike on more than 28 mi (45 km) of trails (closed to dogs and bikes). The most popular hike is the McCallum Trail, an easy, level trail across the desert to a spectacular series of oasis pools. To extend the hike, continue onto the Moon Country Loop and wind through the Colorado Desert, a barren and desolate 4 mi (6.4 km) round-trip in combination with the McCallum Trail and oasis. Note that the pond is closed periodically for restoration efforts.

Santa Rosa and San Jacinto Mountains National Monument

www.blm.gov, www.fs.usda.gov

The Santa Rosa and San Jacinto Mountains National Monument encompasses the mountain ranges to the west of the Coachella Valley, towering above the desert floor. With its highest elevation reaching 10,834 ft (3,302 m), it provides a spectacular, sometimes snow-capped, backdrop to the desert communities. An array of destinations and hikes—from lush palm oases to rugged peaks, wilderness areas, and a scenic section of the Pacific Crest Trail—makes the national monument an outstanding destination.

The monument spans more than 280,000 acres (113,000 ha), extending from the Coachella Valley to the alpine hamlet of Idyllwild near Mount San Jacinto State Park. The vast sprawl encompasses two federal wilderness areas (Santa Rosa and San Jacinto), the San Jacinto Ranger District, and public Bureau of Land Management (BLM) lands within the California Desert Conservation Area. The monument's extensive network of trails and backcountry can be accessed from Idyllwild and the Coachella Valley.

Visitor Center

51500 Hwy. 74, Palm Desert; 760/862-9984; 8:30am-4pm Thurs.-Mon.

The ranger-staffed visitor center is your best resource for exploring this region, with maps and books for hikes and recreation. The visitor center is in the Coachella Valley 4 mi (6.4 km) south of Highway 111 in the town of Palm Desert. Interpretive trails ranging from 0.2 mi (0.3 km) to 2.5 mi (4 km) leave from the visitor center and wind through the desert landscape.

Golf

The Coachella Valley is a golfing mecca. Moderate year-round temperatures and spectacular mountain views have given rise to a wealth of golf courses and clubs throughout the valley. Golfing is a lifestyle as well as a destination in the Coachella Valley, and there are a number of courses open to the public, including municipal courses, semiprivate clubs, and resort facilities. Courses vary widely for a range of skill levels and price points, from basic courses for knocking around to luxury resort settings to PGA Classic courses. Many courses enforce dress codes. To immerse yourself in a golfing vacation, stay at one of the Coachella Valley's numerous resorts.

Most golf courses maintain online booking for tee times on their websites. Pricing for many courses is dynamic, reflecting real-time conditions including weather, demand, and other market factors.

Stand-By Golf

760/321-2665; www.standbygolf.com; 7am-7pm daily

Stand-By Golf is a booking resource that offers discounted tee times for Palm Springs, Phoenix and Scottsdale, and Las Vegas. Call for specials and private course access.

Golf Now

www.golfnow.com

Golf Now offers an online tee time retail service for Palm Springs and other international golfing destinations. The comprehensive booking site is able to search for tee times in all Coachella Valley communities, including Palm Springs, Cathedral City, Rancho Mirage, Palm Desert, Indian Wells, La Quinta, and Indio. You can search by desired tee time, price range, and course. Book directly through this website 365 days a year.

Westin Rancho Mirage Golf Resort & Spa

71333 Dinah Shore Dr., Rancho Mirage; 760/328-3198; www.westinranchomiragegolf.com; from $55

Located at the Westin Rancho Mirage Golf Resort & Spa, the Pete Dye Course offers a playable challenge on a well-maintained course with spectacular mountain views. Amenities include club rentals and shared golf carts. The resort also offers a golf lessons and clinics.

Omni Rancho Las Palmas Resort & Spa

42000 Bob Hope Dr., Rancho Mirage; 760/862-4551, ext. 2; www.omnihotels.com; from $39

Also in Rancho Mirage, Omni Rancho Las Palmas Resort & Spa has three distinct layouts across a 27-hole championship course characterized by a gently rolling terrain with palm trees and six lakes.

Golf Courses Around Palm Springs

Course	Location	Status	Holes	Rating	Slope
Westin Rancho Mirage Golf Resort & Spa Pete Dye Course	Rancho Mirage	Public, resort	18	72.2	131
Omni Rancho Las Palmas Resort North Course	Rancho Mirage	Public, resort	9	69.2	124
Omni Rancho Las Palmas Resort South Course	Rancho Mirage	Public, resort	9	70.1	121
Omni Rancho Las Palmas Resort West Course	Rancho Mirage	Public, resort	9	69.8	122
Desert Willow Golf Resort Firecliff Course	Palm Desert	Public, resort	18	74.1	141
Desert Willow Golf Resort Mountain View Course	Palm Desert	Public, resort	18	73.0	132
JW Marriott Desert Springs Resort Palms Course	Palm Desert	Public, resort	18	72.1	130
JW Marriott Desert Springs Resort Valley Course	Palm Desert	Public, resort	18	71.5	127
Indian Wells Golf Resort Celebrity Course	Indian Wells	Public, resort	18	74.3	138
Indian Wells Golf Resort Players Course	Indian Wells	Public, resort	18	75.4	140
Silverrock Resort	La Quinta	Public, resort	18	75.0	139
Dunes Course at La Quinta Resort	La Quinta	Public, resort	18	72.3	134
Mountain Course at La Quinta Resort	La Quinta	Public, resort	18	72.8	135
Greg Norman Course at PGA West (La Quinta Resort)	La Quinta	Semiprivate	18	74.9	138
Stadium Course at PGA West (La Quinta Resort)	La Quinta	Public	18	75.8	148
Nicklaus Tournament Course at PGA West (La Quinta Resort)	La Quinta	Public	18	75.3	143

Desert Willow Golf Resort

38995 Desert Willow Dr., Palm Desert; 760/346-7060; www.desertwillow.com; from $33

Desert Willow Golf Resort in Palm Desert offers two 18-hole regulation courses featuring desert landscaping, large lakes, and bunkers. Amenities include a golf academy with daily golf clinics ($65 pp), PGA instruction, a restaurant with patio dining, a full-service pro shop, and premium club rentals ($75).

JW Marriott Desert Springs Resort & Spa

74855 Country Club Dr., Palm Desert; 760/341-2211; www.marriott.com; from $75

JW Marriott Desert Springs Resort & Spa is a luxury golf resort in the city of Palm Desert that encompasses 36 holes across two championship layouts—the Palms Course (par 72) and Valley Course (par 72). Resort amenities include a clubhouse and pro shop, rentals and lessons, and an 18-hole mini championship putting course designed for all ages and skill levels.

Indian Wells Golf Resort

44500 Indian Wells Lane, Indian Wells; 760/346-4653; www.indianwellsgolfresort.com; from $109

The Indian Wells Golf Resort offers two 18-hole courses. The Celebrity course features undulating fairways, split-level lakes, waterfalls, brooks, and floral details. The Players course features wide playing corridors and sculpted bunkers. A 53,000-sq-ft (4,920-sq-m) clubhouse offers resort amenities as well as a bar and grill. Luxury accommodations, golf packages, and rental clubs are available.

SilverRock Resort

79179 Ahmanson Lane, La Quinta; 760/777-8884; www.silverrock.org; from $107

A former home course of the PGA, SilverRock Resort in La Quinta features an 18-hole regulation course that sprawls over 200 acres (81 ha) with water features and native bunkers. The clubhouse is a historic, renovated ranch hacienda situated amid rocky outcroppings. Amenities include a grill-style restaurant.

La Quinta Resort

50200 Av. Vista Bonita, La Quinta; 760/564-4111; www.laquintaresort.com; from $79

La Quinta Resort offers two 18-hole regulation golf courses—the Dunes Course, with traditional Scottish design, and the Mountain Course, known for its dramatic mountain backdrop and challenging layout. Both courses are open to resort guests

and nonguests. Golf amenities include the Mountain Dunes clubhouse with a grill-style restaurant and a golf shop (6am-6pm daily). Fees include shared cart and unlimited day-of-play use of practice facilities. The resort also offers resort accommodations and golf packages. Golf club rentals are available.

Three 18-hole regulation PGA West golf courses are also part of the luxurious La Quinta Resort ($89-179). Greg Norman Course at PGA West features 60 acres (24 ha) of fairways and nine ponds spanning 18 acres (7 ha). The world-famous Stadium Course at PGA West is considered one of the greatest 100 courses in the world and has been viewed on TV by millions. The Nicklaus Course at PGA West is a more manageable version of the PGA West TPC. Both courses are open to resort guests and nonguests. Tee time reservations are available online. Amenities include two clubhouses with restaurants and golf shops.

Tennis

Like golf, tennis is a big draw to Palm Springs and the Coachella Valley. The lovely weather and year-round sun put Palm Springs on the map even before golf became a favorite pastime. There are a number of public, semiprivate, and resort facilities open to the public.

Indian Wells Tennis Garden

78200 Miles Ave., Indian Wells; 760/200-8200; https://indianwellstennisgarden.com; 7am-8pm Mon.-Fri., 7am-5pm Sat.-Sun.

Play where the pros play at the Indian Wells Tennis Garden, a state-of-the-art facility most famous for hosting the BNP Paribas Open, the world's largest combined men's and women's tennis tournament. The full-service tennis club features 29 concrete courts, 23 lighted courts, and a pro shop. A regular calendar of private lessons, group lessons, clinics, and camps are available for both adults and juniors. Additional services include ball-machine rental ($30), racquet stringing and repairs, and game arrangements.

Spas and Hot Mineral Springs

There is no shortage of opportunity to luxuriate in hot water in the Coachella Valley. The town of Desert Hot Springs, developed over natural hot- and cold-water aquifers, is a haven for spa hounds who flock to the dozens of hotels that have tapped into these rich mineral aquifers to fill their swimming pools and hot tubs. Farther south, in the Coachella Valley south of Palm Springs, big resorts offer on-site spas that specialize in body treatments and give access to a range of amenities.

Azure Palm Hot Springs Resort

67589 Hacienda Ave., Desert Hot Springs; 760/251-2000; https://azurepalmhotsprings.com; weekend day pass $79

The stylishly renovated Azure Palm Hot Springs Resort offers day passes with access to the resort grounds, central swimming pool, and café. Rock paths wander through native landscaping to a series of hot soaking pools, including the thatch roof-covered villa tubs that can be reserved privately. The resort also offers a full menu of spa treatments. Day spa visitors are provided with use of a locker, towel, and robe.

El Morocco Inn

66810 4th St., Desert Hot Springs; 760/288-2527; www.elmoroccoinn.com; 9am-4pm daily; 4 hours $55 pp, free with 1-hour spa treatment

The charming Moroccan-themed El Morocco Inn offers a huge covered hot spa, outdoor mineral pool, and sauna. A range of spa services including massages and body treatments are available by reservation only for guests and nonguests. Day spa visitors are provided with use of a locker, towel, and robe.

Miracle Springs Resort & Spa

10625 Palm Dr., Desert Hot Springs; 760/251-6000; www.miraclesprings.com; 10am-6pm daily; age 21 and over only; $20

The Miracle Springs Resort & Spa offers eight pools and spas for day use. Bring your own towel and locker lock. Towels are available for purchase ($10). They also offer spa services including facials, massages, and body treatments available by reservation only. The on-site Capri restaurant serves breakfast, lunch, and dinner and has full bar and poolside lunch service.

The Spring Resort & Spa

12699 Reposo Way, Desert Hot Springs; 760/251-6700; www.the-spring.com; 4 hours $75

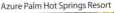

Azure Palm Hot Springs Resort

At The Spring Resort & Spa, day spa guests receive four hours' use of the resort's three mineral pools heated to different temperatures along with a Finnish sauna. They also offer a full menu of spa services, including massage, wellness, body treatments, and facials.

Sam's Family Spa Hot Water Resort

70875 Dillon Rd., Desert Hot Springs; 760/329-6457; www.samsfamilyspa.com; Mon.-Fri. $25, Sat.-Sun. and holidays $30

The setting at family-friendly Sam's Family Spa Hot Water Resort includes a spring-fed swimming pool and a series of hot mineral pools tucked amid palm trees in a parklike setting.

The Spa at Desert Springs

74855 Country Club Dr., Palm Desert; 760/341-1874; www.marriott.com; 10am-6pm daily; $125 per day

If you're looking for something outside Desert Hot Springs, The Spa at Desert Springs, located in the JW Marriott Desert Springs Resort & Spa in Palm Desert, offers unlimited use of its outdoor whirlpools, Finnish sauna, Turkish steam room, fitness equipment, and lounges. They also offer a menu of spa services.

SHOPPING
Desert Hills Premium Outlets

48400 Seminole Dr., Cabazon; 951/849-5018; www.premiumoutlets.com; 10am-9pm Mon.-Sat., 10am-8pm Sun.

A popular stop on the way to or from Palm Springs, the Desert Hills Premium Outlets boast over 180 luxury outlets for clothing, shoes, luggage, and accessories. The collection of outdoor outlets are located just off I-10. Top-tier luxury brands include Gucci, Prada, and Fendi. Other offerings are more within reach for a broader audience, including Theory, Lucky, and Levi's.

Perez Art District

68929 Perez Rd., Cathedral City; 760/770-0090; https://perezartdistrict.com; 11am-4pm Fri.-Sun., shop and gallery hours vary

The hotbed of mid-century home furnishing shopping may be in Palm Springs, but Cathedral City's Perez Art District makes for a vibrant destination in the otherwise uninspired suburban sprawl. The 30,000 sq ft (2,790 sq m) of retail and studio space concentrates a series of vintage and contemporary art and design stores in an unassuming strip mall north of Highway 111. The spaces range from high-ceilinged galleries with vibrant art displays to cluttered estate-sale vibes where you are sure to find a treasure. The highly curated offerings range from vintage mid-century furniture and housewares to new art to draw designers, collectors, and those seeking unique pieces for their homes.

Palm Desert
The Fine Art of Design

73717 Hwy. 111, Palm Desert; 760/565-7388; www.thefineartofdesign.com; 11am-4pm Thurs.-Mon., or by appointment

The Fine Art of Design in Palm Desert features a vintage collection of designer gems. This is not your average vintage shop: They specialize in couture classics from shiny Halston wraps to Alexander McQueen dresses as well as wedding dresses, shoes, jewelry, and handbags.

El Paseo Shopping District

73061 El Paseo, Palm Desert; www.elpaseocatalogue.com; shops open daily

El Paseo Shopping District is the Rodeo Drive, Beverly Hills, of Palm Desert. The walkable outdoor six-block area features luxury shopping set against landscaped desert gardens and mountain views. High-end brands like Ralph Lauren, Burberry, and Gucci along with staples such as Pottery Barn mingle with designer boutiques and restaurants to create a destination. The upscale shopping district begins on El Paseo Drive between Highway 74 and Sage Lane. The shopping and dining district continues another four blocks east, where Hotel Paseo anchors one end.

FOOD
Desert Hot Springs
There are dining options in Desert Hot Springs, but few are destination-worthy. It's worth it to drive or rideshare to Palm Springs, 12 mi (19.3 km) south, or take advantage of the kitchens and barbecues provided at some of the resorts. If you want to stick close to your hotel, casual Mexican is usually a crowd-pleaser.

Delicias Mexican Cuisine
66121 Pierson Blvd.; 760/894-3400; www.ilovedeliciasmexicancuisine.com; 10am-9pm Mon.-Sat., 9am-9pm Sun.; $13-23

Holy mole! Delicias Mexican Cuisine does everything right, including its complex chili sauce. Delicias took over a tired burger joint and watering hole to bring outstanding traditional Mexican cuisine to Desert Hot Springs. Even a humble cheese enchilada is made delicious with the addition of a slow-simmered red sauce and cotija cheese. Try the sizzling molcajetes served in a volcanic mortar or any one of the tacos, tortas, tamales, or specialties.

Palm Desert
Wilma and Frieda
73575 El Paseo, Suite 2310, Palm Desert; 760/773-2807; https://wilmafrieda.com; 8am-2pm daily; $12-25

Wilma and Frieda offers brunch classics in its original location in Palm Desert, including the post-brunch-coma-inducing banana caramel French toast and griddled meatloaf and eggs. Look for the Palm Desert spot on the 2nd floor in El Paseo shopping district. There is a second location in Palm Springs (155 S. Palm Canyon Dr., Suite A21-A27; 760/992-5080; 8am-2pm daily; $12-25).

Alps Village
77734 Country Club Dr., Suite F, Palm Desert; 760/200-5400; www.alpsvillage.com; brunch 10am-1:30pm Fri.-Sat., dinner 4:30pm-8:30pm Mon.-Thurs., 4:30pm-9:30pm Fri.-Sat.; brunch $12-23, dinner $22-44

The mother-daughter chef duo Milka Damjanovic and Blanka Sanin prepare authentic German, Balkan, and Mediterranean dishes in a light brick and knotty wood space reminiscent of a beer hall. The menu ranges wide in a traditional European cooking style. Dishes like cevapcici, a house-made beef sausage with pita bread, schnitzel, and spätzle, anchor it, offset by a range of flavorful salads.

The Nest
75188 Hwy. 111, Indian Wells; 760/346-2314; www.gotothenest.com; 4:30pm-close daily; $33-79

An Indian Wells staple since 1965, The Nest offers a full-service restaurant and lively venue with live music, drinks, and dancing nightly. Around 5pm, the long-timers from the surrounding Indian Wells communities and a smattering of tourists start to roll into the dining room for dinner. At 10pm, some of them may still be there on the dance floor. The restaurant features American specialties like steaks, pastas, and seafood as well as traditional family recipes, including cabbage rolls and moussaka. They also offer an excellent happy hour (4:30pm-6pm daily) at the bar, with a pared-down version of their dining room menu, happy hour prices, and smaller portions. The restaurant is connected to the Sands Hotel but operates as a separate business.

Indio
Tack Room Tavern
81800 51st Ave., Indio; 760/347-9985; www.tackroomtavern.com; 11am-9pm Sun.-Thurs., 11am-10pm Fri.-Sat.; $12-40

On the edge of the Coachella polo fields, where the Coachella Music Festival is held, Tack Room Tavern is open to the public. This fun local watering hole, with a patio and saddle bar seats, serves excellent sandwiches, burgers, and salads, drawing everyone from ladies sipping Manhattans to dudes chanting over the big game.

ACCOMMODATIONS
Resort accommodations in the Coachella Valley tend to go big. Major hotel chains like JW Marriott and the Omni, tribe-owned luxury casino hotels, and a few sleek new or

Desert Hot Springs

(map)

refurbished properties offer grand amenity-filled resorts with multiple swimming pools, on-site restaurants, and other perks. The exception is the small town of Desert Hot Springs, where the lodging tends to be more like an understated Palm Springs, with mid-century architecture and quiet courtyard pools.

Desert Hot Springs

Situated along the San Andreas Fault, Desert Hot Springs's claim to fame is the abundance of hot natural mineral springs that propelled the development of the town's spas and resorts. The 1950s were the heyday, and some of the operating boutique hotels sport the clean lines and neon signs of desert resort mid-century architecture. Desert Hot Springs has never achieved the popularity of nearby Palm Springs. The town has seen growth in recent years but much of it in the form of newer residences. Desert Hot Springs's spas are mixed in amid the more recent housing. The town attracts snowbirds and other visitors looking for a more low-key and affordable experience than that found in Palm Springs. Its spas range from retro-hip to sleekly luxurious.

El Morocco Inn

66810 4th St.; 760/288-2527; www.elmoroccoinn.com; age 21 and over only; from $209

The Casablanca-inspired digs at El Morocco Inn walk the line between kitschy and chic. The hotel is strewn with extravagant Moroccan lamps that the owner brings back from his travels. Rooms in this hideaway feature canopy beds, while the hotel spoils guests with complimentary mint tea, expanded continental breakfast, and a nightly "Moroccotini" hour. There's also a desert garden with hammocks and a bocce ball court. The pool and gigantic covered spa are open 24 hours daily.

Azure Palm Hot Springs Resort

67589 Hacienda Ave.; 760/251-2000; https:// azurepalmhotsprings.com; from $259

Expansive grounds, an on-site spa, a café, and stylish luxury suites draw mineral water seekers to the Azure Palm Hot Springs Resort. Queen and king suites come with private in-room mineral spring soaking tubs as well as 24-hour access to the Himalayan salt room. There are no televisions, but views include Mount San Jacinto, the rooftop Zen garden, and the Santa Rosa mountain range.

The Spring Resort & Day Spa

12699 Reposo Way; 760/251-6700; www.the-spring. com; from $279

The tranquil resort fans out from a central courtyard and offers 12 understated guest rooms in view of the San Jacinto Mountains. Rooms include rain showerheads and Egyptian cotton linens; some have private soaking tubs. The property has one of the hottest mineral spring sources in the area, and its three pools are cooled to various warm temperatures. Guests can also look forward to a complimentary breakfast and a fire pit.

Hope Springs Resort

68075 Club Circle Dr.; 760/329-4003; www. hopespringsresort.com; $260-310

Spare mid-century style and desert chic meet over-polished concrete floors at Hope Springs Resort, which offers 10 rooms with king beds (4 rooms include kitchens) that open onto a communal pool and spa. Guests take advantage of the continental breakfast, communal kitchen, and grill, which means you never have to leave. Children and pets are not permitted.

The Lautner Compound

67710 San Antonio St.; 760/832-5288; www.thelautner. com; from $350

Iconic architectural home turned self-catering boutique hotel, The Lautner Compound was designed by John Lautner in 1947 and features concrete, redwood, lots of glass, and skylights. Four private vacation rental units with a luxury feel offer private patios and share a communal space with a saltwater plunge pool, a fire-pit lounge, and a grilling area. Guests must be age 25 or over.

The Good House

12885 Eliseo Rd.; 760/251-2885; www. welcometothegoodhouse.com; $315-495

Lush, tropical grounds and a naturally heated pool are at the center of The Good House. The small secluded property offers seven stylish guest rooms with king beds and kitchenettes, some with private patios. The property offers a small café for poolside wine, coffee, and other refreshing beverages as well as breakfast, pizzas, sandwiches, and salads.

Two Bunch Palms Resort & Spa

67425 Two Bunch Palms Tr.; 760/329-8791; www. twobunchpalms.com; from $525

Set on 77 lush acres (31 ha), Two Bunch Palms Resort & Spa offers charm dating back to 1930. The original Spring rooms and suites are located in tropical landscaping closest to the pool and soaking tubs, meant for digital detox and equipped with a Bluetooth speaker but no televisions. Radiating outward, the Grove rooms offer double queens or kings with sound systems and televisions. Desert rooms are situated near olive groves on the southern end of the property and offer kings or suites with sound systems and televisions. Suites add a wet bar and a private patio. Villa suites are located next to the pond and offer private front and back patios with jetted tubs, wet bars, and dining space. An on-site farm-to-table restaurant offers breakfast, lunch, and dinner. Hotel and grounds are restricted to guests age 18 and over.

Palm Desert

In the land of shining swimming pools, the town of Palm Springs is the primary destination with its mid-century architectural treasures and small, high-design, luxury boutique hotels. But the sunshine continues beyond the boundaries of Palm Springs, and the Coachella Valley provides a whole different vacation experience that is bigger, grander, resortier, and child-friendlier. If you want swimming pool options, tee times, 38,000-sq-ft (3,530-sq-m) spa facilities, on-site restaurants, outdoor bars, family-friendly rooms, and amenities that compel you to stay on the premises for your entire visit, you may want to shift your vacation digs south to the Coachella Valley.

Hotel Paseo

45400 Larkspur Lane, Palm Desert; 760/340-9001; from $384

Hotel Paseo opened in 2018 next to the upscale El Paseo shopping district (known as the Rodeo Drive of the Desert), creating a destination hub for upscale shopping, dining, and lounging. The sleek luxury hotel differs from the mega-resorts that the Coachella Valley is known for. Instead of offering everything, it prides itself on one well-appointed restaurant, spa, and swimming pool. The hotel's format is open and

airy, encouraging you to explore the shopping, art, restaurants, tennis, golf, hiking, and natural beauty nearby.

Omni Rancho Las Palmas Resort & Spa

42000 Bob Hope Dr., Rancho Mirage; 760/568-2727; www.omnihotels.com; from $411

The 240-acre (97-ha) Omni Rancho Las Palmas Resort & Spa has been fully revitalized from its original Hollywood heyday in the 1950s as the Desert Air Hotel & Resort. It boasts 444 guest rooms, a 27-hole golf course, tennis courts, a full-service spa, and on-site bars and restaurants. The kids will love **Splashtopia,** a 2-acre (0.8-ha) water playground complete with a lazy river, a sandy beach, two 100-ft (31-m) waterslides, and sprinklers. Need some grownup time? An adults-only pool is also on-site, with poolside drink and food service, a cliff-side hot tub, and cabanas.

Sands Hotel & Spa

44985 Province Way, Indian Wells; 760/321-3771; https://sandshotelandspa.com; from $484

A dazzling redesign by renowned interior designer Martyn Lawrence Bullard transformed the historic Sands Hotel & Spa from a nondescript stucco hotel into a luxurious destination with Moroccan influences and a mid-century vibe. Service at the hotel can fall short of the high bar set by the design, but the property's charms are many. The hotel offers 46 guest rooms, each uniquely designed with different color combinations, handcrafted furniture, and custom textiles, many with private patios or balconies. They have taken the concept of the in-room minibar to the next level with vintage crystal stemware and pre-mixed cocktails rivaling ones from the actual bar. Baths are luxurious with Acqua di Parma bath amenities and open showers with soaking tubs. The on-site Pink Cabana restaurant and bar serves breakfast, lunch, and dinner. Guests age 18 and over only are allowed at the hotel.

GETTING THERE AND AROUND

The Coachella Valley sprawls southeast of Palm Springs, encompassing the towns of Desert Hot Springs, Cathedral City, Rancho Mirage, Thousand Palms, Palm Desert, Indian Wells, La Quinta, Indio, and Coachella, all of which are accessed from I-10. A car is the only way to navigate this region surrounding Palm Springs.

Car

Desert Hot Springs is located north of Palm Springs and I-10. To get here, follow North Indian Canyon Drive north from Palm Springs, or take Highway 62 north from I-10 and turn right (east) on Pierson Boulevard.

Cathedral City abuts Palm Springs to the east and is accessible via I-10 by following Vista Chino or Ramon Road east from Palm Springs. Continuing east, **Rancho Mirage** is the next in line, accessible from I-10 via Bob Hope Drive or along Highway 111 from Palm Springs.

Thousand Palms and **Palm Desert** sandwich I-10 north and south, respectively. Monterey Avenue (exit 131 from I-10) links the two.

Tiny **Indian Wells** is off Highway 111 between Palm Desert and La Quinta. To get here from Palm Springs, follow Highway 111 east. To get here from I-10, exit at Cook Street (exit 134) or Washington Street (exit 137) and drive south to Highway 111.

As Highway 111 continues its journey east, it passes through **La Quinta, Indio,** and **Coachella** to connect with Business I-10 in Indio. Note that Business I-10 continues south, merging with Highway 111 and Highway 86 north of Mecca and toward the Salton Sea. To continue on I-10 east and the South Entrance to Joshua Tree, turn northeast on Dillon Road to I-10.

Mount San Jacinto State Park and Wilderness

Subalpine forests, granite peaks, and mountain meadows quilt the 14,000-acre (5,670-ha) Mount San Jacinto State Park and Wilderness in the heart of the San Jacinto Mountains. Craggy San Jacinto Peak, the highest peak in the park and the second highest in the San Jacinto Range (after Mount San Gorgonio), reaches nearly 11,000 ft (3,350 m) and is snow-capped for much of the year. The steep mountain escarpments of the San Jacinto Range plunge 9,000 ft (2,740 m) in less than 4 mi (6.4 km) to the desert floor on the northeast side down.

Hiking trails offer sweeping views toward Palm Springs and over 100 mi (160 km) to the southeast and the Salton Sea.

Orientation

The state park extends from the Palm Springs Aerial Tramway's Valley Station in Palm Springs southwest to the town of Idyllwild, adjoining the San Jacinto Wilderness on its southern boundary. The two main jumping-off points for hiking and camping in the state park and wilderness are the town of Idyllwild and the Palm Springs Aerial Tramway. Follow Highway 243 or Highway 74 up from the Coachella Valley desert floor, and in under an hour you will find yourself in the much cooler San Jacinto Mountains.

Originally the summer home of the Cahuilla people migrating from the desert valleys below, the area began to be settled by homesteaders in the 1890s. Logging and tourism became the primary industries. Tourism won out, and now most of the land surrounding Idyllwild is protected through the Mount San Jacinto State Park, Santa Rosa and San

Jacinto Mountains National Monument, and San Bernardino National Forest. In the 1960s and 1970s an influx of hippies to the area changed the cultural fabric in Idyllwild. Browse the boutique shops in the town center now and you'll find cowboy hats as well as healing crystals.

All sights and hikes in the Mount San Jacinto State Park that are accessed from the Palm Springs Aerial Tramway are covered in the Palm Springs hiking section.

Planning Your Time

Summer is high season, with visitors taking advantage of cooler temperatures, campgrounds, and hiking trails. **Winter** brings snow tourism. Community events such as the Art Walk and Wine Tasting (Oct.) give folks an excuse to visit year-round.

PARK ENTRY
Adventure Pass

www.parks.ca.gov, www.fs.usda.gov

A **Forest Adventure Pass** is required to park at trailheads and day-use areas. Adventure Passes are available at the San Jacinto Ranger Station or at **Nomad Ventures** (54415 N. Circle Dr.; 951/659-4853; www.nomadventures.com; 9am-5pm daily) as well as at other ranger stations and retailers throughout the San Bernardino, Angeles, and Los Padres National Forests. They can also be purchased online (www.myscenicdrives.com). Rules regarding where Adventure Passes are required are somewhat in flux. Pay attention to signage; the default is that Adventure Passes are required.

Hiking and Camping Permits

Hundreds of miles of hiking trails for all ability levels are accessible from the town of Idyllwild. Due to the short hiking season and popularity of the area, there is a **wilderness permit** system in place for all hikes except for the Long Valley Discovery Trail and Desert View Trail, both covered in the Palm Springs section. *Everyone must obtain a wilderness permit prior to day hiking or overnight camping.*

San Jacinto Ranger Station

54270 Pine Crest Ave.; 909/382-2921; 8am-4pm Fri.-Mon., 8am-noon Tues.

Day-use permits are free and available at the San Jacinto Ranger Station in Idyllwild.

Idyllwild Campground

25905 Hwy. 243

Permits are also available at the entrance station for Idyllwild Campground in San Jacinto State Park. Outside business hours you can complete a form available on the porch of the campground's ranger station and drop it in the drop box.

HIKING

The park is a destination for day hiking, backpacking, snowshoeing, and camping. The famous Pacific Crest Trail (PCT), a continuous 2,650-mi (4,267-km) trail system that runs from Mexico to Canada, passes through the San Jacinto Mountains, and Idyllwild is a destination for PCT hikers.

Ernie Maxwell Scenic Trail

Distance: *5.3 mi (8.5 km) round-trip*
Duration: *2-3 hours*
Elevation gain: *550 ft (168 m)*
Effort: *Easy*
Trailhead: *Tahquitz View Drive, at the end of a dirt road on the south end of Idyllwild*
Directions: *From the Idyllwild Ranger Station (Hwy. 243 and Pine Crest Ave., Idyllwild), head south on Highway 243 for 0.7 mi (1.1 km). Turn left onto Saunders Meadow Road just past the Mile High Café and before the Idyllwild School. Follow Saunders Meadow Road for 0.8 mi (1.3 km) and then turn left onto signed Pine Avenue. After 0.1 mi (0.2 km) turn right onto the signed Tahquitz View Road. The trailhead is in 0.6 mi (1 km). The pavement ends 0.2 mi (0.3 km) into Tahquitz View Drive, and the road forks. Follow the left fork, signed for*

1: walkway at Mount San Jacinto State Park
2: views from the Ernie Maxwell Scenic Trail

the Ernie Maxwell Scenic Trail. The trailhead is signed on the right. Park along the dirt road.

Information and Maps: *www.fs.usda.gov*

First off, here's a pro tip: Hike the trail starting from the dirt road trailhead in Idyllwild. This way, you will gain elevation at the beginning stretch and have an easier return.

A gentle elevation gain through a mostly shaded forested trail makes this a good choice for a leisurely but satisfying hike. (This is a good pre-brunch Sunday-morning hike.) Starting from the **Tahquitz View Drive** trailhead, the path climbs gently through a mix of Jeffrey, ponderosa, and Coulter pines all the way to the **Humber Park** trailhead. The trail provides intermittent views toward Idyllwild and the southwest. The real highlight here is the immersive forest experience and the mellow grades. The trail is particularly nice in **September-October.** Once you reach the Humber Park trailhead, turn around and return the way you came.

Devil's Slide

Distance: *5 mi (8.1 km)*
Duration: *2-3 hours*
Elevation gain: *1,300 ft (396 m)*
Effort: *Moderate*
Trailhead: *Humber Park*
Directions: *To get here from the Idyllwild Ranger Station, head northeast on Pine Crest Avenue for 0.6 mi (1 km). Turn left onto Fern Valley Road and continue for 1.8 mi (2.9 km) until you reach Humber Park. The trail begins on the upper level of the parking area.*

Information and Maps: *www.fs.usda.gov*

The Devil's Slide trail offers a scenic climb through idyllic forest. It's a nice day hike on its own merits, but it's also a key connector trail that leads to the PCT as well as routes to San Jacinto Peak and Tahquitz Peak. This busy trail can be congested; **hike in the morning** to beat some of the traffic as well as catch cooler temperatures. Much of the trail is exposed to direct sunlight after noon.

The trail begins in the upper parking level of **Humber Park.** A short climb quickly gives way to stunning views of Tahquitz Rock, a local landmark sometimes called **Lily Rock.**

As the trail continues to climb, you'll have views of Idyllwild and Strawberry Valley to the southwest. You'll climb steadily all the way to **Saddle Junction.** Although Saddle Junction isn't really a destination in and of itself, it's a good goal for a hike that really is about the journey. Return the way you came or continue on to Tahquitz Peak (8.6 mi/13.8 km round-trip), San Jacinto Peak (16 mi/26 km round-trip), or an array of other backpacking or day-hiking destinations.

Tahquitz Peak (via South Ridge Trail)

Distance: *7.6 mi (12.2 km) round-trip*
Duration: *4-5 hours*
Elevation Gain: *2,100 ft (640 m)*
Effort: *Strenuous*
Trailhead: *Via the South Ridge Trail. It can also be hiked via the Devil's Slide Trail and PCT; the trailhead is accessed from Humber Park.*
Directions: *From the Idyllwild Ranger Station at the corner of Highway 243 and Pine Crest Avenue in Idyllwild, head south on Highway 243 for 0.7 mi (1.1 km). Turn left onto Saunders Meadow Road just past the Mile High Café and before the Idyllwild School. Follow Saunders Meadow Road for 0.8 mi (1.3 km) and then turn left onto signed Pine Avenue, also signed for the South Ridge Trailhead. After 0.1 mi (0.2 km), turn right onto the signed Tahquitz View Road, with additional signs for the South Ridge Trailhead. The pavement ends 0.2 mi (0.3 km) into Tahquitz View Drive, and the road forks. Take the right fork, signed for Forest Road 5S11. From here it is 1 mi (1.6 km) to the trailhead. This last stretch is prone to washouts and may require a high clearance vehicle. If you're in doubt, you can park and walk the remaining dirt road or hike Tahquitz Peak using the alternate Devil's Slide Trail via Humber Park (this route is fully paved). Follow the dirt road until one final fork, a few hundred yards from the trailhead. Turn left and park at a small parking area at the trailhead. There are also a few parking spaces at the fork.*

Information and Maps: *www.fs.usda.gov*

If you're going to do one hike in the Idyllwild area and are up for a challenge, hike Tahquitz Peak. This striking granite crag can be seen on the drive in from Highway 243. It stands sentinel over the town, and you'll catch glimpses of it from different vantage points. In addition to experiencing breathtaking views and a trip to a historic furnished fire tower, if you kick off your time in Idyllwild with this spectacular hike, you'll get to feel a sense of smug accomplishment every time you look up.

The South Ridge Trail gives you the most direct route and the most solitude on your trek to Tahquitz Peak. From the trailhead, the trail climbs into the San Jacinto Wilderness region within a few yards; it *feels* like wilderness. Manzanitas with their strange peeling rust-red bark, Jeffrey pine, live oak, and white fir line the trail.

Around 1 mi (1.6 km), views open up to the south toward Garner Valley and Lake Hemet. Impressive views continue for the rest of the hike. Over the next 0.5 mi (0.8 km) you pass along the Desert Divide, a spur ridge that runs through the southern section of the San Jacinto mountain range. Views from here are sweeping to the east.

Take a breather and a water break at Window Rock at 1.5 mi (2.4 km). This unique geologic feature frames rugged granite crags to the north. From here, the trail climbs gently, passing through Lodgepole Pine Forest until about 2.2 mi (3.5 km).

The last 1.5 mi (2.4 km) of switchbacks climb steeply to Tahquitz Peak and the lookout tower.

Climb the steps up to the deck of the lookout tower to get an eyeful. The tower was used historically as a fire lookout, positioned because of its 360-degree views. It has been preserved with historic furnishings, and volunteers maintain the space and greet hikers at the top on some weekends in high season (May-Nov.). It adds a layer of richness to the experience to tap into some of the region's history and pick the volunteers' brains about trails and the surrounding geography as well as enjoy the natural beauty. From the lookout tower deck, the Coachella Valley sprawls to the east, bounded by Joshua Tree National Park and the Little San Bernardino and Cottonwood Mountains. To the north, Marion Mountain looms, blocking views of San Jacinto Peak and the Palm Springs Aerial Tramway. To the southeast, the views extend as far as the Salton Sea.

Tahquitz Peak (Continuing via Devil's Slide Trail)

Distance: *8.6 mi (13.8 km)*
Duration: *5 hours*
Elevation gain: *2,800 ft (853 m)*
Effort: *Strenuous*
Trailhead: *Humber Park*
Directions: *From the Idyllwild Ranger Station, head northeast on Pine Crest Avenue for 0.6 mi (1 km). Turn left onto Fern Valley Road and continue for 1.8 mi (2.9 km) until you reach Humber Park. The trail begins on the upper level of the parking area.*
Information and Maps: *www.fs.usda.gov*

After the South Ridge Trail, the Devil's Slide trail is the next-best option for reaching Tahquitz Peak. It adds 1 mi (1.6 km) and an additional 700 ft (213 m) of elevation gain than the more direct South Ridge Trail, but it achieves the same lofty peak.

Follow the Devil's Slide Trail to Saddle Junction. From this five-way junction, turn right onto the PCT heading south. You will have a slight break from climbing before the trail ascends through pine forest. The climb continues along a ridge, the Desert Divide, with views into the Coachella Valley. After 1.3 mi (2.1 km) along the PCT, turn right onto an access trail and begin the final climb. When you come to a junction with the South Ridge Trail, stay to the right for the last rocky stretch before the lookout tower comes into view.

WINTER SPORTS

Winter Adventure Center

https://pstramway.com; 10am-4pm Fri., 9am-4pm Sat.-Sun. and holidays

While Mount San Jacinto State Park was never developed for skiing (a boon, as this allowed the wilderness to be preserved and the mountain town of Idyllwild to remain peaceful), cross-country skiing and snowshoeing are accessible from Mountain Station at the top of the Palm Springs Aerial Tramway. A Winter Adventure Center is open whenever there is snow. The center offers cross-country ski packages (skis, poles, and boots, $21 per day) and snowshoe packages ($18 per day). Mount San Jacinto State Park is also a good destination for families who just want to have some fun snow frolicking. Snow camping is even available at the hike-in campgrounds along the network of trails in the state park and wilderness.

Idyllwild Regional Park

54000 Riverside County Playground Rd.; 951/659-2656; www.rivcoparks.org; sunrise-sunset daily; $20 per vehicle

There are snow play opportunities at Idyllwild Regional Park. Bring your own sled to enjoy winter snows in a designated section of the park. Call for current conditions.

IDYLLWILD

Idyllwild is a charming mountain town, a forest island nestled 1 mi (1.6 km) high in the San Jacinto Mountains and surrounded by the outlying desert. The artsy, rustic community is nestled amid pines, cedars, manzanitas, and scenic rock outcroppings. Picturesque cabins with A-frame roofs hint at snow, an exciting proposition in contrast with the sleek, flat mid-century desert dwellings below. Seasonal streams and hiking trails crisscross the hills. Inns with chainsaw-carved wildlife sculptures and fireplaces welcome visitors escaping the heat and traffic of the urban areas below.

The adjacent communities of Fern Valley, Pine Cove, and Idyllwild are generally grouped together and are all considered "Idyllwild."

Shopping

Many shops here can feel like they're caught in a time warp catering to the New Age hippie at heart, while other boutique shops cover a range of specialties, including gifts, sweets, art, clothing, and outdoor gear. The majority of the shops in Idyllwild are clustered in a three-block radius on North Circle Drive, where it intersects with Highway 243. The Idyllwild town website (https://idyllwildcalifornia.com) provides a town business directory, including shopping, dining, and lodging.

Nomad Ventures

54415 N. Circle Dr.; 951/659-4853; www.nomadventures.com; 9am-5pm daily

Nomad Ventures provides outdoor gear and equipment covering climbing, mountaineering, backpacking, hiking, trail running, and kayaking. There is a second location in Joshua Tree (61795 Twentynine Palms Hwy.; 760/366-4684; 8am-6pm daily).

Wooley's

54274 N. Circle Dr.; 951/659-0017; www.wooleys.com; 10am-5:30pm Mon.-Thurs., 10am-7:30pm Fri.-Sat., 9am-5:30pm Sun.

Wooley's offers sheepskin products, including sheepskin slippers, boots, and seat covers. They also stock clothing, cowboy hats, and winter hats—great if you're caught in the cooler temperatures of Idyllwild and need to make an emergency fashion purchase. Home furnishings include high-quality cowhide rugs, lambskin throws, and pillows.

Coyote Red's

54225 N. Circle Dr.; 951/659-2305; https://coyoteredsstore.com; 10am-5pm daily

Coyote Red's is a gourmet country store featuring beef jerky and hot sauce. Their signature chipotle sauce rivals the best of them.

Remember When

54225 N. Circle Dr.; 951/659-6456; 11am-4pm Thurs.-Mon.

Remember When stocks nostalgic sweets, sodas, and toys. Its almost 200 specialty sodas, throwback candies, and selection of simple toys are fun for the family.

Food
Red Kettle

54220 N. Circle Dr.; 951/659-4063; https://perrysredkettle.com; 7am-2pm daily; $8-18

The Red Kettle is a great place to fuel up before a

Idyllwild

PALM SPRINGS AND THE COACHELLA VALLEY

MOUNT SAN JACINTO STATE PARK AND WILDERNESS

hike or to savor a casual weekend. They serve up classic American breakfasts like country ham and eggs and lunch specials like chili, burgers, soups, and salads in a quaint cottage setting.

La Casita Mexican Restaurant

54650 N. Circle Dr.; 951/659-6038; www. idyllwildlacasita.com; 11am-9pm daily summer, 11am-8pm daily winter; $13-26

In the Fern Valley neighborhood, La Casita Mexican Restaurant anchors the other end of town with satisfying plates of Mexican food and margaritas served in a rustic, wood-paneled setting with a large patio. Located near the entrance to the hiking trails in Humber Park, the small restaurant can get packed.

Mama's Egg House

54241 Ridgeview Dr.; 951/659-1276; www.
mamasegghouse.com; 8am-4pm Thurs.-Mon.; $13-29

Mama's Egg House serves elevated comfort food in an airy A-frame. Order at the counter, then settle into an indoor or patio table overlooking the action on the town center. Choose from classic diner combinations to chilaquiles. Lunch adds salads, sandwiches, and vegan options. They blend up smoothies and also pour coffee, beer, and wine.

★ Idyllwild Brewpub

54423 Village Center Dr.; 951/659-0163; www.
idyllwildbrewpub.com; 11am-8pm Sun.-Mon. and Wed.-
Thurs., 11am-10pm Fri.-Sat.; $12-40

Idyllwild Brewpub brought Idyllwild into the 21st century (in a good way) for food and drink with the opening of this lively gastropub. They offer a full menu of competently brewed English-, Belgian-, US-, and Canadian-style brews as well as a full bar. The menu offers hearty shareable snacks like brisket nachos and buffalo wings and mains including burgers and fish-and-chips. The upstairs location has an indoor space with tables and a long bar as well as an outdoor patio with forest views. It is both family- and party-friendly.

Gastrognome

54381 Ridge View Dr.; 951/659-5055; www.
gastrognome.com; noon-2pm and 4pm-8pm Mon. and
Thurs.-Fri., noon-8pm Sat.-Sun.; $15-43

Take a 1970s ski lodge and spruce it up with design tips from *The Hobbit* and you've got Gastrognome, the picturesque favorite of locals and visitors. A lengthy dinner menu features fish, chicken, lamb, steaks, and pasta dishes. The lunch menu is equally daunting with sandwiches, fish, seafood, pastas, vegetarian options, and steaks. When in doubt, the French onion soup is a solid choice. The charm of the restaurant might be its biggest selling point, but the food is generally well executed. Reservations are recommended for dinner on weekends.

Ferro Restaurant

25840 Cedar St.; 951/659-0700; www.ferrorestaurant.
com; 3pm-9pm Mon.-Fri., 2pm-9pm Sat.-Sun.; $22-40

Ferro Restaurant offers a lovely alfresco dining experience with a patio, a pine canopy, and Edison lights, with live music some nights; they also offer indoor seating. The wood-oven pizza is a good choice as the dough is excellent. The outdoor pizza oven with bar seating gives you front-row seats. The menu also features pasta, pizza, and panini for lunch, and pasta, risotto, polenta, seafood, chicken, steaks, and small plates for dinner. Reservations are advised for dinner.

Café Aroma

54750 N. Circle Dr.; 951/659-5212; https://cafearoma-
idyllwild.com; brunch 10am-noon Sat.-Sun., dinner
4:30pm-9pm Tues.-Thurs., 4:30pm-10pm Fri.-Sat.,
4:30pm-8:30pm Sun.; $20-46

Café Aroma serves an Italian fusion dinner menu in an eclectic treehouse-like setting with an outdoor patio. Weekends add brunch. A live music schedule adds to the festivity.

Accommodations

The aesthetic here is rustic, and hotel accommodations range from boutique mountain lodges with elaborate amenities to frayed cabin motels with charming exteriors and interiors that have seen better days. A host of cabin rentals through third-party rental sites offer a range, from romantic two-person hideaways with hot tubs to expansive properties for larger groups. Hotels and motels put you closer to town and within walking distance to restaurants, bars, and shopping. Cabins can make for a more secluded weekend. Make reservations in advance, as Idyllwild can book up completely on holiday weekends or when it snows.

Idyllwild Vacation Cabins

54380 N. Circle Dr.; 951/663-0527; www.
idyllwildvacationcabins.com; office 11am-4pm daily

In addition to rentals through Airbnb, Vrbo,

1: Idyllwild Inn **2:** Gastrognome

Homeaway, or other vacation rental platforms, Idyllwild Vacation Cabins is a locally based company with a large selection of rental cabins. You can search by preference: pet-friendly, with views, with hot tubs, on a creek, and rates. Cabins are searchable and bookable on the website, but the company also has an actual physical location in Idyllwild's downtown and an actual real-live human in the office who can assist with booking. The office is convenient for last-minute bookings when your day trip turns into a weekend getaway, and they also offer centralized management assistance.

Creekstone Inn

54950 Pine Crest Ave.; 951/659-3342; https:// creekstoneinn.com; from $180

The Creekstone Inn began life in 1947 as a general store, but a recent reenvisioning turned it into a rustic-chic modern boutique hotel that has upped the lodging game in Idyllwild. Owners Amy and Tim Brinkman had renovated three Palm Springs properties when they acquired the inn in 2020 and brought some of the desert town's flair up the mountain. The result blends mountain style with Palm Springs's clean lines. The property consists of nine luxury suites that sleep two (children are discouraged at the hotel) plus a cottage. For families, the two-story cottage is a better choice with its master bedroom and four-bed sleeping loft.

Idyllwild Inn

54300 Village Center Dr.; 888/659-2552; www. idyllwildinn.com; $150-190

The family-owned Idyllwild Inn dates from 1904 and is a favorite of PCT hikers and repeat visitors. Set on 5 wooded acres (2 ha) in the center of town, it features cabins, suites, and theme rooms. Its 12 one- and two-bedroom rustic cabins are original, with knotty pine paneling, fireplaces, and private decks. Cabin 9 is carved with historic graffiti dating to the 1950s. Eight new rustic cabins are family-friendly, with queen beds and sleeper sofas. New rustic suites offer hot tubs, queen beds, and sleeper sofas. Eight themed rooms are a relatively recent addition.

The Fireside Inn

54540 N. Circle Dr.; 951/659-2966; www.thefiresideinn. com; $199-269

Make sure you know what your spirit animal (or tree) is before you make reservations at The Fireside Inn. They offer eight quaintly named duplex cottages and a separate 1930s lodge, all with fireplaces and most with kitchens. The inn is set in a residential neighborhood in the center of town within easy walking distance to shops and restaurants.

Camping

There are many great camping options in and around Idyllwild, from developed camping close to town to more remote sites. Note that fire restrictions may be in effect during fire season (the summer months), and campfires may not be allowed at local campgrounds. Campgrounds may be closed intermittently due to drought and fire conditions. Check online for current conditions.

Mount San Jacinto State Park (www.parks. ca.gov) operates two campgrounds near Idyllwild: Idyllwild Campground and Stone Creek Campground.

Idyllwild Campground

25905 Hwy. 243; 951/659-2607; www.parks.ca.gov, reservations www.reservecalifornia.com; year-round; $25

Idyllwild Campground has 28 sites under a canopy of pine and amid manzanitas for tent camping, RVs, and trailers. Showers, flush toilets, water, picnic tables, and fire rings are on-site. Since the site is walking distance to Idyllwild shops and restaurants, campers can spend time enjoying the stars instead of washing dishes.

Stone Creek Campground

Hwy. 243; www.parks.ca.gov, reservations www. reservecalifornia.com; May-Oct.; $25

Stone Creek Campground is off Highway 243, about 6 mi (9.7 km) north of Idyllwild. The campground offers 44 sites for tent camping as well as trailer and RV sites (24 ft/7.3 m maximum, no hookups or dump stations). Amenities include fire rings, picnic tables, water, and vault toilets.

Idyllwild Regional Park Campground

54000 Riverside County Playground Rd.; 951/659-2656; www.rivcoparks.org; $30-70

Idyllwild Regional Park Campground is less than 1 mi (1.6 km) south of the state park campground. Its 88 sites are situated amid shaded pine forest and are available year-round for tent, RV, and trailer camping. Amenities include picnic tables, fire rings, flush toilets, and showers. Sites 1, 23, and 39 are designated accessible. These sites also have a grill. Reservations are accepted by phone (800/234-7375 8am-5pm Mon.-Thurs.) or online (www.rivcoparks.org) year-round. The park also offers a nature center and interpretive trails and is within walking distance to shops and restaurants.

San Bernardino National Forest

909/382-2921; www.fs.usda.gov

Other seasonal campgrounds are open in summer only; these are in the vicinity of the Stone Creek Campground and are operated by the San Bernardino National Forest. Most sites require advance reservations (www.recreation.gov), but a few sites are open to walk-ins.

Fern Basin

www.recreation.gov; May-Oct.; $10

At Fern Basin, about 6.5 mi (10.5 km) north of Idyllwild, 22 reservable sites are set amid manzanitas, oaks, and conifers at 6,400 ft (1,950 m). Amenities include vault toilets,

fire rings, and picnic tables, but there is no drinking water.

Marion Mountain Campground

www.recreation.gov; June-Nov.; $10

Up the road from Fern Basin, Marion Mountain Campground has 25 reservable campsites set in two loops amid a cedar and ponderosa pine forest. Amenities include vault toilets, fire rings, drinking water, and picnic tables. Marion Mountain is located about 7 mi (11.3 km) north of Idyllwild.

Boulder Basin Campground

www.recreation.gov; end of May-mid-Oct.; $10

Boulder Basin Campground is a secluded forested campground pitched at 7,300 ft (2,225 m) elevation. The campground is accessed from Highway 243 via a dirt road 8 mi (12.9 km) north of Idyllwild. The road is rough and steep; a high clearance vehicle is recommended, and 4WD may be necessary. Allow extra time for this 5-mi (8.1-km) stretch. The campground offers 16 reservable shaded tent-only campsites with vault toilets, fire rings, and picnic tables. There is no drinking water available. There are bouldering opportunities nearby, and the campground is popular with rock climbers, hikers, and campers who like the solitude. A hike from the campground via dirt road takes you to the Black Mountain Lookout Tower with spectacular views of the area.

Getting There and Around

There is no public transportation available in Idyllwild—no buses, taxis, or ride-sharing services. Idyllwild is a small town of less than 3 mi (4.8 km) from end to end, and it is easy to get around by driving or walking. The town center has sidewalks and lighting, and if you are staying directly in town, it is no problem to do everything on foot.

Outside the town center, the sidewalks and lighting disappear. Both Highway 243 and

Highway 74 have steady traffic, and it can be a little nerve-wracking to be a pedestrian walking along the narrow shoulders of these dark roads at night. Carry a flashlight so that you are visible to drivers.

Car

The town of Idyllwild is located in the San Jacinto Mountains above Palm Springs. To get here from Palm Springs, take North Palm Canyon Drive (Hwy. 111) north to I-10. Take I-10 west for 3 mi (4.8 km) to the town of Banning. At Banning, take Highway 243 and drive the twisting mountain road 25 mi (40 km) south to the town center. Note that Highway 243 may close due to snow or other inclement weather.

From the Coachella Valley, take Highway 74 west from its intersection with Highway 111 and continue onto Highway 243 north to reach Idyllwild in 41 mi (66 km).

The closest hospital is in Hemet, 23 mi (37 km) west of Idyllwild, or Banning, 29 mi (47 km) to the north, along I-10.

Background

The Landscape

The Landscape	185
Plants and Animals	190
History	194
Government and Economy	199
People and Culture	199

GEOGRAPHY
Mojave and Sonoran Deserts

Joshua Tree National Park straddles the Mojave and Sonoran Desert ecosystems. The Mojave Desert covers an area of 35,000 sq mi (90,650 sq km) and extends into Nevada and southern Utah. It encompasses the northwest section of Joshua Tree National Park, the most popular and heavily visited portion of the park for good reason. A drive through Joshua Tree's Mojave Desert reveals a surreal landscape of shattered boulder piles, fields of spiky Joshua trees, and broken mountains

ringing broad valleys. The Mojave is characterized by higher elevations (3,000-5,000 ft/915-1,520 m) and temperatures that can be 15-25°F (8-14°C) cooler than its neighboring Sonoran Desert ecosystem, which spans elevations below 3,000 ft (915 m). The Mojave Desert is marked by distinct vegetation, including large swatches of Joshua trees. Above 4,000 ft (1,220 m), juniper and piñon pine woodlands take over, lending a more forested feel. Desert gardens that blend yucca plants, Joshua trees, junipers, and piñons are not unusual. On the lower end of the elevation range, cacti such as barrel cactus dot the rocky hillsides.

The Coachella Valley lies south of Joshua Tree National Park and encompasses Palm Springs. The valley extends northwest-southeast for approximately 45 mi (72 km), outlined in the west by the San Jacinto Mountains and then the Santa Rosa Mountains continuing south. On the north and east, the Little San Bernardino Mountains frame the valley. The San Andreas fault follows the foothills of the Little San Bernardino Mountains, spouting up at major fissures in a series of hot springs. The Coachella Valley lies within the Sonoran Desert system, which covers southeastern California, much of Arizona, and northwestern Mexico. This "low desert" encompasses the eastern section of Joshua Tree National Park as well as Palm Springs. It is lower and hotter than the neighboring Mojave, with elevations below 1,000 ft (305 m) and starker landscape. The plants that grow here are hardy, able to withstand searing heat and a lack of water. Spindly ocotillos resemble fingered sticks until they bloom with flame-like flowers in wet springs, while fuzzy cholla cacti spread out into strange armies of plants. Bushy creosote, an indicator of the Sonoran Desert, does well here too.

The section of the Sonoran Desert that blankets eastern Joshua Tree National Park and the Coachella Valley is also referred to as the Colorado Desert. A subregion of the Sonoran Desert, the Colorado falls south of the Mojave Desert, extending east to the Colorado River, which marks the boundary between California and Arizona. The Colorado Desert covers more than 7 million acres (2.8 million ha), spanning the Coachella Valley and the heavily irrigated agricultural Imperial Valley, also the location of the Salton Sea, to the south.

Joshua Tree Geology

The strange, jumbled rock formations that make up the labyrinthine Wonderland of Rocks and other striking formations in the northwest of Joshua Tree National Park are captivating. The cracked granite is strangely contorted: giant piles of melted rock are somehow thrown together in otherworldly piles. They rise up in seemingly random clusters, massive sculptures with rocks that resemble skulls or hollowed-out space stations.

The forces that sculpted the monzogranite boulders, peaks, and domes date back two billion years, about half the present age of the Earth. Eroded sediment washed off of ancient continents into the ocean, forming thick layers that fused into sedimentary rock. Around one billion years ago, fragments of ancient continents collided to form a massive supercontinent, Rodinia. As mountain chains rose from the collision, some of the offshore sedimentary rock was buckled by heat and pressure, causing it to metamorphose into granitic gneiss. Joshua Tree has gneiss similar to types found in Australia and Antarctica, suggesting that a mountain chain once connected the three continents. When Rodinia broke apart, the North American continent drifted toward the equator. Likely part of a continental shelf, Joshua Tree lay underwater for 250 million years.

Another supercontinent formation (Pangaea) and breakup 210 million years ago finally forced Joshua Tree above water as

Previous: Sonoran Desert views with Cottonwood Spring and mill ruins.

North America drifted west and collided with the massive Pacific tectonic plate. The shifting plates caused intense friction, and rising magma bubbled up, reaching the gneiss layer (the Pinto gneiss) before cooling into granite.

The rock formations you see in the park are this bubbling magma turned into granite after millions of years of erosion of the overlying rock—sediment, volcanic ash, and metamorphic rock. Their cracked and sculpted shapes are the result of upheaval as rocks were squeezed to the surface and expanded as top layers eroded. When Joshua Tree was much wetter, trickling groundwater also eroded the granite along the crisscrossed fissures that had been formed during the tectonic plate shifts. As the climate in what is now Southern California became drier, this type of erosion slowed, and surface erosion increased, revealing the surreal formations we see today.

San Andreas Fault and Transverse Mountain Ranges

The famous San Andreas fault extends 800 mi (1,290 km) from the Salton Sea (south of Palm Springs in Imperial County) to Cape Mendocino in Northern California's Humboldt County. The fault marks the zone where two massive tectonic plates—the North American Plate and the Pacific Plate—come into contact. These plates, mostly rigid slabs of rock that make up the earth's mantle, are generally stable, but when they shift, they cause earthquakes. The North American Plate is slowly drifting south, and the Pacific Plate is creeping north. The most famous shift was the 1906 San Francisco earthquake.

The San Andreas fault is also responsible for the unique transverse mountain system that dominates the Joshua Tree and Coachella Valley regions. The east-west-trending mountain ranges are a geologic anomaly in North America, where most ranges are oriented north-south. This is because the San Andreas fault is not completely straight; north of the Coachella Valley, near the coastal town of Santa Barbara, the fault makes a clear-cut east-west bend. This bend concentrated geologic pressure and forced up the transverse ranges in Southern California. These east-west-trending ranges form the boundaries of the Coachella Valley—the San Jacinto Mountains and Santa Rosa Mountains on the west and Little San Bernardino Mountains to the north. In Joshua Tree National Park, the transverse formations are reflected in the Little San Bernardino Mountains that run along the park's southern border as well as

monzogranite boulders and Joshua trees, characteristic of the Mojave Desert

the remote Eagle Mountains in the eastern wilderness of the park.

The San Andreas fault is also responsible for some of the natural beauty of Coachella Valley as well as its profusion of natural hot springs. The fault runs 10 mi (16 km) deep, connecting the surface with geothermal activity and underground water. You can see the fault as a dark green line of native California fan palms running along the foot of the Little San Bernardino Mountains. At times, these fan palms are clustered around surface pools and oases, such as the shaded pools in the Thousand Palms Oasis of the Coachella Valley Preserve.

Hot springs are largely responsible for making Palm Springs the destination it is. In particular, hot springs abound in Desert Hot Springs, feeding the mineral pools of the area's many resorts. Palm Springs's history as a resort town began around these natural mineral springs that bubbled up to the surface.

CLIMATE

When distinguishing between Joshua Tree National Park (and surrounding towns) and Palm Springs (and the Coachella Valley), locals refer to the "high desert" and the "low desert." These designations actually refer to their respective elevations and the two different desert zones that encompass them. Elevation is the largest factor in the two region's very different climates.

Joshua Tree mostly lies within the Mojave Desert, a transition desert between the hot Sonoran Desert to the south and the cold Great Basin Desert to the north. The Joshua Tree section of the Mojave has elevations generally between 3,000 and 5,000 ft (915-1,520 m). The highest point in Joshua Tree National Park is Quail Mountain at 5,816 ft (1,773 m). At these elevation levels, the Mojave is considered a high desert, cooler than the neighboring low desert. Joshua Tree's climate is characterized by wild temperature swings, and the region experiences cold winters and blazing-hot summers. Rainfall in the area is generally only about 3-5 inches (8-13 cm)

per year, but Joshua Tree can receive late-summer storms that produce flash floods. Occasionally, Joshua Tree receives a very light blanketing of snow in winter.

Below 3,000 ft (915 m), the Sonoran Desert encompasses the eastern part of the park as well as the Coachella Valley and Palm Springs to the south. With its lower elevation, it is significantly hotter than the Mojave; depending on where you are, this can be up to 10-15°F (5-8°C) hotter. Palm Springs is only 479 ft (146 m) above sea level. This low elevation means that temperatures are fairly mild in the winter. Summers, however, can be brutally hot, with temperatures holding fast in the triple digits (over 38°C) for much of June-September. October-April are the most temperate months, with temperatures ranging from the high 60s to the low 90s F (20-34°C) during the day.

In the desert, there is also the wind to contend with; the San Gorgonio Pass on the northern end of the valley is one of the windiest places on Earth. (The vast wind farms there give testament to this claim.) Temperatures in the Coachella Valley drop at night due to the dry air and lack of cloud cover, which allows temperatures to plummet with the sunset. However, plummeting from 115°F (46°C) during the day in summer to 90°F (32°C) at night is still pretty warm. In contrast, the towering peaks of the San Jacinto Mountains to the south and San Bernardino Mountains to the west (Sand to Snow National Monument) are often snowcapped through late spring, offering a dazzling contrast to the sometimes blow-dryer-like heat below. This snowmelt feeds the streams in the Indian Canyons and percolates into ravines, natural rock tanks, and springs.

ENVIRONMENTAL ISSUES
Air Quality

In 2024, Joshua Tree National Park earned the dubious distinction of being in the top four most ozone-polluted national parks in the country. The reporting system was based on three main categories: unhealthy air, harm to nature, and hazy skies. The ranking, conducted by the National Parks Conservation Association, surveyed 399 national parks. Joshua Tree was the second worst, just behind popular Sequoia and Kings Canyon National Park in the southern Sierra Nevada, and followed by the Mojave National Preserve and iconic Yosemite. Population growth in the Coachella Valley, as well as pollution coming from the Los Angeles Basin, has created reduced air quality, affecting views and quality of life. In addition to being unhealthy, smoggy and hazy air can diminish the park experience. People come for the area's beauty and sweeping views, which can stretch for 200 mi (320 km) on a clear day. That natural visibility has been seriously impacted with poor air quality that has limited views to about 90 mi (145 km) on average.

Adding to the problem are dust particulates from the Salton Sea at the southern end of the Coachella Valley. The 350-sq-mi (907-sq-km) Salton Sea is shrinking due to rapid evaporation amid the region's high summer temperatures and a decrease in the agricultural runoff that supplied the water. The agricultural water source contains pesticides, which makes the dust blowing in from the Salton Sea even more polluted. Without an environmental intervention, the Salton Sea has the potential to become a huge dust bowl as the playa becomes more and more exposed.

Overuse and Vandalism

Though the desert may seem impervious to visitors, it is a delicate and fragile ecosystem relying on tiny amounts of rainfall to sustain life in extreme conditions. Joshua Tree welcomed 3.2 million visitors in 2023, a heavy concentration of visitors for the park's size. The park spans just under 800,000 acres (323,800 ha), approximately 1,200 sq mi (3,240 sq km), and while it is twice as big as the median size for US national parks, most of its traffic is concentrated in the popular western section. This is partially because it is where the striking rock formations and Joshua trees for which the park is known are concentrated, and partially because the only developed roads run through this section. This is not by accident—most of the remote eastern (Pinto Basin) section of the park is being preserved as wilderness.

At its most benign, the park's heavy visitation can translate into crowded park entrances, a lack of solitude on trails and at picnic areas, and a dearth of camping spots during the busy fall and spring seasons. At its most hostile, it can mean a higher likelihood of vandalism, graffiti, and general abuse of the land and cultural resources. Vandalism and graffiti have become an increasing problem in Joshua Tree and other national parks. In 2020, the National Park Service (NPS) reported vandalism at several popular sites. Social media has played a role in the increase in graffiti; people want it to be seen and often post graffiti pics on Instagram and other online venues. On the flip side, posting vandalism and graffiti on social media sometimes offers a way to identify the location and report it. The NPS asks visitors to report any vandalism and graffiti by emailing jotr_graffiti@nps. gov with a detailed description. Photos and GPS coordinates are also helpful.

To minimize your impact on Joshua Tree National Park while hiking, camping, and driving, follow a few general rules advised by the NPS:

- Leave only footprints; take only pictures. Do not leave trash, even organic material (e.g. fruit peels). Do not take any rocks, plants, or cultural artifacts.

- Respect wildlife. Give them space and do not feed them. Keep trash and food scraps secured.

- Make campfires only in designated campfire rings in campgrounds and only when there is no campfire ban.

- Do not scavenge for firewood. This includes park vegetation, living or dead.

- Respect speed limits. They are lower in national parks to protect wildlife.

- Park only in designated parking spots or on graded shoulders along the road.
- Stay on designated roads with vehicles, street-legal motorbikes, and bicycles. They are not allowed on trails or open desert.
- Stay on established hiking trails and do not cut switchbacks.
- Share the trail. Be mindful of your noise level and give others space.
- Graffiti is illegal. Report incidents of graffiti.

Water and Drought

The Coachella Valley is one of the fastest-growing regions in California, and it is also one of the driest places in North America, receiving only 3-4 inches (8-10 cm) of rain annually. This tension surrounding competition for resources is growing in a region that is known for luxury resorts, golf courses, and swimming pools. In 2015 the state ordered the region to cut water use by 36 percent, and resort cities like Palm Springs and Rancho Mirage have adopted strict conservation measures. For now, the region continues to take full advantage of its water rights, receiving billions of gallons annually from the Colorado River and other sources to replenish its underwater aquifer and feed the growing number of housing developments as well as the recreation industry. The valley's population continues to grow even as resources shrink into a hotter and drier future, representing the challenges that California faces as a whole.

Plants and Animals

Joshua Tree and the Coachella Valley are home to a wide range of desert plants and animals, including 700 plant species, more than 50 mammal species, and 40 reptile species, a thriving ecosystem existing within the seemingly stark landscape.

MOJAVE DESERT FLORA

Referred to as piñon-juniper woodland or piñon-juniper forest, a mix of low, bushy evergreens occurs at higher desert elevations above 4,000 ft (1,220 m). The woodlands span vast regions of the Southwest, including northern Arizona and New Mexico, the Canyonlands region of Utah, and the Sierra Nevada. A good place to find this piñon-juniper forest mix in Joshua Tree is along the Pine City Trail in the Queen Valley.

Joshua Trees

The signature plant of the Mojave Desert and Joshua Tree National Park, the spiky Joshua tree *(Yucca brevifolia)* favors the higher elevations. You can find the trees in large stands on the western side of Joshua Tree National Park.

With their sharp demeanor, these specimens resemble cacti but are actually members of the agave family. They were named by Mormon explorers who thought their jaunty shapes resembled the upstretched arms of the prophet Joshua pointing them toward the promised land. Joshua trees can reach more than 40 ft (12 m) and, although dating is difficult due to their fleshy interior (no tree rings), several hundred years old.

Mojave Yucca

The bayonet-like Mojave yucca *(Yucca schidigera)* thrives at elevations of 1,000-4,000 ft (305-1,220 m) and is often found mixed in with Joshua trees in transition zones leading to the higher-elevation piñon-juniper forests, creating a desert garden feel. The fibers of the yucca were a staple Native Americans used to weave rope, sandals, baskets, and other items.

SONORAN DESERT FLORA

There are clear contrasts between the Mojave and Sonoran Deserts as vegetation differs

Fan Palm Oases

Palm Canyon fan palms

Where the San Andreas fault runs through the Coachella Valley, native California fan palms cluster around surface pools, forming shaded oases worth seeking out for their natural beauty—and their relief from the desert heat.

- **49 Palms Oasis:** Hike to this mirage-like fan palm oasis (page 57).
- **Lost Palms Oasis:** From lush Cottonwood Spring, this trail crosses desert ridges to the largest collection of fan palms in the park (page 62).
- **Lower Palm Canyon:** The world's largest fan palm oasis lies at the bottom of a rocky gorge in Palm Springs's Indian Canyons (page 129).
- **Thousand Palms Oasis Preserve:** Across the preserve, clusters of native California fan palms flash in the glaring sun, protecting hidden pools (page 163).

at lower elevations in the desert valleys and floors.

Smoke Trees

Ephemeral in appearance, smoke trees inhabit low washes, their gray-green leaves puffing from spindly branches. These natives of the eastern Mojave Desert and Colorado Desert subsection of the Sonoran Desert are most prevalent in Joshua Tree National Park. The best place to find them is along the Pinto Basin Road north of Cottonwood Spring.

Mesquite

If you're wandering in the low desert and see a plant that you want to identify, mesquite is a good guess. Drought-tolerant mesquite, the most common shrub of the Southwest, survives in harsh environs via its long taproot, which it can use to suck water out of a very low water table. It was an integral resource for Native Americans, who ground the mesquite pods and seeds into flours that were turned into cakes. Hard-up settlers ate the beans roasted or boiled.

Ocotillo

The whip-like funnel shapes of the ocotillo dot the low-desert landscape, its spindly branches bare for most of the year but flaming out in red bloom each spring. It favors the Sonoran Desert of southeastern California, extending to Texas and Mexico.

Creosote

The creosote bush can be found from California to West Texas and Mexico, dominating the Mojave, Sonoran, and Chihuahuan Deserts. The creosote is hardy, surviving in regions with temperatures of more than 120°F (49°C) and surviving through periods of intense drought with waxy leaves that maintain moisture and roots that choke off the water supply of surrounding plants by releasing toxins. The creosote was valued by Native Americans for its medicinal properties; indeed, it emits a medicinal smell when slightly wet. Maybe the strangest thing about the creosote is its propensity for longevity. To reproduce, new plants grow from a single progenitor. The creosote ring dubbed King Clone in the Mojave Desert is thought to be 11,700 years old, making it one of the oldest living organisms on earth.

Cholla

The cholla cactus, also known as the jumping cholla, may look fuzzy and cuddly, but it is known for its spiny stems, which easily detach when brushed, clinging to unsuspecting visitors who have gotten too close. If you see one cholla cactus, you will likely see them all because new plants grow from stems that have fallen from an adult. Their bristly ranks extend across the desert in mini cactus gardens.

WILDFLOWERS

Spring wildflowers begin to color the lower elevations of the Pinto Basin in February, climbing to higher elevations in March-April. Above 5,000 ft (1,520 m), desert regions may see blooms as late as June. The colorful display varies each year depending on winter precipitation and spring temperatures. Optimal conditions include a good soaking of rain and warm spring temperatures.

The staunch barrel cactus offers beautiful blooms in spring; pink and yellow crowns form at the top of the cactus. Barrel cacti are highly ornamental, cultivated by nurseries for their symmetric and easy-growing properties. But they are also dangerous, easily puncturing skin. The beavertail has broad, flat stems growing in clusters and can be identified by its vivid magenta flowers.

Brittlebush is ubiquitously cheerful across the lower elevations. Vibrant yellow flowers bloom on the silvery gray bushes that dot washes and hillsides. The tiny purple flowers of the sand verbena have been known to quilt large areas, favoring dunes, washes, and sandy areas.

MAMMALS
Bighorn Sheep

The most dramatic sight in Joshua Tree may be bighorn sheep. It is estimated that there are 100-200 in the park across three herds. The largest herd ranges through the remote Eagle Mountains in the southeastern section of the park. The second largest lives in the Little San Bernardino Mountains along the park's western boundary. The smallest herd lives in the Wonderland of Rocks. The numbers are down from an estimated 200-300 animals in 2015, when a respiratory disease began to spread through the population; the illness is not transmissible to humans. Bighorn sheep prefer steep, rocky terrain in order to elude predators, and they are able to navigate canyons and cliffs, bounding as far as 20 ft (6 m) from ledge to ledge. Their distinctive concave hoofs have a hard outer shell and a softer interior sole perfect for gripping the steep canyon walls. Scan the hillsides to make a sighting; male sheep in particular have impressive curved horns and can weigh more than 220 lbs (100 kg).

Mountain Lions

Mountain lions, also known as cougars or pumas, are the second-largest wild cats in the western hemisphere (jaguars are the largest). Mountain lions historically ranged across all of the contiguous 48 states but were hunted almost to extinction. Conservation efforts have brought their populations back in the West. Mountain lions are lethal hunters; they often stalk animals before they pounce, and they can span more than 30 ft (9 m) in one leap. Solitary hunters, mountain lions range over a large home territory and generally go out of their way to avoid humans. If you do happen to encounter a mountain lion, maintain eye contact, back away slowly, and make yourself appear larger; make loud noises and speak slowly, firmly, and loudly.

Coyotes

Coyotes roam all across Joshua Tree and are common wildlife sightings. Even if you don't see them, you may hear their howling at night—a diabolical-sounding series of yips and yaps when they are in a pack. Coyotes mainly eat small mammals and rodents, but they are scavengers that have been known to get into trash receptacles looking for food.

Jackrabbits

Another commonly spotted animal in Joshua Tree is the jackrabbit, originally called the "jackass rabbit." It is distinguished by its long ears, which give it exceptional hearing to help protect it from predators.

REPTILES
Desert Tortoises

The largest reptile in the Mojave and Sonoran Deserts is the desert tortoise, which can weigh up to 50 lbs (23 kg). Desert tortoises were plentiful until the 1950s; since then, populations have drastically declined due to several factors, including development causing habitat loss as well as speeding and off-road vehicles. Studies estimate that until the 1950s, the desert tortoise population maintained at least 200 adults per square mile; these numbers have dropped to only 5-60 adults per square mile. The desert tortoise is on both the California and federal endangered species lists. Desert tortoises survive the heat by staying cool in burrows and rehydrating after a rainstorm. If you come across a desert tortoise, do not disturb it—even getting close can stress a tortoise, causing it to void vital water stored in its bladder.

Chuckwalla

The chuckwalla is an iguana distinctive for its potbelly. After the Gila monster, it is the second-largest lizard in North America. The chuckwalla inflates when frightened, puffing up its lungs to three times their normal capacity. Native Americans hunted them for food,

Chuckwalla lizards can inflate to ward off predators.

and there is at least one account of a later settler serving up chuckwalla. "Chuckwalla Bill," a would-be miner who lived in a canyon south of Desert Hot Springs in the 1930s, earned his nickname by serving chuckwalla to a priest and trying to pass it off as fish. The priest was not fooled, and the nickname stuck.

Rattlesnakes

The Mojave and Sonoran Deserts have their share of venomous creatures, although only the rattlesnake poses a real health threat. Of the 11 rattlesnake species in North America, 6 reside in the region around Joshua Tree National Park, including the Mojave rattlesnake—one of the most toxic of all rattlesnakes. Fortunately, it is highly unlikely you will encounter a rattlesnake; they prefer open rocky habitat with crevices in which to hide and plentiful rodents. Still, if you do hear the rattle of a snake, consider it a warning and back away, giving it a wide berth.

INSECTS AND ARACHNIDS

Hairy tarantulas are the largest spiders in the world, and while they may look creepy, the reality is that their venomous bites, which paralyze insects, lizards, and small mammals, are harmless to humans. Also misunderstood is the giant hairy scorpion, with its famous stinger. Although stings are painful, they are generally harmless to humans (similar to a bee's sting). The giant hairy scorpion is the largest in the United States and common in the Joshua Tree region. However, because it is nocturnal, it is rarely seen.

BIRDS

Joshua Tree and the Coachella Valley are in the direct path of the Pacific Flyway, a major north-south flight path for migratory birds extending from Alaska to Patagonia in South America. The Salton Sea, at the south end of Coachella Valley, is a notable stop on the migratory path. Joshua Tree National Park and the surrounding desert are also home to many nesting bird species, including the golden eagle. This predatory bird has an 8-ft (2.4-m) wingspan, which makes it the largest bird of prey in North America. You may also see the long-legged roadrunner dashing across roads (seriously!) and the open desert in Joshua Tree National Park and Coachella Valley neighborhoods. What they lack in flying abilities they make up for with ground speed and maneuverability.

History

JOSHUA TREE
Ancient Culture

The first known people to inhabit Joshua Tree were the Pinto culture, dating as far back as 8,000 years. The Pinto occupied today's Pinto Basin, the stark rolling landscape in the southern part of the park. At the end of the last ice age, roughly 10,000 years ago, California's deserts were lush and filled with rivers and lakes; large mammals such as mastodons, camels, and mammoths wandered the grassy landscape, and a river flowed through the Pinto Basin. By the time the Pinto people arrived, however, many of the ice age mammals had gone extinct and the river was dry. Still, the Pinto persisted for as long as 4,000 years. Though very little is known about them, what we do understand is based on archaeological finds from the 1930s, which include stone tools and spearpoints. These artifacts suggest that the Pinto people were mobile and mostly dependent on large game for survival.

Serrano and Cahuilla Indians

The Serrano and Cahuilla people moved into the region several thousand years after the Pinto people had left. They used the area that is now the park seasonally, moving to where food sources were plentiful. The largest village was at the Oasis of Mara (near the modern-day 29 Palms Inn), the winter home of the Serrano people. In summer, the Serrano moved west to the pine forests of the San Bernardino Mountains. The Cahuilla people occupied the southern reaches of the park (their northernmost boundary) and regions farther south in Palm Springs and the Indian Canyons.

The harsh landscape and climate dictated the daily activities of the Indigenous desert dwellers. They were primarily hunters and gatherers living in seasonal small villages of 25-100 individuals. The most important food sources were pine nuts, acorns, and mesquite beans as well as small animals like jackrabbits and rodents. Villages consisted of communal structures for storage, a sweathouse, and a ceremonial room; family houses were circular thatched huts made of palm fronds. Serrano and Cahuilla women were expert weavers, crafting baskets, netting, rope hats, sandals, and other items from palm trees and yuccas. Pottery made by these desert people included earthenware vessels called ollas for food and water storage.

The Mission Era

The 1771 construction of the Spanish Mission San Gabriel Archangel in present-day Los Angeles marked the start of a land and power shift away from the Indigenous people of the California desert to European control, although it would be another 100 years before the full impact was felt. The mission was just one of 21 that Spanish officials had ordered constructed along the California coast. The Spanish largely avoided the deserts, seeing them as remote and dangerous. With the dominance of Spanish missions on the coast, Native Americans fled inland, sharing the land with groups who were already living in the Joshua Tree region. The Spanish built a second chain of missions inland; the closest to what is now Joshua Tree National Park was erected in 1819 in Redlands, less than 40 mi (64 km) away, impacting the Serrano and Cahuilla people within its reach. More far-flung villages like the one at Oasis of Mara evaded the mission's control.

Miners, Ranchers, and Homesteaders

The year 1848 was eventful for California. It became a US state, handed over from Mexico, and the gold rush had started in Northern California. As goldfields tapped out, prospectors chased the precious metal farther afield into California's deserts, which until this point had been mostly untouched. Gold was discovered near the Oasis of Mara in 1863. This discovery, plus a smallpox epidemic that swept east from Los Angeles and wiped out whole villages of the Indigenous population, marked the breakdown of traditional Native American life, including political and social structures, and shifted the culture of the desert. Indigenous people at the Oasis of Mara hung on for several decades, sharing their precious water resources with the Chemehuevi people, who had been driven from their traditional lands to the east, as well as with gold prospectors, all the while locked in a land dispute with the Southern Pacific Railroad. By 1912 the last holdouts were gone, and there were no Native Americans remaining at the oasis.

Prospectors had been poking around Joshua Tree for decades following the initial discovery of gold in California, but 1883 marked the defining moment for mining when one discovered rich deposits in the Pinto Mountains east of the Oasis of Mara. Prospectors flocked to the boomtown named Dale that at its peak claimed over 1,000 residents. Over time, the town moved, following the gold. Other mines sprang up. Today the region, called the Old Dale Mining District, is located just north of the Joshua Tree National Park boundary. It is littered with old mining camps and crisscrossed by a series of rugged roads.

It may be easy to think of Joshua Tree National Park as a pristine land, preserved in its natural state, but the reality is that ranching, mining, and homesteading were deeply entrenched in the region in the 1900s. The area was used for ranching; the sparse landscape required 17 acres (7 ha) per animal for grazing. The presence of concrete dams at places like Barker Dam and Twin Tanks are reminders of Joshua Tree's ranching days.

The most notable settler was resourceful homesteader, rancher, and miner Bill Keys, who arrived in 1910 and thrived for decades on his property within the current Joshua Tree National Park boundary. He got his start as supervisor of the Desert Queen Mine. When the mining company he worked for went bankrupt, Keys gladly accepted their offer of a deed to the mine. From there he settled a 160-acre (65-ha) homestead and built a ranch. On a trip to Los Angeles he met his future wife, and they raised a family on the ranch. Keys was a legendary scavenger, collecting machinery and spare parts from abandoned mines and other desert sites. His resourcefulness served him well in this hardscrabble desert environment. The couple lived at the ranch until well into the 1960s, when Joshua Tree had already become a national monument. It is possible to visit the still-standing Desert Queen Ranch via tours offered by the National Park Service.

Joshua Tree National Monument

The 1930s brought the seemingly conflicting goals of settlement and preservation to Joshua Tree. In many of the western states, including Arizona, California, Nevada, New Mexico, and Utah, the federal government was promoting development of "useless" lands unsuitable for ranching or farming; the 1938 Small Tract Act offered dirt-cheap land to individuals for settlement. To earn a right to purchase at the government's rates, applicants had to build a simple dwelling within three years. This homestead act tapped into a deep American desire to claim a piece of territory, even if the land was deemed unprofitable. Some of these "jackrabbit homesteads" are evident north of the park, particularly in the area of Wonder Valley, east of Twentynine Palms. In this scrubby desert, the tiny shacks stand in various degrees of preservation and decay, some housing a burgeoning artist community. The homestead program was not disbanded until 1976.

While the federal government was encouraging settlement, activists were calling for the preservation of Joshua Tree's unique geography. Beginning in the 1920s, Minerva Hoyt, a wealthy Pasadena widow, led the conservation effort to protect Joshua Tree. Following the untimely death of her husband and infant son, she made frequent trips to the California desert, taking solace there. While Joshua Tree had caught on as a tourist destination, the prevailing mentality was that the desert was indestructible. Landscapers catering to a desert garden craze in Los Angeles looted the area, uprooting plants by the acre and doing lasting damage to the ecosystem. Travelers setting up camp routinely set fire to Joshua trees at night to guide motorists coming in after dark. Hoyt, an active gardener, designed desert conservation exhibits that were showcased in New York and London to address the ecological damage she had witnessed on her trips. This got her elected president of the newly created Desert Conservation League, through which she campaigned for protected lands to encompass the Southern California deserts. In 1936 President Franklin Roosevelt signed a proclamation that established Joshua Tree National Monument. It spanned privately owned land, including massive swathes owned by the Southern Pacific Railroad and more than 8,000 existing mining claims, some operating and profitable, within its boundaries.

Joshua Tree National Park

Over the next decades, the National Park Service negotiated and maneuvered, obtaining deeds and purchasing real estate. In 1964, Congress authorized the Wilderness Act, protecting federally managed lands from mechanized vehicles and equipment. In 1994, President Bill Clinton signed the Desert Protection Act, upgrading Joshua

Tree to national park status and transferring 3 million acres (1.2 million ha) for protection in Joshua Tree, Death Valley National Park, and the Mojave National Preserve. Today Joshua Tree National Park is wildly popular and receives more than three million visitors a year.

Keeping pace with the visitation to the national park, the gateway towns have grown from rural desert outposts to burgeoning scenes for shopping, art, and music. In the tiny town of Morongo Valley on the edge of the Sand to Snow National Monument, a defunct saloon turned popular spaghetti restaurant steadily draws locals and tourists. Yucca Valley, the biggest and most suburban town, has a growing old town with destination-worthy shopping for clothing, jewelry, housewares, and vintage. The addition of two stylish bars has added to the draw.

The reenvisioning of the Joshua Tree Trading Post in downtown Joshua Tree as well as the addition of high-end shops for coffee and provisions has changed the nature of the town from artist outpost with tumbleweeds blowing down Highway 62 to style mecca. On weekends in-season, pop-up shops with vintage clothing, jewelry, bespoke hats, food, and drink keeps the tiny downtown bustling with foot traffic. In addition, the airstream camp Auto Camp added an outpost here, making Joshua Tree a glamping destination. Until fairly recently in the town of Twentynine Palms, the historic 29 Palms Inn was the only tourist game in town. Now there are destination restaurants and shopping in the historically no-frills Marine base town and outsider artist hideout. An increasing number of boutiques and restaurants have taken advantage of downtown Twentynine Palms's "good bones" to set up shop.

In 2024, Joshua Tree National Park also opened a brand-new visitor center in downtown Twentynine Palms, further solidifying its status as a tourist-friendly destination. Short-term rentals have proliferated in the area, with old homesteads and local housing snapped up to satisfy tourism demands.

PALM SPRINGS
Agua Caliente Band of Cahuilla Indians

The first inhabitants came to Palm Springs 2,000 years ago, establishing complex communities in the well-watered canyons at the base of the San Jacinto Mountains. These people fished, trapped, and gathered as well as developed agricultural systems by diverting streams to irrigate crops. Named after the natural hot springs in the canyons, the Agua Caliente (hot water) Band of Cahuilla Indians still owns these canyons. You can see evidence of the ancient habitation in Tahquitz Canyon, Chino Canyon, and the Indian Canyons. Ancient artifacts, including baskets and pottery, can be viewed at the Palm Springs Art Museum.

In 1876, the federal government deeded land to both the Southern Pacific Railroad and the Cahuilla Indians in a checkerboard of alternating tracts. The Native American land turned out to be highly valuable real estate. The next year the Southern Pacific Railroad built a line linking Yuma, Arizona, with Los Angeles running through the Cahuilla reservation.

The Birth of Tourism

The presence of water is what set Palm Springs's course. In the mid-19th century, there was a plan to irrigate the area around Palm Springs to create an agricultural valley, but grander things were in store. A railroad engineer "discovered" mineral springs in 1853, calling them "Agua Caliente." With the railroad in place, tourists began to visit the hot climate for their health, hiking the canyons and learning about Native American culture. The first structures were canvas-and-wood huts clustered together.

In 1884, pioneer settler "Judge" John Guthrie McCallum built the first permanent structure. McCallum had come seeking a climate to aid his young son's tuberculosis. His adobe homestead is still standing, now home to the Palm Springs Historical Society. Right next door is the Cornelia White House, built entirely of railroad ties. The White House was part of the town's first hotel, the Palm Springs Hotel, built in 1893 by Welwood Murray. He drummed up business by having a local Indigenous people dress in Arabic clothing and ride a camel to the railroad station to greet passengers as they stopped at the railroad watering stop. The timing of the hotel was inopportune, coinciding with a drought that lasted until 1905.

Palm Springs as a destination didn't take off until 1915 when "Mother" Nellie Coffman built the Desert Inn. Stars of the silent screen, including Fatty Arbuckle and Rudolph Valentino, spent winter months at her hotel for their health, establishing Palm Springs as a destination for shooting desert- and Wild West-themed movies.

Another game changer, the Oasis Hotel, was built in 1928 and had the first swimming pool in Palm Springs. The building of the luxurious Spanish-Moorish-style El Mirador, as well as the opening of the ranch-style accommodations at Smoke Tree Ranch, ushered in the era of Palm Springs as a glitterati destination, hosting stars like Marlene Dietrich, Clark Gable, Bette Davis, and Errol Flynn, and Hollywood moguls such as Samuel Goldwyn and Walt Disney.

Palm Springs's Heyday

Following World War II, tastes moved from the traditional adobe-and-stucco construction into a more futuristic style. Palm Springs has an astonishing collection of first-tier modernist architecture, one of the highest concentrations in the world. The sleek lines and use of glass, concrete, and metal distinguish hotels, public buildings, and private homes throughout the chic resort town. Beginning in the 1930s, Hollywood began decamping to the desert; the 1950s and 1960s were the zenith of the legendary Hollywood party scene as well as architectural style.

Noted architects Albert Frey, E. Stewart Williams, William F. Cody, Donald Wexler, John Lautner, Richard Neutra, John Porter Clark, and others literally shaped the town, commissioned to build celebrity homes, businesses, civic buildings, and stylish and affordable tract homes.

Many of these houses were second homes, and so architects did not have to adhere so much to the daily functionality required of a main residence. The architectural lines, like the lifestyle out in Los Angeles's desert backyard, were freer. The optimism of the 1950s also inspired creative risk taking, and architectural designers began playing with the modern form. Modernism was an international trend, but it was a brilliant match with the austere landscape and sun-soaked climate of the California desert. Architects were able to erase barriers between indoors and outdoors, opting for open spaces that integrated with the landscape. Palm Springs's magnificent scenery, such as the striking escarpment of the San Jacinto Mountains, inspired clean lines and low designs that deferred to the views, creating a harmony of nature and culture.

Soon iconic celebrities like Frank Sinatra, Marilyn Monroe, Sammy Davis Jr., Bing Crosby, and Bob Hope were regulars in Palm Springs. Frank Sinatra and Bob Hope even built houses here.

The 1970s and 1980s were a low point for Palm Springs, as modernist design (and as a result, the town) fell out of fashion, and celebrities and vacationers gravitated toward luxurious resorts in Rancho Mirage and points farther south. Palm Springs limped along as a seedy spring break destination with much of its downtown shuttered. As a resort town, Palm Springs stagnated, and developers did not care enough to even raze and rebuild it to conform with newer ideas of luxury (ahem, Las Vegas). It was this apathy that saved Palm Springs. When members of the fashion world started to buy properties in the late 1990s, it turned out that the town was a trove of architectural treasure waiting to be rediscovered and rehabbed.

Government and Economy

Although Palm Springs may seem like a glimmering vacation mirage, removed from the mundane details of daily life, it is in fact a functioning municipality. Palm Springs is a city in Riverside County governed by a mayor and city council. In 2018 the city drew national attention when they elected the nation's first city council entirely comprising members of the LGBTQ+ community. In this progressive desert haven, it was a fact that went almost entirely unremarked by the council members or the community.

The Agua Caliente Band of Cahuilla Indians, a federally recognized Native American tribe historically based in Palm Springs, also has landholdings in the area, most prominently the well-watered Indian Canyons on the south end of town. The tribe has its own governing body. The Tribal Council sets policy makes laws and implements the direction voted on by Tribal membership. They have several different administrative branches, including a water authority, emergency services, a legal department, cultural tourism, and a historic preservation office.

Once a seasonal destination, Palm Springs is on the upswing as a year-round inclusive resort destination that attracts a wide variety of visitors. You may still see caftan-wearing golden-agers dining on shrimp cocktail and martinis or golfers whiling away the mornings on the greens, but there's also an infusion of newer generations visiting Palm Springs. Hip hotels like the Arrive hotel draw a stylish millennial set (as well as the young at heart) to deejay- and craft cocktail-fueled pool parties.

Palm Springs has almost a century of attracting A-listers, stars, and architects to the desert home haven. It continues to attract the Hollywood set buying homes (Leonardo DiCaprio purchased entertainer Dinah Shore's old mansion) or hiding out at desert retreats like the Korakia Pensione.

Like many resort towns, the short-term rental market ballooned in 2020-2021 with investors snapping up properties and taking them off the market for full-time residents. In 2022, the Palm Springs City Council capped the number of homes that can be used at short-term rental properties in each neighborhood and restricting how many times a property can be rented this way in a year. The regulations shifted the buyer profile back to the traditional demographic, including second-home buyers and retirees.

People and Culture

JOSHUA TREE AND AROUND

Like many desert regions, the land around Joshua Tree National Park has grappled with competing visions for its use. In the 1930s, when the park was made a national monument, the monument status blanketed a patchwork of homesteads and mining claims. It took the better part of the 20th century to fold these tracts into what eventually became Joshua Tree National Park. If you look at a map even now, you will see the strategically excluded district east of Twentynine Palms where the Dale Mining District once thrived.

Native American groups were not considered in the national monument status effort, having been driven out of the region in the early 20th century amid pressure from the Southern Pacific Railroad and other hardships.

The region's identity as an outdoors destination was emphasized in 2016 by conservation efforts resulting in three newly established national monuments to protect desert lands. The 154,000-acre (62,320-ha) Sand to Snow National Monument (www.fs.fed.us) links Joshua Tree National Park to the east and the Santa Rosa and San Jacinto Mountain National Monument to the south with several preserves by folding in previously unprotected land.

The gateway towns of Yucca Valley, Joshua Tree, and Twentynine Palms draw a wide cast of characters, and each town has its own distinct vibe. Joshua Tree is funky, artsy, and outdoorsy, luring park visitors, locals, and seasonal rock climbers. It's a tiny town with a saloon, outdoor outfitters, and a few small hotels to anchor its small main street. It functions as the main gateway to Joshua Tree National Park (the popular West Entrance is accessed via Joshua Tree) but feels like an authentic town instead of a tourist trap. Yucca Valley is more suburban, home to big-box stores and chain restaurants. It does not have a direct entrance to the park, but it does provide access to the Black Rock Canyon Campground as well as the Covington Flats area of the park, making it a strange mix of suburban sprawl and natural beauty. Yucca Valley also supports a burgeoning boutique and vintage shopping market; for a visitor to the area, the city is not without its charms. Twentynine Palms operates as the eastern gateway to the park and the North Entrance. There are a few excellent hotels, but the town is not the gateway tourist destination that Joshua Tree or even Yucca Valley are. The town of Twentynine Palms is home to a US Marine base, which forms the backbone of the community.

The region around Joshua Tree National Park has long been a haven for musicians and artists. Musicians from Los Angeles and elsewhere come to record albums, shoot music videos, and soak up the silence and stunning landscape. The music scene is alive and well, with small music festivals drawing some big names throughout the year. Many visual artists are also based here, showcasing their work in galleries across the Morongo Basin and in yearly open studio art tours every October.

The communities in the Joshua Tree region are slowly growing as escapees from urban centers like Los Angeles find their way here. There is even a growing homestead movement in which people are attempting to rehab old homesteads, sometimes even creating permaculture systems.

PALM SPRINGS AND THE COACHELLA VALLEY

Palm Springs began its current incarnation as a seasonal resort town in the 1920s. The 1930s to the 1970s mark the halcyon years for Palm Springs, as Hollywood celebrities and others flocked to the stylish resorts springing up. In the 1970s, the city of Palm Springs began its fall from favor as visitors gravitated to increasingly grandiose resorts in Rancho Mirage and farther south in the Coachella Valley. As Palm Springs languished, the Coachella Valley became known as a golfing and retirement destination. Palm Springs itself veered into a seedy spring break destination and many of its downtown businesses were boarded shut. In the 1990s, some of the fashionable set began buying up the area's mid-century architectural gems, breathing new life into Palm Springs as a resort destination.

Today, the town of Palm Springs is a connected community of entrepreneurs with a forward-looking vision and passionate interest in the town's history. Palm Springs has a vested interest in preserving its mid-century architectural heritage while refreshing its hotels and businesses to be current and chic. New retail shops and restaurants continue to pop up in the town's stylish Uptown Design District. It's hard to keep up with the burgeoning business scene. Old hotels and residences are continually being shined and styled.

The LGBTQ+ community is well represented in Palm Springs's year-round residents, with many gay-owned hotels and retail shops. Palm Springs is also an international

LGBTQ+ destination. Visitors come for resorts that cater specifically to men (there are no hotels that cater to an all-women clientele), as well as destination parties like the all-male White Party and the all-female The Dinah, the largest gay and lesbian music festival parties in the world.

Native American groups in Palm Springs and the Coachella Valley have the corner on some of the region's stunning natural beauty as well as resort casinos. The Agua Caliente Band of Cahuilla Indians owns the land and allows visitors access (for a fee) to the gorgeous palm tree- and stream-filled Indian Canyons, as well as Tahquitz Canyon's creek and waterfall. The tribe also owns and manages several casinos in the Coachella Valley. The Morongo Band of Cahuilla Mission Indians operates a casino at the foot of the San Gorgonio and San Jacinto Mountains west of Palm Springs.

Essentials

Transportation 202
Travel Hub:
    Los Angeles 205
Travel Tips 211

Transportation

GETTING THERE
Air
Palm Springs International Airport
PSP; 3400 E. Tahquitz Canyon Way, Palm Springs; 760/318-3800; https://flypsp.com
The Palm Springs International Airport is in metro Palm Springs less than 3 mi (4.8 km) from downtown. The airport provides service via 12 major airline carriers. It is also convenient to the Joshua Tree area, 40 mi (64 km) and less than an hour's drive from Palm Springs. Several Palm Springs hotels offer airport shuttle service. The major car rental

carriers are located here, including Enterprise, Hertz, Dollar, Avis, Budget, National, Thrifty, and Alamo.

Ontario International Airport

ONT; 2500 Terminal Way, Ontario; 909/937-2700; www.flyontario.com

Ontario International Airport is another good option. It is located off I-10 in the city of Ontario, about 90 mi (145 km) southwest (a 1.75-hour drive) from Joshua Tree and 70 mi (113 km) west of Palm Springs (a 1-hour drive via I-10). Ontario Airport has all the major rental car companies on-site.

The two closest major cities to Joshua Tree and Palm Springs are Los Angeles to the west and San Diego to the southwest. Both airports provide flight options, though a car rental will be required to reach Joshua Tree and Palm Springs.

Los Angeles International Airport

LAX; 1 World Way, Los Angeles; 424/646-5252; www.flylax.com

Los Angeles International Airport is a major international airport with many carriers and flight options, as well as car rentals. Airport shuttles, hotel shuttles, long-distance vans, rideshare vans, and taxis can all be accessed at the lower arrivals level directly outside the baggage claim area. A **FlyAway Bus** service (no reservations; 24 hours daily) offers the best public transportation from LAX to limited destinations around the city, including Union Station (downtown) and Van Nuys (San Fernando Valley). The drive from LAX to Joshua Tree and Palm Springs takes 2-4 hours, as traffic congestion can increase travel time significantly.

San Diego International Airport

SAN; 3225 N. Harbor Dr., San Diego; 619/400-2404; www.san.org

San Diego International Airport is the farthest option, 140 mi (225 km) and about a 2.5-hour

drive southwest in the city of San Diego. Major airline carriers include Southwest, American, United, Alaska, and Delta, and there is a consolidated rental car center on-site.

Car

A car is necessary to visit Joshua Tree National Park and towns in the high desert and the Coachella Valley. Within the town of Palm Springs, it is easy to get around without a car as rideshares are prevalent and much of the town is walkable.

From Los Angeles

If you're lucky and time your trip outside rush hour, the drive from Los Angeles can take less than two hours via I-10. Getting out of LA can be a slog, though, so you may need to factor in extra time, up to 2-3 hours more during rush hour or on Friday afternoon. From Los Angeles, take I-10 east for approximately 100 mi (160 km) to Highway 62 (exit 117), and continue 27 mi (43 km) north to the town of Joshua Tree. To reach the West Entrance to Joshua Tree National Park, follow Park Boulevard southeast into the park.

Palm Springs is about 100 mi (160 km) east of Los Angeles via I-10. From I-10, take Highway 111 south toward Palm Springs. Highway 111B continues south to reach the Palm Springs city limit in just over 10 mi (16 km), turning into North Palm Canyon Drive, the main road through Palm Springs.

The I-210 and Highway 60 freeways can sometimes provide good eastbound alternatives if I-10 is jammed. Both I-210 and Highway 60 join up with I-10 west of Palm Springs.

From San Diego

From San Diego, take I-15 north for about 50 mi (80 km). When I-15 splits off with I-215, follow I-215 and signs for Riverside/San Bernardino. Continue north on I-215 for 30 mi (48 km) until it intersects with Highway

Previous: Hidden Valley Campground in Joshua Tree National Park.

60. Take the exit for Highway 60, heading east for 18 mi (29 km). Merge onto I-10 and continue east for another 22 mi (35 km) to Highway 62 (exit 117), then continue 27 mi (43 km) north to the town of Joshua Tree. To reach the West Entrance to Joshua Tree National Park, follow Park Boulevard southeast into the park.

To reach Palm Springs, take the Highway 111 exit from I-10, about 18 mi (29 km) east of the Highway 60 junction. Highway 111B continues south to reach the Palm Springs city limit in just over 10 mi (16 km), turning into North Palm Canyon Drive, the main road through Palm Springs.

Car Rental

Car rentals are available from all area airports. Approximately 20 car rental companies operate at Los Angeles International Airport; all vehicle rental companies are located offsite. The major rental companies provide courtesy shuttles to meet arriving customers under the purple Rental Car Shuttle sign on the Lower/Arrival Level outside baggage claim. To reach other car rental agencies, take the **Metro Connector** shuttle under the pink LAX shuttle sign on the lower/arrivals level in front of each terminal to reach the **Remote Rental Car Depot.** Check with your car rental agency when making a reservation to make sure you know how to get there.

In addition to Palm Springs and LAX, **Enterprise Rent-A-Car** (55255 29 Palms Hwy.; 760/369-0515; www.enterprise.com; 8am-5pm Mon.-Fri., 9am-noon Sat.) is located in the gateway town of Yucca Valley.

RV Rental

A few RV and camper van rental agencies have offices in Los Angeles convenient to LAX, including **Cruise America** (800/671-8042; www.cruiseamerica.com). Direct rental RV shares are also available through companies like **Outdoorsy** (www.outdoorsy.com) or **RVshare** (rvshare.com). Camper van rentals are available through **Escape Campervans** (4858 W. Century Blvd., Inglewood; 877/270-8267, international 310/672-9909; www.escapecampervans.com), and **Lost Campers** (8820 Aviation Blvd., Inglewood; 888/567-8826, international 415/386-2693; www.lostcampersusa.com).

Train and Bus

For point-to-point travel, **FlixBus** (www.flixbus.com) is the best option for public transportation between Los Angeles and Palm Springs. The company was founded as a German start-up in 2013 and offers routes in the United States. It relies on technology and regional partners to offer direct routes between popular destinations. FlixBus offers five buses daily between downtown Los Angeles (Union Station or the Flix bus lot) and North Palm Springs (from $22 one-way), with daytime and evening booking times that make sense for hotel check-in. Book tickets online or via an app. There is no station; pickup is curbside.

There are no direct train routes to Palm Springs.

GETTING AROUND

In and around Joshua Tree National Park, the towns of Yucca Valley, Joshua Tree, and Twentynine Palms are all accessed from Highway 62. Public transit in this area is limited. Travel in this region requires that you have your own vehicle.

Palm Springs is immensely walkable. When you're not walking or driving, rideshares are the easiest way to get around. There are plenty of Uber and Lyft options.

Travel Hub: Los Angeles

Los Angeles has a lot to offer as a gateway hub to Palm Springs and Joshua Tree, including a thriving downtown, beaches, a wealth of foodie neighborhoods, shopping, and cultural sightseeing. However, LA's reputation as a difficult driving destination precedes it. The number of freeways crossing the city, a rush hour that never ends, and the sheer sprawl of the metro region mean that it's best to come to Los Angeles with a plan. If you only have a day or two, set up your base camp in one of the three major areas listed below.

The official visitor website for Los Angeles (www.discoverlosangeles.com) is an excellent resource.

DOWNTOWN LOS ANGELES

Los Angeles's historic downtown is a vibrant destination for food, culture, and events. Located on the northeast side of Los Angeles, downtown is an excellent jumping-off point for exploring and continuing east to Palm Springs and Joshua Tree.

Sights and Activities
Walt Disney Concert Hall
111 S. Grand Ave.

Los Angeles has a wealth of outstanding architecture. Downtown is home to notable landmarks such as the Walt Disney Concert Hall, designed by Frank Gehry. This distinctive building, home to the Los Angeles Philharmonic, draws focus with the striking stainless steel curves of its exterior.

Bradbury Building
304 S. Broadway

The Bradbury Building is an architectural landmark built in 1893, commissioned by gold mining millionaire Lewis L. Bradbury. The Broadway Theater District stretches for six blocks from 3rd Street to 9th Street along South Broadway and includes 12 movie theaters built between 1910 and 1931, many of them in the process of being restored. Walking tours are available through the **Los Angeles Conservancy** (www.laconservancy.org).

Olvera Street
www.olvera-street.com; hours vary

A Mexican marketplace that is part of El Pueblo de Los Angeles Historic Monument, Olvera Street features historic structures, restaurants, and shopping along the oldest street in Los Angeles.

MOCA Grand
250 S. Grand Ave.; 213/626-6222; 11am-5pm Tues.-Wed. and Fri., 11am-8pm Thurs., 11am-6pm Sat.-Sun.; $18 adults, $10 students and seniors, free under age 12

The Museum of Contemporary Art (MOCA) has three distinct locations in the greater Los Angeles area. MOCA Grand is the main branch in downtown Los Angeles, on Grand Avenue near the Walt Disney Concert Hall. It features a prominent collection of post-1940s works.

Broad Museum
221 S. Grand Ave.; 213/232-6200; 11am-5pm Tues.-Wed. and Fri., 11am-8pm Thurs., 10am-6pm Sat.-Sun.; free, reservations required

The Broad Museum was financed by philanthropists Eli and Edyth Broad to house their prominent and world-renowned collection of postwar and contemporary art in a stunning $140 million building.

Griffith Park Ranger Station
4730 Crystal Springs Dr.

Griffith Park spans 4,310 acres (1,744 ha) of surprisingly rugged landscape in the hills of northeast Los Angeles, 9 mi (14.5 km) north of downtown. Its 53 mi (85 km) of trails are popular, as are its acres of picnic and recreation areas. Hiking trail maps are available from the Griffith Park Ranger Station as well as online (www.laparks.org).

Los Angeles Zoo and Botanical Gardens

5333 Zoo Dr.; 323/644-4200; www.lazoo.org; 10am-5pm daily; $22 adults, $19 seniors, $17 ages 2-15, free under age 2

Griffith Park also features the Los Angeles Zoo and Botanical Gardens, a 133-acre (54-ha) zoo that's home to 1,100 animals and a botanical collection that features more than 800 plant species.

Griffith Observatory

2800 E. Observatory Rd.; 213/473-0800; www.griffithobservatory.org; noon-10pm Tues.-Fri., 10am-10pm Sat.-Sun., free

The Griffith Observatory is an art deco landmark with a planetarium and grounds that feature stunning views of the city. The instantly recognizable Hollywood sign was made part of Griffith Park to protect the area from development. Hikes lead to the views of the city from above the sign.

Autry Museum of the American West

4700 Western Heritage Way; www.theautry.org; 323/667-2000; 10am-4pm Tues.-Fri., 10am-5pm Sat.-Sun.; $18 adults, $14 students and seniors, $8 ages 3-12, free under age 3

The Autry Museum of the American West features exhibits that tell the stories of the peoples and cultures of the American West.

Travel Town Museum

5200 Zoo Dr.; 323/662-5874; www.traveltown.org; 10am-5pm daily; free

Travel Town Museum highlights railroad history in the western United States from 1880s to the 1930s. A miniature train once owned by Gene Autry takes passengers on a loop around the museum grounds.

Sunset Ranch Hollywood

3400 N. Beachwood Dr.; 323/469-5450; www.sunsetranchhollywood.com; day tours 9am-3pm daily, evening tours 4pm, 4:30pm, and 5pm daily; $75-175

The only horse ranch in Los Angeles, Sunset Ranch Hollywood offers a unique Griffith Park outing in the form of one- and two-hour trail rides featuring spectacular views of the Hollywood Sign, Griffith Observatory, and downtown Los Angeles.

Food

Grand Central Market

317 S. Broadway; 213/624-2378; www.grandcentralmarket.com; 8am-9pm daily

A landmark food and retail emporium established in 1917, Grand Central Market is an incredible mix of old classics and exciting new chef-driven fare, with casual counter seating, on-site dining, takeout, and market groceries.

Eateries include the Asian sandwich shop **Moon Rabbit** featuring banh mi and katsu sandwiches (11am-5pm daily), the rustic Italian menu at **Knead & Co Pasta Bar & Marketplace** (213/223-7592; 11am-5pm Sun.-Wed., 11am-8pm Thurs., 11am-9pm Fri.-Sat.), the traditional Jewish **Wexler's Deli** (213/620-0633; www.wexlersdeli.com; 8am-4pm daily), breakfast-centric **Eggslut** (213/625-0292; www.eggslut.com; 8am-2pm daily), and seasonal Thai street fare at **Sticky Rice** (323/284-8744; www.eatstickyrice.com; 11am-8:30pm daily).

Several stalls pour a range of craft beers and fine wines in addition to tasty eats: **Olio GCM Wood Fired Pizzeria** (www.oliowfp.com; 10am-9pm daily), **The Oyster Gourmet** (https://theoystergourmet.com; 11am-7pm Mon.-Thurs., 10am-9pm Fri.-Sun.), and **Golden Road Brewing Company** (www.goldenroad.la; 10am-9pm daily).

Phillipe the Original

1001 N. Alameda St.; 213/628-3781; www.philippes.com; 6am-10pm daily; $12-14

Phillipe the Original serves up signature French dips and deli sides in this historic space (established in 1908) with sawdust-covered floors and communal tables.

The Original Pantry

877 S. Figueroa St.; 213/972-9279; www.pantrycafe.com; 7am-3pm Wed.-Fri., 7am-5pm Sat.-Sun.; breakfast $12-20, lunch and dinner $13-31, cash only

An old-school diner that has been operating since 1924, The Original Pantry serves American classics and all-day breakfast.

Bar Amá

118 W. 4th St.; 213/687-8002; www.bar-ama.com; 5pm-10pm Tues.-Sat., 4pm-9pm Sun.; $17-24

Bar Amá serves upmarket Tex-Mex in a warm, industrial space, and it delivers a great daily happy hour called Super Nacho Hour.

Guisados

541 S. Spring St., Suite 101; 213/627-7656; www.guisados.co; 10am-10pm Mon.-Thurs., 9am-11pm Fri.-Sat., 9am-9pm Sun.; $4-7

Local favorite Guisados has a number of locations on the east side of LA, including downtown, serving up homestyle braised tacos on handmade tortillas with meat and veggie options and aguas frescas to wash them down.

Badmaash

108 W. 2nd St.; 213/221-7466; https://badmaashla.com; 11:30am-3pm and 5pm-10pm Mon.-Fri., noon-3pm and 5pm-10pm Sat.-Sun.; $17-29

Badmaash serves Indian classics plus creative inventions like chana masala poutine in a colorful gastropub.

The Little Jewel of New Orleans

207 Ord St.; 213/620-0461; www.littlejewel.net; 11am-4pm. Mon.-Fri., noon-8pm Sat., noon-7pm Sun.; $7-20

The Little Jewel of New Orleans serves giant New Orleans-inspired po' boys and specials in a casual café setting in historic Chinatown, just north of downtown.

Yang Chow

819 N. Broadway; 213/625-0811; www.yangchow.com; 11:30am-8:30pm Sun.-Thurs., 11:30am-9:30pm Fri.-Sat.; $17-24

Family-run Yang Chow is a Chinatown fixture, serving authentic Mandarin and Szechwan cuisine in a stripped-down space. Try the signature slippery shrimp.

Accommodations

The Hoxton

1060 S. Broadway; 213/725-5900; https://thehoxton.com/downtown-la; from $180

The Hoxton boutique hotel offers views of historic Broadway in rooms that blend beachy California with old-school Hollywood glamour. Amenities include two restaurants and a rooftop pool.

Millennium Biltmore Hotel

506 S. Grand Ave.; 213/624-1011; www.millenniumhotels.com; from $200

The home of old Hollywood glamour, the historic 1923 Millennium Biltmore Hotel is a cultural landmark with 683 guest rooms and amenities including a Roman-style pool.

Hotel Figueroa

939 S. Figueroa St.; 213/627-8971; www.hotelfigueroa.com; $270-320

The historic Hotel Figueroa underwent a two-year restoration to restore it to its original Spanish Colonial beauty. The hotel offers 268 guest rooms and suites, a lobby bar, restaurant, and a veranda pool and bar. It is located near LA Live and the Convention Center.

Conrad Los Angeles

100 S. Grand Ave.; 213/349-8585; www.hilton.com; from $524

Conrad Los Angeles is located on historic Bunker Hill directly across from the striking stainless steel Walt Disney Concert Hall. Designed by famed architect Frank Gehry, the hotel offers stunning views of the iconic steel swooshes as well as five restaurants and a spa. For the arts-focused traveler, you are within walking distance of the Broad Museum, the Music Center, and MOCA.

HOLLYWOOD AND MID-CITY

Centrally located between the beaches and downtown, Mid-City gives the easiest access to famous Hollywood and Museum Row.

Sights and Activities

Museum Row, a walkable stretch of Wilshire Boulevard between Fairfax Avenue and La Brea Avenue, is home to four main Los Angeles museums.

Los Angeles County Museum of Art

LACMA; 5905 Wilshire Blvd.; 323/857-6000; www.lacma.org; 11am-6pm Mon.-Tues. and Thurs., 11am-8pm Fri., 10am-7pm Sat.-Sun.; $28 adults, $24 seniors and students, $13 ages 3-17, free under age 3

Visit the Los Angeles County Museum of Art for the largest collection of art spanning ancient to contemporary in the western United States.

Petersen Auto Museum

6060 Wilshire Blvd.; 323/930-2277; www.petersen.org; 10am-5pm daily; $21 adults, $19 seniors, $13 ages 12-17, $12 ages 4-11, free under age 4

The Petersen Auto Museum celebrates the automobile with over 25 exhibitions, including automobiles in the movies and hot rods.

La Brea Tar Pits

5801 Wilshire Blvd.; 213/763-3499; www.tarpits.org; 9:30am-5pm daily; $18 adults, $14 seniors, students, and ages 13-17, $7 ages 3-12, free under age 3

Kids and adults alike will love the La Brea Tar Pits, a museum and archaeological excavation where extinct animals were trapped and preserved in tar.

Craft Contemporary

5814 Wilshire Blvd.; 323/937-4230; www.craftcontemporary.org; 11am-5pm Tues.-Sun.; $9 adults, $7 students and seniors, free under age 12

With a focus on the edge of craft and design, the Craft Contemporary cycles exhibitions in a range of media, including glass, metal, paper, ceramics, photography, and textiles.

Original Farmers Market

6333 W. 3rd St.; 323/933-9211; www.farmersmarketla.com; 9am-9pm Mon.-Fri., 10am-9pm Sat., 10am-7pm Sun.

Established in 1934, the Original Farmers Market is a destination gourmet market with more than 100 grocers and restaurants.

The Grove

189 The Grove Dr.; 323/900-8080; www.thegrovela.com; 10am-9pm Mon.-Thurs., 10am-10pm Fri.-Sat., 11am-8pm Sun.

Adjacent to the Original Farmers Market is the Grove, an upscale shopping, entertainment, and dining complex.

Hollywood Walk of Fame

The highlight of Hollywood is the star-studded sidewalks of the Hollywood Walk of Fame. Beginning at La Brea Avenue (to the west), the famous pavement runs for 18 blocks to Gower Street on the east. You can also find the sidewalk stars along three blocks of Vine Street, running north and south of Hollywood Boulevard.

Grauman's Chinese Theatre

6925 Hollywood Blvd.; www.tclchinesetheatres.com

Two historic cinema palaces, TCL Chinese Theatre, originally Grauman's Chinese Theatre, and Grauman's Egyptian Theatre, are cultural landmarks worth a stop on your walking tour.

Grauman's Egyptian Theatre

6706 Hollywood Blvd.; www.egyptiantheatre.com

The intricately designed Grauman's Chinese Theatre opened to celebrity fanfare in 1927 and is still sought after for movie premieres and events. Its renovated theater has a regular movie schedule.

Amoeba Records

6200 Hollywood Blvd.; 323/245-6400; www.amoeba.com; 11am-8pm daily

The world's largest independent record store, Amoeba Records, is a bustling outlet with a massive collection of vinyl records as well as CDs, videos, and live shows.

Hollywood Farmers Market

Selma Ave. and Ivar Ave., between Hollywood Blvd. and Sunset Blvd.; www.hollywoodfarmersmarket.net; 8am-1pm Sun.

If you're in town on a Sunday, the Hollywood Farmers Market is an outdoor street market offering impressively stacked blocks of fresh produce and goods from local farmers, ranchers, and vendors.

Food
Musso and Frank
6667 Hollywood Blvd.; 323/467-7788; www.mussoandfrank.com; 5pm-11pm Tues.-Sat., 4pm-10pm Sun.; $22-63

At Hollywood's oldest eatery, Musso and Frank, tuxedoed waiters serve steaks, pastas, and American specialties in a classic setting.

Canter's Deli
419 N. Fairfax Ave.; 323/651-2030; www.cantersdeli.com; 6am-11:30pm Mon.-Thurs., 24 hours 6am Fri.-11:30pm Sun.; $11-25

Canter's Deli is an iconic Jewish deli serving up a vast menu of sandwiches and deli fare. The adjacent **Kibbitz Room** (323/651-2030; 10:30am-1:40am daily) offers an old-school cocktail lounge with a full bar and a small stage.

Pink's Hot Dogs
709 N. La Brea Ave.; 323/931-4223; www.pinkshollywood.com; 9:30am-1am Sun.-Thurs., 9:30am-2am Fri.-Sat.; $7-14

The lines at Pink's Hot Dogs attest that it is worth the wait at this landmark 1939 roadside stand.

Trejo's Tacos
1556 N. Cahuenga Blvd.; 323/461-8226; www.trejostacos.com; 11:30am-9pm Sun.-Thurs., 11:30am-10pm Fri.-Sat.; $6-16

Celebrity-owned Trejo's Tacos is a casual taqueria offering meat and vegan specialty tacos with kombucha, aguas frescas, and beer and wine in a bright industrial-sleek setting.

Jon & Vinny's
412 N. Fairfax Ave.; 323/334-3369; www.jonandvinnys.com; 8am-10pm daily; breakfast $12-24, lunch or dinner $15-30

Jon & Vinny's features Italian-inspired fare, including creatively topped pizzas and pastas in a relaxed contemporary setting.

Accommodations
Hotel Wilshire
6317 Wilshire Blvd.; 323/852-6000; www.hotelwilshire.com; $245-325

Hotel Wilshire, a Kimpton property, is a sleekly contemporary, glass and steel boutique hotel with a rooftop pool, restaurant, and bar near Museum Row.

Roosevelt Hotel
7000 Hollywood Blvd.; 323/856-1970; www.thehollywoodroosevelt.com; from $293

The glamorous Roosevelt Hotel, established in 1927, is located along the Walk of Fame, offering a stunning pool and on-site restaurants and bars.

Magic Castle Hotel
7025 Franklin Ave.; 323/851-0800; www.magiccastlehotel.com; $299-519

The family-friendly Magic Castle Hotel offers rooms and suites and a ton of amenities, including a 24-hour heated pool, complimentary continental breakfast, snacks, and robes. Rooms book fast.

SANTA MONICA AND VENICE

Los Angeles's beaches are a destination in and of themselves, and they're a great place to visit if you only have a day or two. The beach cities are also conveniently located near Los Angeles International Airport.

Sights and Activities
Santa Monica Beach
www.venicebeach.com

Along the coastal towns of Venice and Santa Monica, Venice Beach and Santa Monica Beach offer a gorgeous, recreational 3-mi (4.8-km) stretch of coastline along the Pacific Ocean, with the Santa Monica Mountains creating a dramatic backdrop. In the immediate vicinity, the funky Venice Beach Boardwalk is good for a stroll and people-watching.

Venice Skate Park
www.veniceskatepark.com

ESSENTIALS
TRAVEL HUB: LOS ANGELES

An oceanfront skate park, the Venice Skate Park, has a fun vibe and is a great place to watch the talented kids.

Santa Monica Pier

www.santamonicapier.org

The Santa Monica Pier has an amusement park and offers good strolling on its weathered timbers. Rent bikes at one of several beach bike rental shops along the boardwalk connecting Venice and Santa Monica. A paved bike path connecting the two communities makes for an easy ride with gorgeous oceanfront views.

3rd Street Promenade

www.santamonica.com/shopping

Downtown Santa Monica offers retail shopping and dining on its 3rd Street Promenade, a few blocks from the beach.

Abbot Kinney

www.abbotkinneyblvd.com

For exploring Venice, check out the cool Abbot Kinney neighborhood. This walkable 1-mi (1.6-km) stretch between Westminster Avenue and Venice Boulevard is a hub of fashionable retail shopping, restaurants, art galleries, and nightlife.

Santa Monica Farmers Market

Arizona Ave. and 2nd St.; 8:30am-1:30pm Wed., 8am-1pm Sat.

If you're in town on a Wednesday or Sunday, don't miss the weekly downtown Santa Monica Farmers Market, where local chefs regularly shop. It's a great place to grab coffee and breakfast and be dazzled by the array of seasonal produce, meats and dairy, artisanal goods, and flowers.

Food
The Waterfront

205 Ocean Front Walk, Venice; 424/404-8470; www.waterfrontcafe.com; 11am-10pm Tues.-Fri., 10am-10pm Sat.-Sun.; $15-27

The Waterfront revamped a casual tourist and local boardwalk spot to add tacos, burgers,

salads, and fresh seafood. The ocean views and great people-watching remain the same.

The Galley

2442 Main St., Santa Monica; 310/452-1934; www.thegalleyrestaurant.net; 5pm-close daily; $16-70

Opened in 1934, The Galley is Santa Monica's oldest restaurant, serving seafood and steaks amid nautical decor.

Gjusta

320 Sunset Ave., Venice; 310/314-0320; www.gjusta.com; 7am-4pm daily; $10-42

At Gjusta, choose from the mouthwatering sandwiches, breakfasts, dinner plates, and cases of freshly made salads and sides at this artisanal gourmet bakery, market, and café housed in a hip industrial space.

The Albright

258 Santa Monica Pier; 310/394-9683; https://thealbright.com; 11:30am-9pm Mon.-Fri., 11am-9pm Sat.-Sun.; $12-23

The Albright reinvented a seafood joint on the Santa Monica Pier as a casual, rustic-chic eatery with a raw bar, burgers, sandwiches, and seafood specials.

Milo and Olive

2723 Wilshire Blvd., Santa Monica; 310/453-6776; www.miloandolive.com; 7am-10pm daily; $10-31

Milo and Olive elevates everyday food with small plates, pastas, salads, wood-fired pizzas, and fresh baked goods served in a communal space.

Accommodations
The Shore Hotel

1515 Ocean Ave., Santa Monica; 310/458-1515; www.shorehotel.com; from $222

Contemporary, eco-conscious The Shore Hotel overlooks the beach opposite the Santa Monica Pier, with a heated outdoor pool and hot tub.

Hotel Erwin

1697 Pacific Ave., Venice; 310/452-1111; https://hotelerwin.com; from $305

Hotel Erwin looks down on the Venice scene from its boardwalk-front location, offering a low-key restaurant and rooftop cocktail lounge.

Venice V

5 Westminster Ave., Venice; 310/912-6488; www. venicevhotel.com; from $339

Venice V has design-forward rooms that capture the neighborhood's boho, artsy, surf vibe while preserving historic details of the Waldorf, originally opened in 1915 for Hollywood A-listers.

Casa del Mar

1910 Ocean Way, Santa Monica; 310/581-5533; www. hotelcasadelmar.com; from $344

Inspired by grand Mediterranean villas, iconic Casa del Mar offers oceanfront lodging with private patios and an inner courtyard.

Georgian

1415 Ocean Ave., Santa Monica; 310/395-9945; www. thegeorgian.com; from $387

The 1930s art deco Georgian hotel offers a retro-luxe vibe with a horseshoe lobby bar and art-filled rooms, all just steps from the sand.

The Surfrider

23033 Pacific Coast Hwy., Malibu; 310/526-6158; https://thesurfridermalibu.com; from $636

Airy and design-forward The Surfrider is a 20-room boutique beach house hotel located across from the world-famous Surfrider surf beach, with beach views and a fire pit.

Travel Tips

WHAT TO PACK

Joshua Tree has cold winters (it's been known to snow) and hot summers (over 100°F/38°C). Always carry layers and be prepared for temperature fluctuations throughout the day. Nighttime temperatures can drop as much as 40°F (20°C). For hiking and touring around the desert, wear sturdy shoes, a brimmed hat, and sunglasses. The gateway towns around Joshua Tree are very casual; no formal attire is required.

It's possible to pack lightly for the resort town of Palm Springs. Temperatures are usually mild year-round, if cooler at night and subject to cooler weather and temperature fluctuations in winter. Pack for poolside and dress up for dinners or brunch. Most hotels provide pool towels, and some provide sunscreen, water, snacks, or other amenities.

INTERNATIONAL TRAVELERS

The closest gateway city for international travelers to fly into is Los Angeles (LAX). The drive from Los Angeles to Joshua Tree or Palm Springs takes 2-4 hours, depending on traffic. There are no stops, checkpoints, or special concerns along this route, which sticks to I-10.

Palm Springs International Airport (PSP) has updated from a regional to an international airport with limited international flights. PSP is centrally located in Palm Springs, with taxis and rideshares available from the airport.

Visas and Passports

Visitors from most other countries must have a valid passport and a visa or visa waiver to enter the United States. Citizens of Canada and Bermuda need a passport but not a visa or a visa waiver. To learn more about visa and passport requirements, visit https://travel.state.gov.

In most countries, the local US embassy or consulate should be able to provide a **tourist visa.** The average fee for a visa is $185. While a visa may be processed as quickly as 24 hours on request, plan for at least a couple of weeks, as there can be unexpected delays, particularly during the busy summer season (June-Aug.).

Los Angeles is home to **consulates** from

many countries around the globe. If you should lose your passport or find yourself in some other trouble while visiting California, contact your country's offices for assistance. To find a consulate or embassy, check online (www.state.gov) for a list of all foreign countries represented in the United States. A representative will be able to direct you to the nearest consulate.

Customs

Before entering the United States from another country by air, you'll be required to fill out a customs form. Check with the US embassy in your country or **US Customs and Border Protection** (www.cbp.gov) for an updated list of items you must declare. Prescription medications should be in their original containers accompanied by a doctor's prescription. Carry only the quantity needed for personal use for a condition. For information about current regulations on domestic flights, visit the website of the **Transportation Security Administration** (www.tsa.gov).

If you are driving into California along I-5 or another major highway, be prepared to stop at **Agricultural Inspection Stations** a few miles inside the state line. You don't need to present a passport or a driver's license; instead, you must present any fruits and vegetables you have in the vehicle. California's largest economic sector is agriculture, and a number of the major crops grown here are sensitive to pests and diseases. In an effort to prevent known pests from entering the state and endangering crops, travelers are asked to identify all the produce they're carrying in from other states or from Mexico. If you are carrying produce, it may be confiscated on the spot. You'll also be asked about fruits and veggies on the US Customs form that you fill out on the plane before reaching the United States.

Money

California businesses use the **US dollar** ($). Most businesses also accept the major credit cards Visa, MasterCard, Discover, and American Express. ATM and debit cards work at many stores and restaurants, and ATMs are available at banks and in some local businesses like convenience or grocery stores. Within the Joshua Tree area and Yucca Valley, ATMs are limited. Currency exchange offices are available at any international airport. Some businesses accept card or mobile pay only and do not accept cash.

TOURIST INFORMATION

Palm Springs Visitors Center

2901 N. Palm Canyon Dr., Palm Springs; 760/778-8418; www.visitpalmsprings.com; 10am-5pm daily

Entering the city of Palm Springs from the north via I-10, you will be greeted by the Palm Springs Visitors Center, a good stop for books and information.

Joshua Tree Visitor Center

6554 Park Blvd., Joshua Tree; 760/367-5500; 7:30am-5pm daily

When visiting the Joshua Tree area, make sure to stop at one of the park's four visitor centers for maps and information. Three of these correspond to the park entrances: The Joshua Tree Visitor Center is in the town of Joshua Tree near the West Entrance to the park.

Joshua Tree National Park Visitor Center

6533 Freedom Way, Twentynine Palms; 760/367-5500; 8:30am-5pm daily

The Joshua Tree National Park Visitor Center is in downtown Twentynine Palms, en route to the park's North Entrance.

Cottonwood Visitor Center

Cottonwood Spring Rd.; 760/367-5500; 8:30am-4pm daily

The Cottonwood Visitor Center is at the remote South Entrance to the park.

Black Rock Nature Center

9800 Black Rock Canyon Rd., Yucca Valley; 760/367-5500; 8am-11am and noon-4pm daily winter, hours vary in summer

In addition, the Black Rock Nature Center

is a small visitor center used primarily as a check-in for campers to the Black Rock Canyon Campground.

City of Twentynine Palms Visitor Center

6847 Adobe Rd., Twentynine Palms; 760/358-6324; 10am-4pm Mon.-Fri., 10am-3pm Sat.-Sun.

Other area visitor centers include the City of Twentynine Palms Visitor Center, en route to the North Entrance in the gateway town of Twentynine Palms.

ACCESS FOR TRAVELERS WITH DISABILITIES
Joshua Tree
Access Pass

www.nps.gov; free

An Access Pass permits free entrance to Joshua Tree National Park for US citizens and permanent residents with permanent disabilities. Passes can be obtained online or in person at the park.

All Joshua Tree National Park **visitor centers** are ADA complaint, and all have accessible ranger desks. The Joshua Tree Visitor Center has low displays in its natural history areas.

There are also several **accessible nature trails.** The Bajada Trail (near the South Entrance) is a 0.3-mi (0.5-km) loop with a packed dirt and gravel surface that leads through exposed Colorado Desert featuring interpretive panels. The trail is 5.6 mi (9 km) south of the Cottonwood Spring Ranger Station and 0.5 mi (0.8 km) north of the south park entrance. The Cap Rock Nature Trail leads 0.4 mi (0.6 km) along packed dirt and gravel through eroded boulder formations. Parking is available at the junction of Park Boulevard and Keys View Road. At the end of Keys View Road, Keys View lookout is wheelchair-accessible and offers sweeping views of Palm Springs, Coachella Valley, and the San Jacinto Mountains. At the historic Oasis of Mara, a 0.5-mi (0.8-km) paved trail winds through native vegetation and fan palms in an area that was used extensively by Native American groups.

A bounty of paved **pullouts** along Park Boulevard also offer close-up views of boulder piles, rock formations, and other spectacular scenery. A few sites worth admiring include Skull Rock (on Park Boulevard near the Jumbo Rocks Campground entrance) and the Cholla Cactus Garden along the Pinto Basin Road. At the Intersection Rock parking area and the Hidden Valley picnic areas, sidewalks give access to wayside exhibits and vault toilets. Intersection Rock parking area also has an accessible sidewalk for access to wayside exhibits and pit toilets.

ADA-compliant **campground** sites include Jumbo Rocks Campground (site 122) and Black Rock Campground (site 61).

Palm Springs

The Palm Springs Aerial Tramway is fully ADA compliant, including the rotating tram cars and both tram stations. At Valley Station on the desert floor, an outdoor lift takes visitors from the parking area to the ground-floor station. There is an accessible viewing area outside the back of the station giving a look at tram cars as they ascend and descend Chino Canyon. At Mountain Station, there is an accessible outdoor patio and viewing area. From the back of Mountain Station, a paved path leads down to forest level; however, this path is steep and not necessarily appropriate for all wheelchairs.

The Living Desert Zoo and Gardens, in the Coachella Valley, has paved paths meandering through the main exhibits of the park.

While none of the trails in the Indian Canyons are accessible, there is a beautiful picnic area in the parking area at the head of Andreas Canyon set next to a stream and palm groves.

TRAVELING WITH CHILDREN

Joshua Tree is a great family destination. Children will enjoy being able to clamber around on the rocks and boulders, and there

Desert Survival Tips

Vast spaces, remote roads, and weather extremes can create potentially risky situations, but traveling in a desert is not any more dangerous than in other national parks if you are prepared for the unique environment. Know what weather to expect and where you're going and be prepared for the unexpected.

TELL SOMEONE WHERE YOU ARE GOING

Whether you're hiking, driving, or a combination, make sure you tell someone where you are going and when to expect your return. The desert covers a huge area, and in the event that you are stranded, the search effort can be pinpointed. Permits are required for all backcountry camping. Obtain a backcountry permit ahead of time in one of three ways: (1) book through www.recreation.gov; (2) call 877/444-6777 to book through a recreation.gov agent; (3) visit the permit office at Joshua Tree National Park Visitor Center (6533 Freedom Way, Twentynine Palms; 8am-4pm daily).

Follow desert safety tips when hiking.

BRING SUPPLIES

Temperatures can fluctuate 40°F (20°C) between day and night. Bring a sleeping bag or emergency blanket even if you do not plan to be out overnight. Pack appropriate clothing for a range of temperatures, and be prepared for cold temperatures at night. Always bring extra water and extra nonperishable food that does not have to be cooked. GPS navigation is notoriously unreliable in the park. Be prepared with a paper map or an electronic offline map and a charger. Cell phones do not work in much of the park. Be prepared to survive until help arrives if you are stranded.

VEHICLE BREAKDOWNS

Sharp rocks, long bumpy roads, and heat can cause your vehicle to break down on backcountry roads. Always drive with a full-size spare tire. A fix-a-flat tire kit may also be helpful. If you are stranded, stay with your car until help arrives. It is much easier to spot a big metal car that flashes in the sunlight than a person walking. Also, it is dangerous to overexert yourself in the heat of the desert, so hiking out to safety is not generally the best option. Be prepared with extra supplies, including food, water, and warm clothes.

---

are a number of easy short hikes that families can enjoy. The Junior Ranger Program allows young visitors (typically ages 5-13) to earn a badge by completing a series of activities, including drawing, writing, attending a ranger program, and picking up trash in the park. Ranger programs such as the guided walks are geared toward families and can help kids earn a Junior Ranger badge. Joshua Tree also participates in national Junior Ranger programs, including Junior Paleontologist, Junior Ranger Night Explorer, and Wilderness Explorer. Booklets are available at park visitor centers.

While it is possible to have a great family vacation in Palm Springs, many hotels are adults-only and do not allow guests under age 21. Be sure to check the individual policy of any hotel when booking a room. The Parker Palm Springs and the Ace Hotel are two hotels that welcome children and offer separate swimming pools geared toward families.

Check out the city's tourism website (https://visitpalmsprings.com) for family fun ideas.

SENIOR TRAVELERS

Senior Pass

https://store.usgs.gov; lifetime pass $80, annual pass $20

A Senior Pass is available to US citizens and permanent residents over age 62 who are visiting Joshua Tree National Park. The Senior Pass is available online or in person at park visitor centers. The lifetime pass has a one-time fee. The annual pass is good for one year; if an annual pass is purchased for three consecutive years, the fourth pass can be traded in for a lifetime pass.

LGBTQ+ TRAVELERS

Palm Springs is an international gay-friendly resort destination and a mecca for gay and lesbian travelers. Several accommodations cater exclusively to gay male travelers; however, all lodgings in Palm Springs are open to gay and lesbian visitors. In addition to a range of gay bars and clubs, the spring festival season draws thousands of visitors annually to the all-male music and dance White Party weekend (https://whitepartyglobal.com) and the all-female The Dinah music and party weekend (www.thedinah.com). The city's tourism website (https://visitpalmsprings.com) offers an LGBTQ+ Travel Guide with recommendations. The largest concentration of LGBTQ+ businesses in Palm Springs, including resorts, shopping, bars, and restaurants, are located in South Palm Springs on East Arenas Road between South Indian Canyon Drive and South Calle Encilia.

Consider visiting the following websites for more information:

- **Purple Roofs** (www.purpleroofs.com)
- **Out Traveler** (www.outtraveler.com)
- **Visit Palm Springs** (https://visitpalmsprings.com/palm-springs-visit/gay-palm-springs)
- **Queer in the World** (https://queerintheworld.com/gay-palm-springs-california-travel-guide)

TRAVELERS OF COLOR

Palm Springs celebrates diversity through its LGBTQ+ residential community and its status as an LGBTQ+ traveler destination; however, its racial and ethnic demographics are far less diverse. Surrounding the main downtown tourist area, you will find historically white residential areas and gated retirement communities. As of 2021, the city of nearly 49,000 was 82 percent white, with 15 percent of residents identifying as Asian, Black or African American, or Other. Despite its lack of racial diversity, Palm Springs is generally a polite and welcoming town open to visitors, who form the foundation of the Palm Springs economy.

Consider visiting the following websites for more information:

- **Travel Noire** (https://travelnoire.com)
- **Palm Springs Black History Committee** (https://palmspringsblackhistory.org)

TRAVELING WITH PETS

Many hotels in Palm Springs accept well-behaved pets for a fee; check with the individual hotel when booking. However, it is best to leave your pet at home when visiting Joshua Tree National Park. Pets are allowed in Joshua Tree, but they are not allowed on any trails and cannot be left unattended in a car, since desert temperatures can soar. Pets must be on a leash at all times and cannot be more than 100 ft (30 m) from a picnic area, road, or campground.

HEALTH AND SAFETY

As a desert park, Joshua Tree National Park is no more dangerous than any other national park. However, there are a few extra precautions you should take to stay safe.

ESSENTIALS
TRAVEL TIPS

Heat

Heat is the biggest health threat in the desert. The hottest conditions occur at the lower elevations during summer and can be dangerously hot **May-October.** Many visitors choose to visit the park in summer, and it is possible to do so safely if you take some precautions. Avoid hiking or other outdoor exertion at low elevations during summer. In summer, confine hiking to high elevations or go out early in the morning (plan to be off the trail by 10am) or late in the evening; stick to paved roads for touring at low elevations. When hiking or exploring outdoors, wear a wide-brimmed hat, sunglasses, and proper sun protection. Lightweight, light-colored breathable clothing can offer better protection than sunscreen—wear both.

Dehydration

Dehydration is a serious health concern in Joshua Tree. Daytime temperatures can soar. Always carry plenty of water—at least 2 gallons (9 liters) per person per day, and more than you think you will need, especially when hiking or engaging in other physical activity. Signs of heat exhaustion include dizziness, nausea, and headaches. If these occur, get into the shade and drink plenty of water or sports drinks.

Water Safety

Visitors should expect to buy bottled water and take it into the park. There are no water stations in the national park. There are refillable water stations at the Joshua Tree National Park Visitor Center in downtown Twentynine Palms. Potable water for camping is available at Cottonwood and Black Rock Campgrounds. All available water is suitable for drinking.

Getting Lost

With its wide network of popular trails, it is easy to underestimate potential dangers when hiking in Joshua Tree National Park. Attempt to keep track of distant landmarks when hiking; the landscape, with its sweeping boulder piles and Joshua trees, can be extremely disorienting. This is especially important because trails in Joshua Tree's sandy soil are easily erased with wind and water, making them hard to follow across open landscape. Watch for trail markers, such as a row of rocks or downed Joshua trees marking trail boundaries. Also, because of the sandy soil, trails and washes can look alike. It is easy to get off-course and follow a wide sandy wash instead of a trail. This may account for the prevalence of social trails (informal trails established by use) in Joshua Tree. Often these trails are made by people who have gone off-course or are attempting a shortcut. Avoid social trails if possible; they have the potential to get you lost, and they damage the landscape.

Resources

Suggested Reading

GUIDEBOOKS

MacKay, Pam. *Mojave Desert Wildflowers: A Field Guide to Wildflowers, Trees, and Shrubs of the Mojave Desert.* Guilford, CT: Morris Book Publishing, 2013. An excellent field guide to Mojave flora.

HIKING

Cunningham, Bill, and Polly Cunningham. Revised by Bruce Grubbs. *Best Easy Day Hikes Joshua Tree National Park.* 3rd ed. Guilford, CT: Falcon Guides, 2019. A short, lightweight version of a classic hiking guide that includes hiking highlights of Joshua Tree National Park for hikers of all abilities and interests.

Cunningham, Bill, and Polly Cunningham. Revised by Bruce Grubbs. *Hiking Joshua Tree National Park: 38 Day and Overnight Hikes.* 3rd ed. Guilford, CT: Falcon Guides, 2019. An update of this classic hiking guide provides detailed trail descriptions for a wide range of hikes for hikers of all abilities and interests in Joshua Tree National Park.

Ferranti, Philip, and Hank Koenig. *140 Great Hikes in and near Palm Springs: 25th Anniversary Edition.* Golden, CO: Colorado Mountain Club, 2020. A reissue of this hiking guide offers a thorough overview of hiking near Palm Springs, including trail descriptions of hikes in the Coachella Valley, San Jacinto Mountains, Santa Rosa Mountains, and Palm Springs and the Indian Canyons.

Harris, D. M., and J. M. Harris. *Afoot & Afield Inland Empire: A Comprehensive Hiking Guide.* Berkeley, CA: Wilderness Press, 2018.

Robinson, J. W., and David Money Harris. *San Bernardino Mountain Trails: 100 Hikes in Southern California.* 7th ed. Berkeley, CA: Wilderness Press, 2016.

Salabert, Shawnté. *Hiking the Pacific Crest Trail: Southern California: Section Hiking from Campo to Tuolumne Meadows.* Seattle: Mountaineers Books, 2017.

ROCK CLIMBING

Gaines, Bob. *Best Climbs, Joshua Tree National Park: The Best Sport and Trad Routes in the Park.* 2nd ed. Guilford, CT: Falcon Guides, 2019. A selection of more than 280 of the best routes in this climbing destination.

Miramontes, Robert. *Joshua Tree Rock Climbs.* 3rd ed. Silt, CO: Wolverine, 2017. An in-depth guide to rock climbing the entire park, this guide features 3,000 of Joshua Tree's easy and moderate routes and recommended bouldering circuits.

Vogel, Randy. *Rock Climbing Joshua Tree West.* Guilford, CT: Falcon Guide, 2006. Focusing on the popular western part of the park, this guide covers climbs from Quail Springs to Hidden Valley Campground.

Winger, Charlie, and Diane Winger. *The Trad Guide to Joshua Tree: 60 Favorite Climbs from 5.5 to 5.9.* Golden, CO: Colorado Mountain Club Press, 2004. This classic rock climbing guide details climbs for a moderate trad climber in Joshua Tree National Park.

CULTURE AND HISTORY

Shulman, Julius, Michael Stern, and Alan Hess. *Julius Shulman: Palm Springs.* New York: Rizzoli, 2008. This photography book captures more than 60 iconic Southern California modernist buildings by 15 notable mid-century architects through the lens of photographer Julius Shulman.

Stringfellow, Kim. *Greetings from the Salton Sea: Folly and Intervention in the Southern California Landscape, 1905-2005.* Santa Fe, NM: Center for American Places, 2005. An artistic mix of cultural geography, history, and photography, this book provides a fascinating glimpse into the dissolution of California's Salton Sea.

NONFICTION

Nyala, Hannah. *Point Last Seen: A Woman Tracker's Story.* New York: Simon & Schuster, 1997. A compelling story of a woman who fled personal danger to become a tracker in Joshua Tree National Park. The author describes her time spent as a tracker and its intersection with her personal narrative.

MAPS

Joshua Tree National Park. San Rafael, CA: Tom Harrison Maps, 2017. A shaded-relief topographic map of Joshua Tree National Park with detailed hiking trails including mileages, road networks, campgrounds, picnic areas, and ranger stations. This map can be the backbone for hiking and driving tours.

Joshua Tree National Park Trails Illustrated Topographic Map. Evergreen, CO: National Geographic, 2023. A topographic map that details hiking trails with mileages, paved and dirt roads, campgrounds, picnic areas, and ranger stations in Joshua Tree National Park.

A Map of Modern Palm Springs. Palm Springs Modern Committee. This foldout map to mid-century modern landmarks includes location, address, architect, and the year built. The map is available through the Palm Springs Historical Society.

San Gorgonio Wilderness Map. San Rafael, CA: Tom Harrison Maps, 2019. Trailheads, trail mileages, topographic details, campgrounds, towns, roads, and ranger stations make this map indispensable for casual or backcountry travel.

San Bernardino Mountains Recreation Map. 7th ed. Berkeley, CA: Wilderness Press, 2016. Good overall area map to get the lay of the land with trailheads, roads, campgrounds, and towns.

Internet Resources

Coachella Valley Preserve
www.cnlm.org/portfolio_page/
coachella-valley

The website includes preserve information, including hours, location, conservation, and flora and fauna as well as up-to-date information on the status of the preserve's 25 mi (40 km) of hiking trails.

Joshua Tree National Park
www.nps.gov/jotr

The main park website is a good resource for planning your visit, including up-to-date visitor center hours and event calendars, an overview of the park's main sights, campgrounds, and climate, as well as information about permits, fees, and park rules.

Sand to Snow National Monument
www.fs.usda.gov

The monument is managed by multiple agencies, but the US Forest Service website provides a good overall description of the monument as well as listings for visitor centers and ranger stations as well as special destinations within the region.

Visit Gay Palm Springs
www.visitgaypalmsprings.com

The official gay and lesbian guide to hotels, resorts, nightlife, clubs, bars, and events that cater to a gay and lesbian clientele, as well as attractions and activities that may be appealing for all visitors.

Visit Palm Springs
www.visitpalmsprings.com

The official visitor website provides recommendations for where to dine, stay, shop, and explore as well as event listings and basic visitor information on traveling to Palm Springs.

Whitewater Preserve
www.wildlandsconservancy.org

The website lists visitor information, including trail maps and descriptions, hours, program information, and plant and animal checklists.

Big Morongo Canyon Preserve
www.bigmorongo.org

An overview for visiting the preserve as well as trail maps and detailed information about the preserve's ecosystem, including birds, plants, and wildlife.

Index

A

accessibility: 213
accommodations: Coachella Valley 169–172; Hi-Desert towns 86, 88; Idyllwild 180, 182; Joshua Tree town 96–97; Palm Springs 153–158; Sand to Snow National Monument 108–110, 111–112; Twentynine Palms 100–101
Agua Caliente Cultural Museum: 121–122
Agua Caliente people: 124, 197
airports: 16, 73, 158–159, 202–203
air quality: 188–189
American Documentary and Animation Film Festival: 137
Andreas Canyon Loop: 131
Annenberg Theater: 136
Araby Trail: 128
architecture: 12, 119–121, 136–137, 138–139
Architecture and Design Center, Edwards Harris Pavilion: 121
Arch Rock Nature Trail: 55
around Joshua Tree: 14, 74–112; maps 76–77, 81, 103
art galleries: Joshua Tree town 90–92; Twentynine Palms 98
Astro Domes: 51

B

Barker Dam: 49
bars/nightlife: Hi-Desert towns 86; Joshua Tree town 94, 96; Palm Springs 151–153; Twentynine Palms 100
Berdoo Canyon Road: 42
Big Bear Lake: 110–112
Big Falls: 104
bighorn sheep: 192
Big Morongo Canyon Preserve: 105
biking: Joshua Tree National Park 63; Palm Springs 133–135
BIPOC travelers: 215
birds: 194
Black Eagle Mine Road: 43
Black Rock Canyon: 37; camping 70; hiking 58–61; map 59; scenic drives 40
Black Rock Nature Center: 34–35, 212–213
Black Rock Ranger Station: 58
Black Rock Spring: 58
BLM camping: 72
Bob Hope Residence: 128
Bootlegger Tiki: 151–152
boulder piles: 42, 45, 49, 51, 52, 55, 63–65

Boy Scout Trail: 48–49
bus travel: 204

C

Cabot's Pueblo Museum: 160, 162
Cahuilla people: 194–195
California Riding and Hiking Trail: 57–58
camping: Idyllwild 182–183; Joshua Tree National Park 21–22, 67–72; Joshua Tree town 96–97; Sand to Snow National Monument 108–110
Canyon View Loop Trail: 107
Cap Rock: 54, 65
car travel: 203–204
Central Palm Springs: 119–122, 143, 145, 148–150, 152, 154–155; map 120
Cheeky's: 146
Chef Tanya's Kitchen: 151
children, traveling with: 213–215
cholla cactus: 192
Cholla Cactus Garden: 39
chuckwalla: 193–194
Cinema Diverse: 141
City of Twentynine Palms Visitor Center: 35, 213
Clandestino: 149–150
climate: 188
climbing: see rock climbing
Coachella Valley: 160–173
Coachella Valley Music and Arts Festival: 15, 162
Colony Palms Hotel: 118
Conan's Corridor: 65
Contact Mine: 55, 57
Copley's: 146
Cornelia White House: 121
Cottonwood Spring: 37, 39; camping 70; hiking 61–63; map 62; scenic drives 42–43
Cottonwood Visitor Center: 17, 34, 212
Covington Flats: 40
coyotes: 193
creosote: 192
Crossroads Café: 93
culture: 199–201
customs at the border: 212
cycling: see biking

DE

day trips: 19
dehydration: 216
Del Marcos Hotel: 154–155
Desert Hot Springs: 160, 162, 170–172; map 170
Desert Queen Mine: 37, 52

Desert Queen Mine and Wash: 52
Desert Queen Well: 51
desert survival: 214
Desert View Trail: 132
Desert X: 163
Devil's Slide: 176
Dinah, The: 140
disabilities, access for travelers with: 213
Disney petroglyphs: 49
diversity: 215
driving: 203–204; see also scenic drives
drought: 190
economy: 199
Eight4Nine Restaurant and Lounge: 146
entrance stations, Joshua Tree National Park: 16–17, 35
equestrian camping: 67
Ernie Maxwell Scenic Trail: 174, 176
Eureka Peak: 40, 60–61
Eureka Peak Overlook: 37

FG

family travel: 213–215
fan palm oases: 191
Faye Sarkowsky Sculpture Garden: 162
festivals/events: Coachella Valley 162–163; Joshua Tree town 92–93; Palm Springs 15, 136–137, 140–142
food: Coachella Valley 169; Hi-Desert towns 84–86; Idyllwild 178–180; Joshua Tree town 93–94; Palm Springs 146–151; Sand to Snow National Monument 108, 110–111; Twentynine Palms 98, 100
Forest Falls: 105
49 Palms Oasis: 23, 57
Frey House II: 121
gay travelers: see LGBTQ+ travelers
geology: 186–187
Geology Tour Road: 40, 42, 63
Giant Rock: 80, 83
Gold Hill Mine: 52
golf: 126, 164–166
government: 199

H

Harmony Motel: 91
health: 215–216
Heyday, The: 146, 148
Hidden Valley: 35–37; camping 68–69; hiking 43–57; maps 36, 50; scenic drives 39
Hidden Valley Campground: 64
Hidden Valley hike: 49
Hi-Desert towns: 78, 79–101; map 81
high season: 16
hiking: Indian Canyons 24, 128–131; Joshua

Tree National Park 10, 23–24, 43–63; Mount San Jacinto State Park and Wilderness 24, 131–133, 174–177; Palm Springs 127–133; San Bernardino National Forest 107–108; Sand to Snow National Monument 105–108; San Gorgonio Wilderness 105–107; Santa Rosa and San Jacinto Mountains National Monument 163–164; Thousand Palms Oasis Preserve 163; Whitewater Preserve 24, 107
history: 47, 124, 138–139, 194–198
Hi-View Nature Trail: 58
Holiday House: 154
Hollywood Rat Pack: 118
horseback riding: 66–67, 135
hotels: see accommodations
hot springs: 25, 167–168
House of Tomorrow: 119
Humber Park: 176

I

Idyllwild: 178–184; map 179
Indian Canyons: 24, 128–131
Indian Cove: 57–58
Indigenous heritage: 124
Indio: 162
information/services: Joshua Tree National Park 72; Palm Springs 160; Sand to Snow National Monument 102–3; Twentynine Palms 100–101
Ingleside Inn: 155
insects: 194
Integratron, The: 80
international travelers: 211–212
Intersection Rock: 64
itinerary ideas: 18–22, 26–27, 33

JK

jackrabbits: 193
Johnny Lang Canyon: 45
Joshua tree forests: 37, 40, 42, 44, 48, 52, 63, 186, 190
Joshua Tree Inn: 90–91
Joshua Tree Music Festival: 92–93
Joshua Tree National Park: 14, 28–73; camping 67–72; information/services 72; maps 30–31, 36, 44, 46, 48, 50, 53, 54, 59, 62; recreation 43–76; scenic drives 39–43; transportation 73
Joshua Tree National Park Visitor Center: 17, 34, 212
Joshua trees: 190
Joshua Tree Saloon: 93–94
Joshua Tree town: 78, 89–97
Joshua Tree Visitor Center: 17, 32, 34, 212
JT Country Kitchen: 94
Jumbo Rocks Campground: 69
Keys Ranch: 35
Keys View: 37
King's Highway: 150

INDEX

222

L

Landers: 78, 79–88
LGBTQ+ events: 137, 140–141
LGBTQ+ hotels: 157–158
LGBTQ+ nightlife: 152–153
LGBTQ+ travelers: 215
Living Desert Zoo and Gardens: 162
Long Valley Discovery Trail: 132
Los Angeles: 205–211
Los Angeles International Airport: 16, 158, 203
Lost Horse Mine: 23, 45–46; map 46
Lost Palms Oasis: 24, 62–63
Lower Palm Canyon Trail: 129, 131
low season: 16
Lucky Boy Vista: 37, 52–54

M

Malapai Hill: 40
Mastodon Mine: 61
Mastodon Peak: 61–62
McCallum Adobe: 121
McCallum Trail: 163
Melvyn's: 152
mesquite: 191
mid-century modern architecture: 12, 26–27, 138–139
mining history: 47, 195–196
Mission era: 195
Modernism Week: 15, 136–137
Mojave Desert: 185–186
Mojave yucca: 190
Momyer Creek Trail: 106
money: 212
Moorten Botanical Garden: 122–123
Morongo Valley: 78
morteros: 53
mountain lions: 192–193
Mount San Jacinto State Park and Wilderness: 131–133, 173–184
Mr. Lyon's: 150
Murray Canyon: 131

NO

Nine Peaks Challenge: 107
Noah Purifoy Outdoor Desert Art Museum: 89–90
North Entrance: 17, 35, 73
North Palm Springs: 116–119, 142–143, 146, 148, 151–154; map 117
North View Maze Loop: 43–45; map 44
oases: 57, 62–63, 128–129, 163, 191
ocotillo: 191–192
Old Dale Mining District: 43
Old Dale Road: 42–43
Ontario Airport: 159, 203
Optimist Mine: 46

PQ

Paac Kŭvŭhŭ'k: 42
Pacific Crest Trail: 107
packing tips: 211
Palm Canyon overlook: 129
Palm Desert: 162
Palm Springs: 14, 113–160; accommodations 153–158; bars/nightlife 151–153; entertainment/events 136–141; food 146–151; information/services 160; maps 115, 117, 120, 123; recreation 125–136; shopping 142–145; transportation 158–159
Palm Springs Aerial Tramway: 116–117, 119
Palm Springs Air Museum: 122
Palm Springs Art Museum: 119–121
Palm Springs Historical Society: 121
Palm Springs International Airport: 16, 73, 158, 202–203
Palm Springs International Film Festival: 15, 137
Palm Springs International ShortFest: 137
Palm Springs Museum Trail: 127
Palm Springs Visitors Center: 17, 160, 212
Panorama Loop: 58, 60
Pappy & Harriet's Pioneertown Palace: 80, 85, 86, 88
Park Boulevard: 39, 63
Parker Palm Springs: 156
passports: 211–212
Paul Bar: 148
permits: 43, 102–103, 132, 174, 214
pets, traveling with: 215
Phylum: 143
Pine Canyon overlook: 52
Pine City Site: 51–52
Pinocchio in the Desert: 148–149
Pinto Basin Road: 42, 63
Pioneertown: 78, 79–88
plants: 190–192
Pleasant Valley: 40, 42
pool-hopping: 13, 140–141
Pride Weekend: 15, 141
Purple Room: 118
Quail Mountain: 45
Quail Springs: 64
Quail Springs Historic Trail: 45
Queen Valley: 37; biking 63; map 53; scenic drives 39–40

R

racism: 215
Rancho de la Luna: 91
ranger programs: 72
rattlesnakes: 194
recreation: Joshua Tree National Park 43–67; Palm Springs 125–136; see also specific activity

Red Dome: 24, 107
Reef, The: 155
reservations: 17
restaurants: see food
Roadrunner Grab + Go: 34
rock and roll history: 90–91
rock climbing: 10, 63–66
Round Valley Loop to Wellman Divide: 132–133
RVs: 204
Ryan Mountain: 23, 54; map 54
Ryan Ranch: 36–37

S

safety: 214, 215–216
San Andreas Fault: 187–188
San Bernardino National Forest: 107–108
San Diego International Airport: 159, 203
Sand to Snow National Monument: 79, 101–112; map 103
San Gorgonio Mountain: 103
San Gorgonio Wilderness: 103–104, 105–107
San Jacinto Peak: 133
Santa Rosa and San Jacinto Mountains National Monument: 163–164
scenic drives: 11, 39–43
senior travelers: 215
Serrano people: 194–195
Seymour's: 152
Shields Date Garden: 162
shopping: Coachella Valley 168; Hi-Desert towns 83–84; Idyllwild 178; Joshua Tree town 93; Palm Springs 11, 142–145; Yucca Valley 83–84
Shops at Thirteen Forty-Five: 142
Skull Rock: 54–55
Sky's the Limit Observatory and Nature Center: 97
smoke trees: 191
Sonoran Desert: 185–186
South Carl Lykken Trail: 127–128
South Entrance: 17, 35, 73, 145
South Fork Meadows: 108
South Palm Springs: 122–125, 150–151, 155–158; map 123
Spa at Séc-he: 125
Sparrows Lodge: 156–157
spas: 25, 125, 167–168
speakeasies: 118, 148, 152, 153
Splash House: 137
Split Rock Loop: 55
Split Rock Region: 65
sports and recreation: see recreation
Stagecoach Festival: 15, 162–163
Sunnylands Center and Gardens: 124–125
swimming: see pool-hopping

T

Tac/Quila: 150
Tahquitz Canyon: 129
Tahquitz Peak: 24
Tahquitz Peak (Continuing via Devil's Slide Trail): 177
Tahquitz Peak (via South Ridge Trail): 176–177
tennis: 166
The Tropicale Restaurant and Coral Seas Lounge: 149
Thousand Palms Oasis Preserve: 163
tortoises: 193
tourist information: see visitor centers, information/services
train travel: 204
Tramway Gas Station: 138
transportation: 16, 202–204; Joshua Tree National Park 73; Palm Springs 158–159
Twentynine Palms: 78, 97–101
Twin Palms Frank Sinatra Estate: 119

UV

Uptown Design District: 116–119, 142–143, 146, 148, 151–152, 153–154, 157
Valley of the Falls: 105
vandalism: 189–190
Victory Palms: 63
vintage shopping: 11, 83–84, 93, 142–143, 145
visas: 211–212
visitor centers: 212–213; Joshua Tree National Park 17, 32, 34–35; Palm Springs 17, 160; Sand to Snow National Monument 102; Twentynine Palms 101
Vivian Creek Trail: 106

WY

Wall Street Mill: 49, 51
Wall Street Mine: 37
Warren Peak: 60
water: 190, 216
waterfalls: 129, 131
West Entrance: 17, 35, 73
White Party: 140–141
Whitewater Preserve: 104–105, 107
wildflowers: 192
Willow Hole Trail: 23, 46–48; map 48
Willows, The: 118
Winona Mill: 61
winter sports: 136, 177–178
Wonderland of Rocks: 36
Wonderland Ranch: 51
Wonderland Wash: 51, 64
Wonder Valley: 97–98
Yucca Valley: 78, 79–88

List of Maps

Front Map
Joshua Tree & Palm Springs: 2–3

Joshua Tree National Park
Joshua Tree National Park: 30–31
Hidden Valley: 36
North View Maze Loop: 44
Lost Horse Mine: 46
Willow Hole Trail: 48
Hidden Valley Trail: 50
Queen Valley: 53
Ryan Mountain: 54
Black Rock Canyon: 59
Cottonwood Spring: 62

Around Joshua Tree
Around Joshua Tree: 76–77
Hi-Desert Towns: 81
Sand to Snow National Monument: 103

Palm Springs and the Coachella Valley
Palm Springs and the Coachella Valley: 115
North Palm Springs: 117
Central Palm Springs: 120
South Palm Springs: 123
Mid-Century Modernism: 138
Desert Hot Springs: 170
Idyllwild: 179

Photo Credits

All interior photos © Jenna Blough except: title page photo © Anton Foltin | Dreamstime.com; page 5 © (left middle) Laure Joliet; (right middle) Vladans | Dreamstime.com; page 8 © NastiaPhoto | Dreamstime.com; page 10 © Sburel | Dreamstime.com; page 11 © (top) Marcie Blough; page 12 © Photographerlondon | Dreamstime.com; page 13 © Bonandbon Dw | Dreamstime.com; page 14 © (bottom) Marcie Blough; page 15 © William Lee Bowman | Dreamstime.com; page 18 © Roman Slavik | Dreamstime.com; page 19 © Wirestock | Dreamstime.com; page 20 © (top) Kip Dawkins; page 21 © (top) Meinzahn | Dreamstime.com; (bottom) © Jim Cottingham | Dreamstime.com; page 22 © (bottom) © Kelly Vandellen | Dreamstime.com; page 23 © (bottom) David Lockeretz | Dreamstime.com; page 24 © Andreistanescu | Dreamstime.com; page 25 © Patricia Marroquin | Dreamstime.com; page 27 © bonandbon | Dreamstime.com; page 28 © Michael Ver Sprill | Dreamstime.com; page 29 © (top right) Brian Flaigmore | Dreamstime.com; page 34 © Andreistanescu | Dreamstime.com; page 38 © (right middle) Gjwsphotography | Dreamstime.com; page 41 © (bottom) Ryan Jones; page 47 © Pancaketom | Dreamstime.com; page 56 © (top) Grace Fujimoto; (bottom) Grace Fujimoto; page 74 © Jon Bilous| Dreamstime.com; page 75 © (top left) Stephen Minkler | Dreamstime.com; (top right) Kip Dawkins; page 82 © (top) Kip Dawkins; page 87 © (bottom) Kip Dawkins; page 104 © Stevehymon | Dreamstime.com; page 113 © Laure Joliet; page 114 © (top left) Chon Kit Leong | Dreamstime.com; page 118 © Marcie Blough; page 119 © Marcie Blough; page 134 © Marcie Blough; page 147 © (bottom) Marcie Blough; page 161 © (bottom) Jane Chapman | Dreamstime.com; page 167 © Azure Palm Hot Springs; page 202 © Goldilock Project | Dreamstime.com; page 214 © Laina Babb.

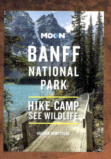

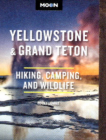

Spending only a few days in a park?

Try our Best Of guides.

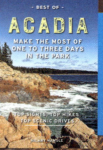

Embark on a transformative journey along the historic Camino de Santiago with Moon Travel Guides!

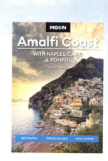
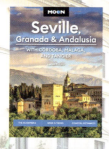

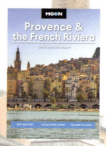

CREATE AN EPIC TRAVEL BUCKET LIST

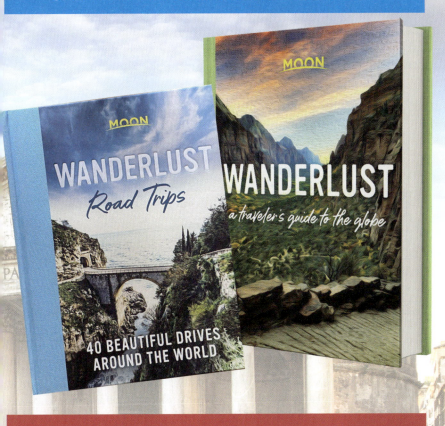

EXPLORE CITY NEIGHBORHOOD WALKS

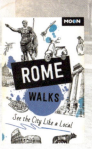

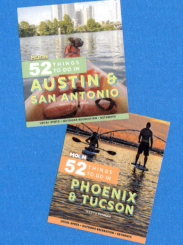

Explore local spots and day trips with Moon's **52 Things**, or make the most of short trips to top national parks with our **Best Of Parks** travel guides.

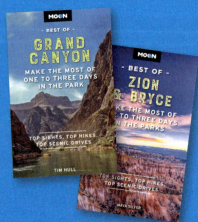

MOON.COM | @MOONGUIDES

MAP SYMBOLS

Highway	○ ○ City/Town	Information Center	Park
Primary Road	● State Capital	✈ International Airport	Golf Course
Secondary Road	⊛ National Capital	✈ Regional Airport	Place of Worship
Unpaved Road	● Highlight	Train Station	▲ Mountain
Walkway	★ Sight	Ⓜ Metro/Bus Stop	✦ Unique Feature
Stairs	● Accommodation	Ⓟ Parking	✦ Hydro Feature
Trail	▼ Restaurant/Bar	Trailhead	Waterfall
Bike Trail	■ Other Location	Camping	Ski Area
Ferry		Winery/Vineyard	Glacier
Railroad			

CONVERSION TABLES

°C = (°F - 32) / 1.8
°F = (°C x 1.8) + 32
1 inch = 2.54 centimeters (cm)
1 foot = 0.304 meters (m)
1 yard = 0.914 meters
1 mile = 1.6093 kilometers (km)
1 km = 0.6214 miles
1 fathom = 1.8288 m
1 chain = 20.1168 m
1 furlong = 201.168 m
1 acre = 0.4047 hectares
1 sq km = 100 hectares
1 sq mile = 2.59 square km
1 ounce = 28.35 grams
1 pound = 0.4536 kilograms
1 short ton = 0.90718 metric ton
1 short ton = 2,000 pounds
1 long ton = 1.016 metric tons
1 long ton = 2,240 pounds
1 metric ton = 1,000 kilograms
1 quart = 0.94635 liters
1 US gallon = 3.7854 liters
1 Imperial gallon = 4.5459 liters
1 nautical mile = 1.852 km

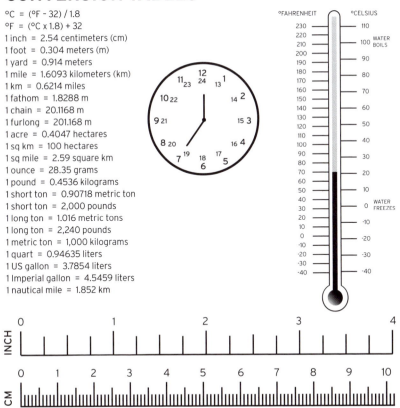

MOON JOSHUA TREE & PALM SPRINGS
Avalon Travel
Hachette Book Group, Inc.
555 12th Street, Suite 1850
Oakland, CA 94607, USA
www.moon.com

Acquisition Editor: Devon Lee
Editorial Assistant: Ajà Miller
Managing Editor: Hannah Brezack
Copy Editor: Christopher Church
Graphics and Production Coordinator: Rue Flaherty
Cover Design: Toni Tajima
Interior Design: Avalon Travel
Map Editor: Karin Dahl
Cartographers: Abby Whelan, Lohnes + Wright, Karin Dahl
Proofreader: Courtney Packard

ISBN-13: 979-8-88647-104-5

Printing History
1st Edition — 2016
4th Edition — July 2025
5 4 3 2 1

Text © 2025 by Jenna Blough.
Maps © 2025 by Avalon Travel.
Some photos and illustrations are used by permission and are the property of the original copyright owners.

Hachette Book Group, Inc. supports the right to free expression and the value of copyright. The purpose of copyright is to encourage writers and artists to produce the creative works that enrich our culture. The scanning, uploading, and distribution of this book without permission is a theft of the author's intellectual property. If you would like permission to use material from the book (other than for review purposes), please contact permissions@hbgusa.com. Thank you for your support of the author's rights.

Front cover photo: Keys Point in Joshua Tree National Park © Caryn Becker / Alamy Stock Photo

Back cover photo: Joshua Tree © Lhb Companies | Dreamstime.com

Printed in China by RR Donnelley

Avalon Travel is a division of Hachette Book Group, Inc. Moon and the Moon logo are trademarks of Hachette Book Group, Inc. All other marks and logos depicted are the property of the original owners.

All recommendations, including those for sights, activities, hotels, restaurants, and shops, are based on each author's individual judgment. We do not accept payment for inclusion in our travel guides, and our authors do not accept free goods or services in exchange for positive coverage.

Although every effort was made to ensure that the information was correct at the time of going to press, the author and Hachette Book Group, Inc. do not assume, and hereby disclaim, any liability to any party for any loss or damage caused by any information or recommendations contained in this book, including any errors or omissions regardless of whether such errors or omissions result from negligence, accident, or any other cause.

Hachette Book Group, Inc. is not responsible for websites (or their content) that are not owned by Hachette Book Group, Inc.